Pottery and Chron

Pottery and Chronology at
ANGEL

Sherri L. Hilgeman

THE UNIVERSITY OF ALABAMA PRESS

Tuscaloosa and London

1 2 3 4 5 6 7 8 9   08 07 06 05 04 03 02 01 00

∞

The paper on which this book is printed meets the minimum requirements of American
National Standard for Information Science-Permanence of Paper for Printed Library
Materials, ANSI Z39.48-1984.

Library of Congress Cataloging-in-Publication Data

Hilgeman, Sherri Lynn, 1958–
Pottery and chronology at Angel / Sherri L. Hilgeman.
p. cm.
Includes bibliographical references and index.
Contents: Introduction—Pottery studies in Mississippian archaeology—Decorated
plates, bottles, bowls, and jars—Closed and open handles—Angel negative painted
plates—Chronology of the Angel site and phase.
ISBN 0-8173-1035-5 (pbk. : alk. paper)
1. Angel Mounds State Historic Site (Ind.) 2. Indians of North
America—Indiana—Antiquities. 3. Mississippian culture—Indiana.
4. Indiana—Antiquities. I. Title.

E78.I53 H56 2000
977.2'33—dc21

                                                                    99-050763

British Library Cataloguing-in-Publication Data available

Contents

Illustrations

Figures

Tables

Acknowledgments

I found my first shell-tempered potsherd when I was about ten years old. It came from a hillock in a field that was used to grow strawberry plants less than a half mile from my house. The hillock was also the location of a small Mississippian farmstead or hamlet overlooking the East Fork White River, in an equally small farming hamlet (population fifty-six in 1967) in southwestern Indiana. When I asked my grandmother or grandfather, I forget which, what it was, the answer was a piece of asphalt. (The road that ran through the site was rock.) That site and a child's book (with a yellow cover; I forget author and title) on famous archaeological discoveries were the beginnings of my interest in archaeology and the people who had lived "around here" hundreds or thousands of years ago. I still visit the site occasionally, just to make sure it is okay.

This book is a revised version of a dissertation completed at the Graduate School of Indiana University, Bloomington. I wish to thank the members of my dissertation committee for uncounted hours of conversation and help: Christopher S. Peebles, R. Berle Clay, Karen D. Vitelli, Robert J. Meier, and Daniel C. Knudsen. Chris Peebles made available to me the resources of the Glenn A. Black Laboratory of Archaeology (GBL) at Indiana University. Berle Clay encouraged me to return to the study of Mississippian and pottery after a brief excursion into Woodland and lithics. K. D. Vitelli seemed to enjoy hearing about a pile of potsherds other than her own Neolithic sherds. Dan Knudsen kept my usage of statistics reasonable. Bob Meier let me ramble on about something other than potsherds. James Kellar, director emeritus of the Glenn A. Black Laboratory of Archaeology, helped me understand many details of the history of Angel archaeology and was always willing to discuss opera and IU basketball, in equal measure, whenever I needed a break.

My student colleagues at the GBL—Ed Smith, Mark Schurr, Brian Redmond, Shawn French, Chris Borstel, Leslie Bush, Steve Ball, and Bret Ruby—were willing to discuss anything from the minutiae of a single sherd to more grandiose revisionist archaeological theory. Minnie Headdy helped me with the administrative issues, and she and Ed were also participants in many welcome basketball discussions.

A heartfelt thank you is due to Rachael Freyman, who produced the majority of the sherd illustrations, including the wonderful (and popular!) assemblage reconstruction in Chapter 6. This document is far more valuable because of Rae's illustrations. Another artist who contributed to this volume is Richard Montgomery, artist during the WPA project, who completed the whole vessel drawings. Karin Stafford unpacked, from boxes approximately 11 × 11 × 17 inches and filled to the brim with sherds, approximately one-third of the sherds—almost all of the closed and open handles—I studied. The year and a half Karin helped me represented a considerable amount of backbreaking labor and dedication on her part.

A number of scholars have also been sources of insight. They are William Autry, Raymond DeMallie, John Kelly, Kit Wesler, Kenneth Carstens, Lawrence Conrad, Jon Muller, Brian Butler, and Barry Lewis. Kit Wesler and Ken Carstens allowed me to study sherds from Chambers and Stone housed at Murray State University, and Larry Conrad allowed me to study the deep rim plate sherds from Crable housed at Western Illinois University Archaeological Laboratory. I also want to thank Barry Lewis, William Autry, Chris Peebles, and Prudence Rice, who reviewed the dissertation and made suggestions that helped transform it into a book manuscript, and Judith Knight and the two anonymous reviewers who helped me complete the transformation.

My family—parents, brother, and nephews, Jon and Andrew—have been very patient over the years, and I want to thank them for all the love and support.

Finally, I want to dedicate this book to Fran Weinberg. Every grad student should have a skilled volunteer like Fran. She helped, anywhere from eight to twenty hours a week, throughout the academic year and for many weeks in the summer, for almost the entire time it took to finish the dissertation. She sorted, resorted, numbered, listed, packed, unpacked, and repacked the twenty-two-thousand-plus piece analytic collection until she knew the sherds as well as I. And to this day she remains a good friend and favorite shopping buddy. Thanks, Fran.

Pottery and Chronology at Angel

1 Introduction

The prehistoric town of Angel, located on the Ohio River in Vanderburgh County, Indiana, was the central community of a Late Prehistoric, Mississippian Tradition chiefdom. It was one of four such towns, larger and smaller, in the lower Ohio Valley (Figure 1.1). Angel has been the subject of professional archaeological scrutiny for more than a half century. After its purchase by the Indiana Historical Society, Glenn A. Black, archaeologist for the society, excavated at the site from 1939 until his death in 1964. These and subsequent excavations examined habitation areas, substructure pyramidal mounds, stockade (defensive wall) lines, and the plaza within the one-hundred-acre town. Approximately 4 percent of the area within the outer stockade line was excavated, and more than two million artifacts were collected.

In addition to Black's (1967) own report on the site, other studies have summarized the more recent periods of excavation (Ball, Senkel, and French 1990; Schurr 1989a, 1992; Wolforth 1983), various artifact classes (Curry 1950; Kellar 1967; Rachlin 1954), the biology of the prehistoric inhabitants (Hilgeman 1988a; Johnston 1957; Schurr 1989a), and the settlement pattern of the Angel system (Green 1977; Green and Munson 1978; Honerkamp 1975; Power 1976).

These many studies have provided a great deal of information concerning the Angel society; however, they lacked the chronological dimension with which to examine the growth and decline of Angel. For many years, very few radiocarbon dates were available, and there was no pottery or other artifactual chronology in place. Researchers were forced to treat the three or four centuries, from A.D. 1100 to 1500, generally thought to encompass the beginning and end of Angel, as a single chronological unit. From a valley-wide perspective, Lewis (1991:293) suggests that this "monolithic" view of Angel hampers cultural-historical and processual studies on the Late Prehistoric societies of the lower Ohio Valley because it has not been possible to incorporate developments within the Angel society into a valley-wide synthesis.

This volume is the result of a research project designed to create a pottery chronology absolutely dated with a series of radiocarbon assays. With this chronology it is possible to divide the occupation of the Angel site into a series of recognizable cultural-historical phases. The results of the project are presented in the seven chapters of this volume. This chapter concludes with a summary description of the Angel site and a little of what is known about the prehistoric Angel society. Chapter 2 considers the contributions that pottery

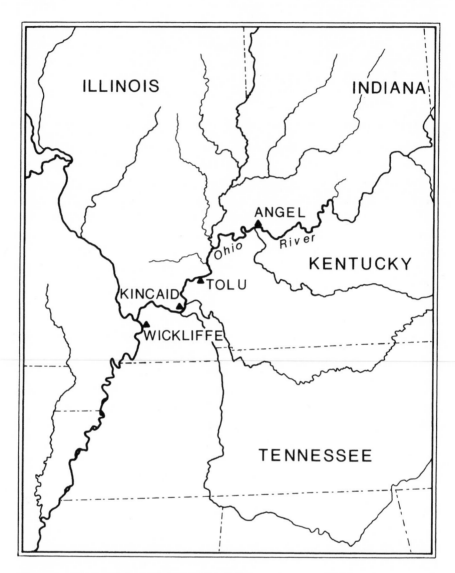

Figure 1.1. The Angel site in the lower Ohio Valley.

studies have made in studying societies such as Angel. Chapters 3 through 5 describe a subset of the Angel pottery assemblage.

Chapter 3 presents a formal classification of the decorated subset of the Angel pottery assemblage. The word "decorated" is used very broadly in this volume. Not only does "decorated" include treatments such as incising, painting, punctating, or modeling, herein it also includes all attachments such as closed and open handles. "Undecorated" or "plain" includes all rim and body sherds that have plain, cord-marked, or fabric-impressed surfaces and no attachments. The decorated pieces are those that have proved useful in creating pottery chronologies for late prehistoric sites elsewhere in the Eastern Woodlands. The chapter is divided into four major sections, each of which covers one of the major Mississippian vessel forms—plates, bottles, bowls, and jars. The fifth Mississippian vessel form, the pan or saltpan, is not included in the analysis or descriptions. Pans have plain or fabric-impressed exterior surfaces and, at least at Angel, do not have handles or other attachments. Each section describes the basic vessel form and its variants, the defined pottery types and varieties, and other kinds of decorations that occur. I organized the classification by vessel form because the presence or form of the types, the secondary shape features, and the other decorations tend not to cross vessel form lines within the Angel pottery assemblage. A final discussion compares the Angel assemblage to other contemporary pottery assemblages in the lower Ohio Valley. The pottery assemblage from Angel is similar to those from other lower Ohio Valley sites in that all include many of the same decorated types. Angel's pottery assemblage differs from other lower Ohio Valley assemblages in that, at Angel, painting is the most important decorative mode and incising is present, but rare. Elsewhere in the valley, the situation is reversed.

Chapter 4 is a description of the closed and open handles. The handles are dealt with in a separate chapter because they are the only large segment of the decorated assemblage that cuts across vessel form lines. Specifically, open handles occur in large numbers on both bowls and jars. The final section of this chapter looks at the ranges of jar sizes (orifice diameters) on which closed and open handles occur and concludes that it is practicality that dictates whether closed or open handles were placed on any particular jar. Jars that were small enough to be moved when full without overtaxing the structure of the jar body or breaking the handle had both open and closed handles attached to them. Large storage jars that were not intended to be moved when full had open handles attached to them; the open handles were sufficient anchors for fastening a flexible cover in place.

Chapter 5 is a history, description of manufacture techniques, and design analysis of the decorated pottery type for which Angel is best known, Angel Negative Painted. Angel Negative Painted is placed stylistically and geographically within the corpus of negative painted pottery types—Nashville Negative Painted, Kincaid Negative Painted, Sikeston Negative Painted, and Angel Negative Painted—and within the corpus of similarly decorated plate types—Wells Incised, O'Byam Incised, and Angel Negative Painted. Replication experiments show that the appearance may be achieved by a smudging technique using clay as a resist. A design analysis indicates that the plates were decorated so that the plate itself was a depiction of a cross-in-circle or suncircle. It is suggested that the plates were used as ritual presentation vessels at a local version of the pan-Southeastern green corn ceremony.

In Chapter 6, I present the pottery chronology for the Angel site. A number of morphological and stylistic pottery attributes that occur relatively frequently in the Angel assemblage and are known to have chronological significance at other Mississippian sites in the lower Ohio and middle Mississippi Valleys are identified. Fifty-six archaeological contexts, including both features and excavation levels, were seriated by their pottery assemblages using the Bonn seriation program (Scollar and Herzog 1991). The validity of the resulting seriation order as a chronological order is corroborated by the applicable stratigraphy, absolute radiocarbon dates, and relative fluorine assays. The radiocarbon dates and cross-dating of the diagnostic pottery suggest that the seriated order represents the A.D. 1200 to 1450 time period. The seriation order is divided into two segments, representing the Angel 2 and Angel 3 phases. The pottery characteristics and absolute dating of these phases, plus a sketch of an earlier phase, are described.

Chapter 7 is the final chapter in this volume. The three major sections of the chapter address three interrelated issues: the possibility of ancestor-descendant relationships between the Angel phase and the preceding Emergent Mississippian Yankeetown phase and the succeeding Terminal Mississippian Caborn-Welborn phase, and the likelihood that the contemporary Angel and Kincaid societies are related polities.

The Angel Site

The one-hundred-acre Angel town is located on the high terrace of the Ohio River just upstream from the mouth of the Green River. Large floodplains lie to the west of the site and across the river in Kentucky.

During the prehistoric occupation of Angel, as today, the Ohio Valley of southwestern Indiana and western Kentucky was characterized by a diversity of physiographic zones and biomes (Green and Munson 1978:297–299).

> According to Indiana land survey records, the area was covered with oak-hickory forest in the early 1800s (T. Green 1972b; Potzger, Potzger, and McCormick 1956). Compared with the central and northern portions of the Indiana, the vegetation of southwestern Indiana has a distinctive southern composition. Many southern plant species are at their most northern distribution in this area. Deam (1953) lists pecan, lowland hackberry or sugarberry, bald cypress, and overcup oak as trees occurring in this area that are typical of the lower Mississippi Valley flora. There are also numerous smaller plant species as well as several small mammals that are at their most northern distribution in this area (Green and Munson 1978:298).

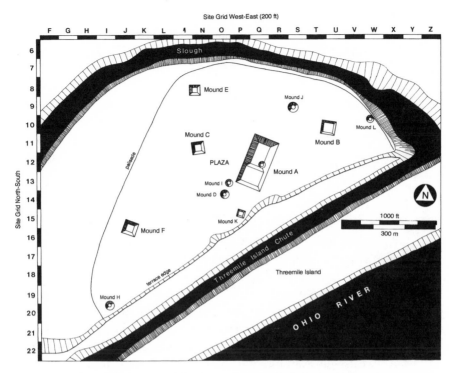

Figure 1.2. The Angel site, 12Vg1 (after Morgan 1980 and Black 1967:Figure 14).

Angel was enclosed by a roughly semicircular bastioned stockade along the eastern, northern, and western margins (Figure 1.2). It is not known whether the river face of the site was enclosed, but the town was screened from the main channel of the Ohio River by a slack water "chute" and a narrow island.

Mound A, a large, centrally placed, multilevel pyramidal mound, dominates the interior of the site. A plaza lies west of Mound A, and the second largest pyramidal mound, Mound F, lies across the plaza. The third pyramidal mound, Mound E, is located in the northwestern corner of the site. Contemporary vegetation differences suggest there may be another smaller plaza east of Mound E. The original shapes of the eight conical mounds cannot be determined with certainty, but their topographies suggest that minimally Mound C, located north of the plaza, and Mound B, located northeast of Mound A, were originally low pyramidal mounds, and their present conical shape is the result of years of cultivation. As the excavation of several of these mounds demonstrate, many were the foundations for special-purpose buildings. At present, archaeological reconstruction of Mississippian society and religion suggests that the buildings were semipublic ritual structures or the dwellings of high-ranking families.

The resident population of Angel at its zenith is difficult to estimate. Black (1967:547) estimated the minimum population of Angel at one thousand persons. He arrived at this figure by estimating that two hundred typical aboriginal Southeastern households, occupied by an average of five persons, would fit in the area—62,500 square feet—upon which there was evidence for intensive occupation. Black considered one thousand persons to be a minimum estimate because it represented only about two hundred adult men to defend a site with a 1.2 mile-long stockade and a 0.8 mile-long river edge. Other estimates have placed the population of Angel as high as 3,000 persons (Green and Munson 1978:312–313) and as low as 240 persons (Muller 1986:207).

Excavations at Angel: 1939–1989

The excavations conducted at Angel from 1939 to 1989 are summarized in a tabular fashion in Appendix A. Black (1967:3–40) brings together the published accounts of investigations of the site prior to 1939 and provides a detailed description of his own excavations and findings from 1939 to 1963. Schurr (1989a:23–57) presents a synopsis of the excavation program reported by Black and brings the story up to date by summarizing the excavations conducted at the site from 1964 to 1983. Ball, Senkel, and French (1990) describe the 1989 testing of the early-nineteenth-century Mathias Angel homestead. The following summary is based on these sources, as well as on unpublished reports and records on file at the Glenn A. Black Laboratory of Archaeology (GBL).

The modern era of archaeological exploration of the site began in 1931, when Eli Lilly visited the site with Warren K. Moorehead, E. Y. Guernsey, and Glenn A. Black. Lilly began negotiations that year to purchase the site for the Indiana Historical Society (Ruegamer 1980:257–297). In 1938, while final negotiations for purchase were being completed, Black submitted a proposal to the Works Progress Administration (WPA) for funding excavations at Angel. The proposal was approved, and archaeological fieldwork began in April 1939 (Black 1967:20–21).

The initial task of the WPA project was to survey the site, establish the site grid, and prepare a topographic map (Black 1967:29–40). The grid established at that time was used in all subsequent excavations, and its designations were a part of feature, burial, and catalog numbers (Black 1967:83–85).

The grid divided the site into 200 × 200 foot squares, or *divisions*. The north-south columns of the grid were identified by the letters of the alphabet, from A to Z, beginning at the western edge of the property. The east-west rows were identified with Arabic numbers, from 1 to 28, beginning at the northern edge of the property. Each division was subdivided into four 100 × 100 foot squares, or *subdivisions*, identified by the letters A to D beginning with the northeastern subdivision and proceeding counterclockwise (Black 1967:Figure 9). Excavations were identified by their division designation, such as J-12, and the subdivision identifier, yielding J-12-A, J-12-B, J-12-C, and J-12-D.

When a subdivision was excavated, it was initially divided into one hundred 10 × 10 foot *blocks*. Each block was identified by a row-and-column designation. The rows of blocks were numbered from 0 to 9, beginning with the southernmost row, and the columns were numbered from 1 to 5 left (west) or right (east) from the subdivision midline. Thus, a block three rows from the south edge of the subdivision and two columns to the left of midline would be designated *2-L-2*.

The only departures from the standard grid were the "mound" grids established for excavations of Mound A and Mound F. The 600 × 600 foot Mound A grid occupied a nine-division block centered on division Q-12 (Black 1967: Figures 11 and 12). The grid midline bisected Mound A along its long axis. The Mound F grid occupied a 220 × 200 ft block within divisions J-15, J-16, K-15, and K-16. The grid midline was established through the approximate center of the mound and was aligned to the site grid, not the mound's axes.

Black directed excavations using WPA workers from April 1939 to May 1942 and Indiana University field schools from 1945 to 1952, in 1954 and 1955, and from 1957 to 1962. Over this two-and-one-half decade period, Black's excavation practices remained consistent.

The darkly colored midden or fill zone of each 10 × 10 foot excavation block was removed in arbitrary 0.4 foot-thick levels until the light yellow-orange sterile subsoil was reached. The fill was troweled through but not screened. Artifacts and other samples were recorded by block and level. Within the midden or fill zone, masses of discolored soil, artifact concentrations, or burials were given feature or burial designations, and the locations were mapped. The contents of the feature or burial were bagged separately from the level fill and given provenance by feature or burial number and occasionally by block and level if the feature was sufficiently large. At the base of the midden or fill zone, features, stockade trenches, and burials intruding into the sterile subsoil were given feature or burial numbers, mapped, and excavated. The location of these latter features comprise the majority of those shown on the published subdivision floor maps (see, for example, Black 1967:Figures 78, 89, 130, 173, 176, 270, and 301). Their contents were treated in the same manner as those located within the midden.

The field school excavations differed from the WPA excavations primarily in scope. The large WPA crews were able to open large areas at a time. The student crews were smaller and participated in the fieldwork for a shorter period of time. Frequently a single field school investigated two or three very small areas in different parts of the site.

The 1961 field school and a project funded by the National Science Foundation from 1962 to 1964 evaluated the use of a proton magnetometer for locating archaeological features. The investigations located the stockade lines on the northern and western edges of the site and the interior stockade line northeast of Mound C (Black 1967; Black and Johnston 1962; Johnston 1964a).

In 1964 and 1965, first Black and Richard Johnston and then John Dorwin used a backhoe to excavate the subprimary mound portion of Mound F (Black 1967:271–272; Dorwin 1965; Johnston 1964b; Schurr 1989a:44–51). Tom Wolforth also used a backhoe to follow a segment of the interior stockade trench south of Mound C in 1983 (Schurr 1989a:55; Wolforth 1983).

Field schools were again held at Angel in 1976, 1977, and 1989. The artifactual remains from 1976 and 1977 have only recently been cataloged, and nothing has yet been published on the areas that were excavated. The 1989 field school investigated a portion of the Mathias Angel farmstead (Ball, Senkel, and French 1990).

Excavation Summary

In the many years of field investigations at Angel, approximately 167,000 square feet, or circa 3.8 percent of the area within the outer stockade, have been excavated. This summary of the excavations is organized in sections on the habitation areas, mounds, and stockades.

Habitation Areas

A total of 55,640 square feet of the excavated area was concentrated in the eastern village, located in the corner formed by the eastern end of the outer stockades and the terrace edge in subdivisions X-11-A, X-11-B, X-11-C, X-11-D, X-10-C, W-11-A, W-10-D, W-10-C, and W-11-B (Figure 1.3). An additional 8,820 square feet were excavated in less intensively used habitation areas elsewhere in the site.

The eastern village represents one of the highest nonmound elevations within the stockades. This height is due to the intensity of use of this part of the site. Midden depths averaged 2.0 feet and were as thick as 2.8 feet in places. Although the midden looked homogeneous, Black (1967:128) believed that it was "possible that thickness of even homogeneous debris layers might reveal subtle changes that could have taken place through time within even a single ethnic group." Even though he was never able to sort out "the problem of structure sequence" (Black 1967:148), he did note that in two subdivisions, X-11-B and X-11-C, "it appeared that a considerable number of inhumations had been made after the dwellings, represented by the multiple wall trench patterns, were no longer standing" (Black 1967:168). He added to this sense of "time elapsed" when he noted that the burials in the northern part of the eastern village excavation, in subdivision W-10-D, had been more disturbed than burials in the other parts of the same area (Black 1967:299). This greater disturbance was the result of greater house-building activity, and Black speculated that areas within the eastern village might have been used for habitation, then for burials and perhaps other purposes, and then for habitation again. Schurr's (1989a) fluorine analysis has generally confirmed this scenario.

Deposits in the other habitation areas elsewhere at Angel tended to be shallower. The midden was thinner in the western portion of the eastern village, in subdivision W-11-B (Black 1967:305). In three smaller excavations conducted between the eastern village and Mound A, subdivisions V-11-A, U-11-D/U-12-A/V-12-B, and S-11-D, deposits were shallower, and there were fewer or no rebuilding episodes (Black 1967:325–337, 393–398, 414–417).

Small portions of three other habitation areas were excavated to the north and south of Mound A and to the east of Mound E, in subdivisions Q-08-C, R-14-B, and O-08-D. Deposits were shallow in the areas south of Mound A and east of Mound E. In the case of the latter area, it seems likely that the soil was borrowed for mound building or for clearing a plaza east of Mound E. Midden deposits were somewhat thicker in the habitation area north of Mound A, and there were more overlapping and rebuilt house patterns in this small area.

Stockades

Excavators investigated a total of 34,790 square feet, which focused on the outer and interior stockade lines. The various stockade lines were traced on the eastern, northern, and western edges of Angel and through the interior west of Mound A.

Two, and possibly three, stockade lines were identified in the eastern village and the northeast stockade excavation (Figure 1.4). The northeast stockade excavation is located in subdivisions U-08-B, U-08-A, U-08-D, V-08-C, V-09-B, V-08-D, and V-09-A. "Palisade trench," "secondary trench," and "heavy trench" are Black's terms for these features (Black 1967:Figures 200 and 206), and I am using them to refer to the same features. I am using "stockade(s)" to refer unspecifically to defensive wall trench(es).

The palisade trench was probably the most recent construction; a number of burials are superimposed on it, but it is not truncated by any house wall trenches. The palisade trench was paralleled on the outside by a curtain wall, the secondary trench. The second stockade, the heavy trench, was an earlier construction than the palisade trench; a number of house wall trenches cut through the heavy trench. A third possible stockade, probably older than the heavy trench and unnamed, is suggested by the bastionlike trench in the southwest corner of W-10-C (Black 1967:Figure 301).

North of Mound J, an interior stockade branches from the course of the palisade trench. The junction, located in subdivisions S-07-C and S-08-B, of these two stockades was excavated, but it was not possible to determine the chronological relationship of the two constructions. A segment of the interior

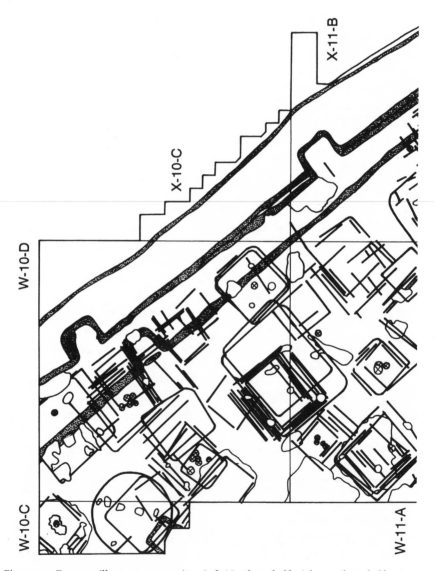

Figure 1.3. Eastern village area excavation. *Left*, Northern half; *right*, southern half.

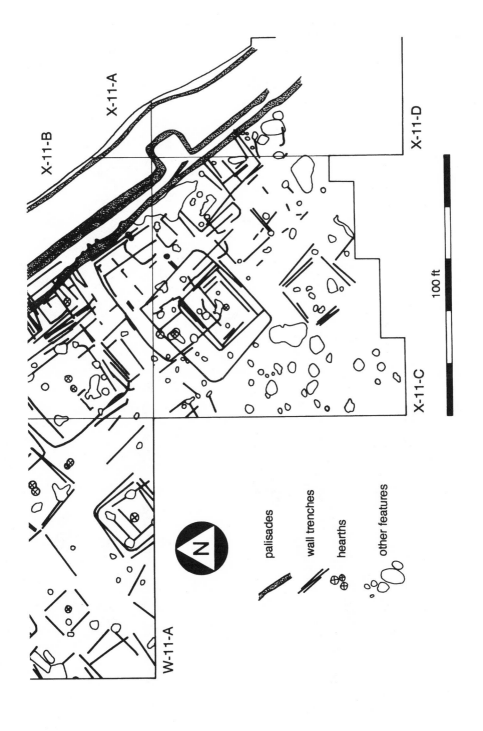

X-11-B

X-11-A

X-11-D

X-11-C

W-11-A

N

100 ft

palisades

wall trenches

hearths

other features

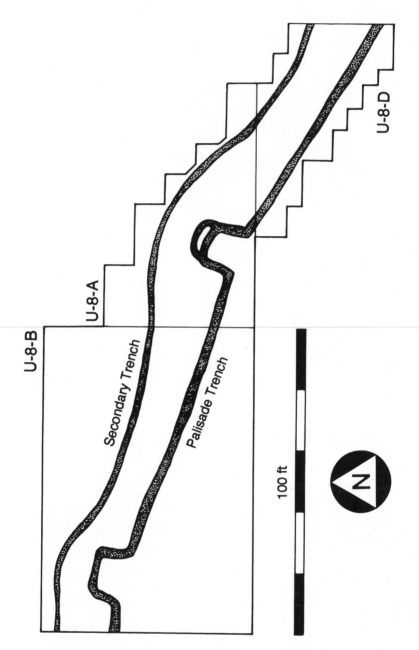

Figure 1.4. Northeastern stockade excavation. *Left*, Western part; *right*, eastern part.

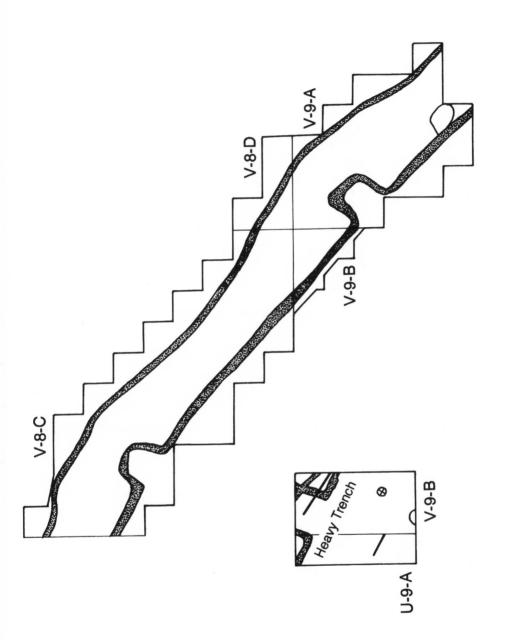

stockade also had a parallel secondary trench. The interior stockade extends to Mound C and then continues south for approximately 300 feet, where it turns south-southeast (Wolforth 1983).

A single outer stockade line, presumably the palisade trench, was traced west of the palisade trench–interior stockade trench junction for more than 1000 feet. There was no evidence of the heavy trench in this area. Two backhoe trenches excavated west of Mound C, in subdivisions K-10-A/L-10-B and K-11-B/K-11-A, uncovered two stockade trenches; they are presumably the palisade trench and the heavy trench. One of these trenches was located in backhoe trenches excavated northwest of Mound F at the southwestern corner of the site in subdivisions J-14-B and H-20-A. A limited search for a stockade along the river edge of the site, east of Mound A in subdivision T-13-C, produced no indications of its existence.

Mounds

Excavators investigated a total of 55,080 square feet, which focused on mound and mound-related areas on Mound A, Mound F, Mound I, and Mound K. All of the excavations were limited tests, except for the complete excavation of Mound F.

The Mound F excavation (Figure 1.5) documented three or possibly four episodes of mound-and-structure construction, as well as earlier, special-purpose premound structures on the old ground surface. The excavations of Mound I, located in adjacent subdivisions O-13-D and P-13-C (Figure 1.6) and Mound K, located in P-15-A, suggested that both had been built over older structures. Mound I may have been surmounted by a circular structure. Excavations on a low eastern ramp of Mound A, in adjacent subdivisions R-12-A and R-11-D, uncovered a possible charnel structure (Black 1967:377–385; Schurr 1987). A limited test of the upper level of Mound A uncovered a double row of postholes (Black 1967:Figure 385), indicating that a large building stood on top of the mound.

Taken together, the excavations suggest that Angel had a complex occupation history. Parts of the interior were occupied so intensely or for so long that almost three feet of midden built up. Other habitation areas were occupied intermittently. In yet other habitation areas, the lack of midden is deceiving. Superimposed wall trenches hint that aboriginal earthmoving activities removed the midden.

The presence of two or three stockade lines around the perimeter argue that defense of the town was an important, protracted issue. The significance of the interior stockade is uncertain; the site may have grown, or contracted, or been segregated in some way.

Excavations of the mounds, especially Mound A and Mound F, confirm that

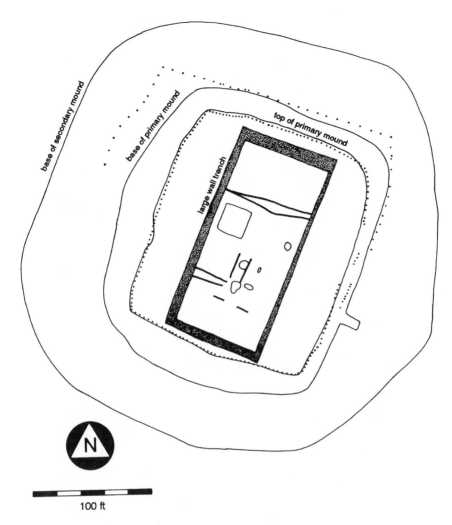

Figure 1.5. Mound F excavation.

mounds functioned at Angel in the same way that they did at other Mississippian mound centers: they were the platforms for important buildings.

Angel Phase

Black (1967:19–20) was well aware that Angel did not exist in splendid isolation on the southwestern Indiana-northwestern Kentucky segment of the Ohio River: "The existence of many small Middle Mississippian sites within a radius of several miles of Angel is known. . . . Providing these are contempo-

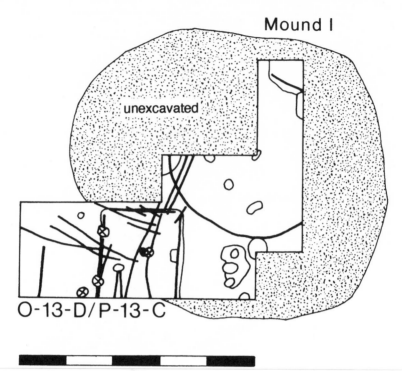

Mound I

unexcavated

O-13-D/P-13-C

50 ft

Figure 1.6. Mound I (O-13-D/P-13-C) excavation.

rary, and many of these surely must be, then Angel was a center—or capital—
for a community of sites involving a rather large area and considerable total
population" (Black 1967:546).

Surveys in the 1940s and 1950s in Vanderburgh, Warrick, Posey, Spencer,
Perry, and Gibson Counties (Adams 1949; Curry 1954; Dragoo 1955; Kellar 1956,
1958) documented the distribution of prehistoric sites with shell-tempered pottery. From the 1960s onward, more site data were collected as a result of federal
projects (Green 1972a; Hoffman 1966) and smaller, problem-oriented surveys
(Burt et al. 1989; GBL n.d.).

In the 1970s, Marjory Honerkamp (1975; Power 1976) defined the "Angel
phase." Known Mississippian sites were assigned to the phase if their shell-tempered pottery assemblages were similar to that of Angel. Sites fitting this criterion are distributed along an approximately 120-river-mile-long segment of

the Ohio River Valley from the mouth of the Anderson River to just beyond the mouth of the Wabash River and then up the Wabash Valley about twenty miles to the vicinity of present-day New Harmony (Figure 1.7). Sites probably extended some distance up the Green River Valley as well. Angel, at the mouth of the Green River, is located at the approximate center of this distribution.

In the late 1970s Thomas Green and Cheryl Munson (Green 1977; Green and Munson 1978) proposed a settlement pattern for the Angel phase. It is composed of a five-tier hierarchy of site classes, with the town of Angel at its apex. Other site classes include, in order of diminishing size and density of occupation debris, small villages (0.6–2.5 acres), hamlets (0.6–2.5 acres), farmsteads (<0.6 acres) and camps (<0.6 acres). The majority of Angel phase sites are located on the floodplains and terrace edges of the Ohio River valley.

Excavations have been conducted at three small Angel phase sites. Ellerbusch (12Vg56), an upland hamlet one and one-half miles northwest of Angel (Green 1977) yielded the remains of four houses. Southwind (12Po265), a six-acre village located on the edge of the high terrace about fifty river miles downstream from Angel (Munson 1994) produced the remains of at least ninety-four houses, fifty-six of which could have been occupied simultaneously. The houses were laid out around a central circular plaza, and the site was enclosed by a rectangular bastioned stockade. Most recently, portions of two houses were excavated at the Stephen-Steinkamp site (12Po33), a multicomponent Angel phase hamlet located about forty river miles southwest of Angel (Hilgeman 1989; Hilgeman and Schurr 1987).

The Angel phase is the middle of three defined Late Prehistoric phases in the region. The earliest of these is the Emergent Mississippian Yankeetown phase, A.D. 750 to 1000. The Yankeetown artifact assemblage includes a number of Mississippian forms and elements. Pottery vessels are grog-tempered, and vessel forms include globular jars with a baglike profile, hemispherical bowls, and pans. The distinctive Yankeetown incised, stamped, and filleted decorations are quite different from later lower Ohio Valley Mississippian pottery decorations. Triangular projectile points are among the more common chipped stone tools. The presence of chipped stone hoes, another Mississippian artifact form, and charred maize remains suggest that Yankeetown people were the first intensive maize horticulturalists in this segment of the lower Ohio Valley. Yankeetown sites are distributed along a 140-river-mile stretch of the Ohio Valley from the mouth of the Anderson River to the mouth of the Saline River in southeastern Illinois, up the Wabash Valley to the mouth of the White River, and up the Green Valley (Redmond 1990:159, Figure 4-2). The proposed settlement pattern includes four site classes: villages (3.2–4.4 acres), hamlets (1.0–2.7 acres), farmsteads (<0.7 acres), and camps (<0.7 acres).

The Terminal Mississippian Caborn-Welborn phase, A.D. 1400 to 1700, postdates the Angel phase (Green and Munson 1978, Pollack 1998, Pollack and

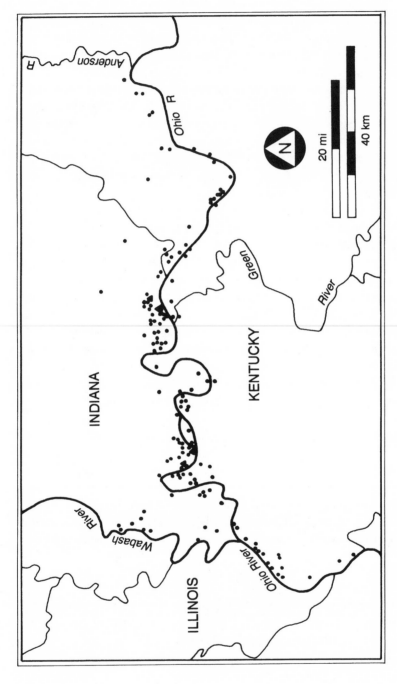

Figure 1.7. Angel phase site distribution on the Ohio River. The large triangle just upstream from the mouth of the Green River marks the location of Angel. The smaller triangles mark the locations of, from east to west, Ellerbusch (12W56), Stephan-Steinkamp (12Po33), and Southwind (12Po265).

Munson 1998). The shell-tempered pottery assemblage is marked by broad-line incised, trailed, and punctated triangular decorations on the upper shoulders of standard Mississippian globular jars. The dominance of incised decorations and the rarity or absence of red-slipped and negative painted decorations typical of the Angel pottery assemblage makes the Caborn-Welborn assemblage distinctive. The presence of historic trade goods on some Caborn-Welborn sites indicates that the phase endures into the protohistoric era. Caborn-Welborn sites are distributed along a less than fifty-river-mile stretch of the Ohio Valley from near the Vanderburgh County–Posey County line in southwestern Indiana to the mouth of the Saline River in southeastern Illinois. The proposed settlement pattern includes five site classes: large villages (7–35 acres), small villages (3.3–7 acres), hamlets (0.6–2.5 acres), farmsteads (0.6–1.2 acres), and blufftop cemeteries.

Dating

Over the years it has been necessary to estimate when Angel was occupied. Many such estimates have been used formally or casually. Some estimates place the beginning of the Mississippian occupation as early as A.D. 1000; others place the final abandonment as late as A.D. 1600. The imprecision of these boundaries is due to two facts. First, there was not a relative artifact chronology—pottery or otherwise—that could be cross-dated by comparison to better-dated chronologies developed in adjacent regions. Second, there were few radiocarbon assays on samples from Angel. Prior to this research, eleven radiocarbon samples from Angel had been assayed, and only six or seven seemed reasonable for a Mississippian occupation (see Appendix B). Three of the seven are from Mound F, and the other four are from habitation areas in the eastern village and north of Mound A (this area is in subdivision Q-08-C). They range from the late A.D. 1200s to about A.D. 1500.

An additional ten radiocarbon samples and two thermoluminescence samples from the three excavated Angel phase sites have been assayed, and five or six have been considered acceptable (see Appendix B). The latter dates range from A.D. 1000 to the mid-A.D. 1300s. This range overlaps with the range of dates from the Angel site.

2 Pottery Studies in Mississippian Archaeology

The manufacture of shell-tempered pottery in the Southeast was described in the early historic period by Dumont:

> The industry of these Indian girls and women is admirable. I have already reported elsewhere with what skill, with their fingers alone and without a potter's wheel they make all sorts of pottery.
>
> After having gathered the earth suitable for this kind of work, and having well cleansed it, they take shells which they grind and reduce to a very fine powder; they mix this very fine dust with the earth which they have provided, and, moistened the whole with a little water, they knead it with the hands and feet, forming a dough of which they make rolls 6 or 7 feet long and of whatever thickness is desired. Should they wish to fashion a dish or a vessel, they take one of these rolls and, holding down one end with the thumb of the left hand they turn it around with admirable swiftness and dexterity, describing a spiral; from time to time they dip their fingers in water, which they are always careful to have near them, and with the right hand they smooth the inside and outside of the vessel they intend to form, which without this care, would be undulated.
>
> In this manner they make all sorts of utensils of earth, dishes, plates, pans, pots, and pitchers, some of which contain 40 or 50 pints. The baking of this pottery does not cause them much trouble. After having dried it in the shade they build a great fire, and when they think they have enough coals they clear a place in the middle where they arrange the vessels and cover them with the coals. It is thus that they give them the baking which is necessary. After this they can be placed on the fire and have as much firmness as ours. Their strength can only be attributed to the mixture which the women make of the powdered shell with the clay (Dumont in Swanton 1946:550).

Pottery has long been one of archaeology's important tools in chronology building, not just in the Southeast or in Mississippian research, but in the case of any prehistoric society that made pots. With few exceptions, pottery sherds comprise the most numerous class of artifacts from a pottery-making society. The many uses people have found for pots, the numerous shapes in which they have been made, and the variety of decorations that were applied to their surfaces make pottery a sensitive medium for tracing both stylistic changes through time and cultural relationships through space. To use an example very relevant here, Fay-Cooper Cole et al. (1951:229) grouped the lower Ohio Valley Mississippian towns of Angel, Kincaid, Tolu, and Wickliffe into the "Kincaid focus." This was a shorthand way of saying that, because their pottery assemblages were stylistically similar, the occupations of all of these sites were roughly contemporaneous and that the peoples living in the sites were culturally closely related.

In the last two decades, however, Southeastern and Mississippian pottery studies have changed their focus as the discipline has changed its focus (Gibson 1993:29, 33). First, pottery typological and chronological studies have shifted from being an end in themselves to being the means to an end. In other words, although most scholars agree that a concern with chronology continues (Emerson and Lewis 1991:ix; Gibson 1993; Milner 1990:27; Watson 1990), the further refining of pottery chronologies should be done to further other research goals. Chronologies, after all, are just the first steps in "doing archaeology" (Thomas 1989:143–144).

The second major change in Mississippian studies is that pottery analysis is addressing new questions—compositional, technological, functional, and stylistic (Gibson 1993:33–34)—in addition to the usual classificatory and chronological ones. The earliest compositional studies, the thin-section analyses conducted by Porter and colleagues (1964a, 1964b, 1966, 1971; Bareis and Porter 1965; Porter and Szuter 1978), focused on cultural-historical issues. The microscopic examination of paste and temper was used to check the macroscopic classification of sherds and to identify nonlocal vessels. However, more recent compositional studies (Cordell 1993; Fischbeck et al. 1990) have as stated goals the investigation of resource use and exchange patterns.

Technological studies have generated much needed information on the manufacture of Mississippian pottery (Gibson 1993:33–34). Million (1975a, 1975b, 1976) and van der Leeuw (1981) have described the ways in which pots were formed. Stimmel et al. (1982) illustrated how sodium chloride improves the workability of some clays and corrects some of the disadvantages of mussel shell temper. Steponaitis (1983, 1984) and Bronitsky and Hamer (1986) investigated the technological significance—resistance to mechanical and thermal stresses—of coarse versus fine shell tempering.

A number of studies have looked at the function of Mississippian pots (Gibson 1993:34). Sears (1973) and Childress (1992) considered the ceremonial versus utilitarian dichotomy in Mississippian pottery assemblages. Smith (1986:54–56) noted that a number of innovations in pottery technology are associated with the cultivation, storage, processing, and preparation of maize. The shift to shell tempering resulted in pastes that allowed the manufacture of larger, stronger globular jars used for cooking and storing. Large, hooded bottles were made for storing seed stock, and Wickliffe funnels and large, fabric-impressed salt pans were used in part for the extraction of salt or lime used in the preparation of maize dishes (Smith 1986:54–56). Hally (1983a) and Pauketat (1987) described relatively complete household assemblages, and Hally (1983b, 1984, 1986) investigated vessel function from the perspectives of vessel morphology, use alterations of the vessel surfaces, and records of aboriginal Southeastern food habits.

Other recent studies have used the make-up of pottery assemblages to address sociocultural issues (Gibson 1993:34–35). Shapiro (1984) looked at social group size and location permanence using the relative frequencies and sizes of storage and serving pieces as measures. Pauketat (1989) attempted to model the relative durations of sites using the amount of pottery refuse as a measure of time elapsed. Blitz (1993) found contrasts in mound and village pottery refuse and evaluated assumptions about elite versus commoner storage and feasting activities.

Stylistic studies have also undergone a change. Interest in the decorations on Mississippian pots may be dated conveniently to Waring and Holder's (1945) article titled "A Prehistoric Ceremonial Complex in the Southeastern United States." They noted that the complex of motifs that occurred on Mississippian pottery and ceremonial objects was widespread over the Southeast. This complex of motifs and objects was termed the "Southeastern Ceremonial Complex," among other things. The Southeastern Ceremonial Complex (SCC) continues to be thought of as related to the social, religious, and political systems of Mississippian societies. From the early days of the formulation of the Southeastern Ceremonial Complex, it was recognized that a limited number of the motifs, specifically the cross-in-circle and suncircle, were common on the painted pottery from Angel and Kincaid (Ford and Willey 1941:358).

More recent studies of Mississippian pottery decorations have moved beyond the rather static viewpoint of the Southeastern Ceremonial Complex (Gibson 1993:34–35). Griffith (1981) described the design structure of Ramey Incised jars from an art historical perspective, and Hardin (1981, 1984) used art historical techniques to detect the products of individual pottery artists in the Moundville Engraved jars. Emerson (1989) and Pauketat and Emerson (1991) characterized the Ramey Incised jars as "utilitarian ritual ware" (Emerson 1989:65) used in elite-sponsored rituals. In similar studies, Hilgeman (1991; Chapter 5, this volume) and Kelly (1991) described the design theme of Angel Negative Painted, O'Byam Incised, and Well Incised plates and argued that they were also ritual serving vessels.

Pottery Classification and Chronology

In spite of the many significant issues that studies of Mississippian pottery have addressed in recent years, Vaillant's comment that "the backbone of most New World chronologies is variation in pottery types" (Vaillant 1930:9) is as true today as it was seventy years ago. Mississippian pottery assemblages exhibit a greater variety of vessel forms, sizes, secondary features, and surface treatments or decorations than do earlier Woodland pottery assemblages. These attributes, singly and in combination, change through time. Once the pattern of stylistic change has been recognized, a relative pottery chronology created, and points in the resulting order anchored by radiocarbon and other absolute dates, sites, and portions of sites, may be ordered from earlier to later on the basis of their pottery assemblages.

At the time of his death, Black (1967) had completed the bulk of the two-volume work *Angel Site: An Archaeological, Historical, and Ethnological Study,* but he had neither established the chronological relationships of the various parts of the site nor had he completely described the material culture (Honer-kamp 1975:iv). The former fact should not be taken to suggest that Black was unaware of the need for chronology building. In Chapter 1 I noted that he outlined a reasonable scenario for the multiple uses of the eastern village area, contemplated the possibility that considerable time was represented by the eastern village deposits, and suggested that the key to dating occupations might lay in those deposits. The latter point—that he had not completely described the material culture—was the result of the fact that he died while in the process of tabulating the pottery assemblage.

Portions of the pottery assemblage were analyzed in a piecemeal fashion. During Black's lifetime, Hilda Curry wrote a master's thesis on the negative painted pottery and later published this work (Curry 1950). Carol Rachlin (1954) described the fabric-impressed pottery. After Black's death, James Kellar (1967) wrote an overview of the artifact assemblage for inclusion in the site report. He was under pressure to complete his summary so that Black's monograph could be promptly published, and his chapter, like Curry's and Rachlin's studies, was primarily descriptive.

The formal pottery classification presented later in this volume and upon which the chronology is based is a combination of typological and attribute approaches. Late Prehistoric Southeastern pottery classifications traditionally have used the "type-variety" system (Gifford 1960; Phillips 1958, 1970; Smith et al. 1960; Wheat et al. 1958). It is an extension of the older type system (binomial nomenclature) used in the Southeast (Phillips, Ford, and Griffin 1951:61–66).

The history of the type-variety system has been reviewed recently by Dunnell (1986) and Gibson (1993). Both agree that the purpose of the system has always been the creation of pottery categories that aid in the establishment of temporal and cultural relationships among prehistoric societies, and as long as its application had adhered to this purpose it has worked well. Dunnell and Gibson also agree that the type-variety system may not be suitable for analyses that are not primarily cultural-historical in intent.

Types are the broader, higher-level categories, and each type includes one or more narrowly defined varieties. Mississippian shell-tempered pottery types are defined and sorted on the basis of three attributes: surface finish (smoothed versus polished finish), temper size (coarse versus fine shell temper), and decorative technique (mode of execution and overall theme), "criteria that can be identified on sherds of average size" (Phillips 1970:26). Types are not restricted in their temporal or spatial distributions. However, division of types into varieties should "reflect specific areal or temporal variations in the norm of the type" and "can be formulated for the investigation of particular problems" (Phillips 1970:25). Varieties are therefore defined to reflect the distinctiveness of the local assemblage, and they often represent variations in the design theme of the type. As Maher (1989:132) notes, varieties are "inherently experimental" and may be "added or dropped as they prove useful in understanding the culture-history of a particular area." The varieties represent the potential flexibility within the type-variety system.

The type-variety system has been little utilized in pottery studies conducted in the lower Ohio Valley. Orr's (1951) classification of the Kincaid pottery, Kellar's (1967) discussion of the Angel pottery, and Clay's (1963) study of the Mississippian pottery assemblages in the lower Tennessee-Cumberland Valleys were completed before the publication of Phillips's (1970) seminal lower Mississippi Valley typology. In recent articles based on his original analysis, Clay (1979, 1984) has adopted the type-variety system, and scholars working on smaller assemblages from the lower Tennessee-Cumberland region (Kreisa 1993; Pollack and Railey 1987; Wolforth 1987) have organized their pottery classifications around the units of the type-variety system. The Kincaid assemblage has not been reanalyzed since Orr's pioneering study, and more recent analyses of smaller Mississippian pottery assemblages from the vicinity of Kincaid (Riordan 1975) have made minimal use of the system. Recent pottery analyses conducted on Mississippian assemblages in the Angel vicinity (Green 1977) likewise have made little or no use of the type-variety system. Kreisa's (1991) analysis of the Andalex assemblage from the Green River valley is an exception to this pattern and does make extensive use of the type-variety system. The most extensive use of the type-variety system has been in an area at the western periphery of the lower Ohio Valley, in Wesler's analyses (1988, 1991a, 1991b, 1991c) of the Wickliffe assemblage and in Lewis and Mackin's (1984) and Lewis's (1986) Mississippian period research in the Mississippi Valley counties of western Kentucky.

The definitions of the types used in this analysis and discussed in Chapter 3 are summarized by the dendritic key in Figure 2.1. Types are divided into one or more varieties, which are not included in the key. In the classification that follows, type and varieties that have been previously defined are used whenever appropriate. In a few cases, new varieties are proposed to point out local variations in the norm of the types, and in a very few cases varieties are elevated to type status.

The type-variety system makes use of variations in only three sets of attributes—surface finish, temper, and decoration—in the definition of its units. However, archaeologists (Phillips 1970; Rouse 1960; Steponaitis 1983) have noted that other attributes also have cultural-historical significance. These singular attributes have been termed *modes,* and their occurrences usually cross the types and varieties. For my purposes, modes include secondary shape features, effigy features, and handle forms and decorations.

Angel Site Collections

In spite of the fact that the earlier portions of the artifact collections and excavation documents from Angel are more than fifty years old, they are in excellent condition. Prior to his death, Black curated the collection and documentation at Angel. After his death and construction of the Glenn A. Black Laboratory of Archaeology at Indiana University, the materials were moved to Bloomington, where they are now curated. The artifactual materials are intact, and the records are complete.

The composition of the Angel artifact assemblage is summarized in Table 2.1. Pottery sherds and vessels, the focus of this study, number more than 1.8 million pieces and make up almost 70 percent of the items that have been catalogued. The other material classes are small only in comparison to the pottery assemblage. In their own rights, they are large, well-documented assemblages and constitute some of the largest Mississippian assemblages of their kind. I hope that the existence of a chronology for Angel will encourage their continued study.

The majority of the pottery sherds, more than 98 percent, are plain, fabric-impressed, or cord-marked rim and body sherds. The remaining 21,453 sherds and vessels, the majority of the decorated pieces, are described in the next three chapters and were used to create the pottery chronology presented in the final chapter.

The analytical unit in this study is the sherd. A sherd may be a pot fragment smaller than a postage stamp, or it may be a whole or reconstructed pot. Comparisons between Mississippian pottery assemblages are usually made in terms of percentages based on the counts of sherds. Sherd counts are just that, the number of pieces assigned to a category or type. They are not estimators of numbers of whole vessels. Furthermore, it is difficult to estimate the number of vessels represented by a count of sherds because there is no simple relation between the size or shape of a vessel and the number of sherds into which it breaks. The problem is compounded in the case of a Mississippian household vessel assemblage (Hally 1983a; Pauketat 1987) that contains fragments of ves-

Table 2.1 Angel Artifact Assemblage n=2,622,737	
class	**count**
pottery sherds and vessels	1,822,583
daub	40,259
other ceramic	15,233
chipped stone (tools+debris)	21,681
ground stone (tools+debris)	3,138
bone and shell tools	2,166
ornaments (various materials)	12,087
rock	132,869
faunal specimens	561,078
botanical specimens	2,510
exotic rocks, minerals, and fossils	766
various sample (soil, etc)	191
historic/modern materials	6,050
other/miscellaneous	2,126

sels of numerous sizes and shapes. In consequence, in only a few cases did I try to estimate the minimum number of vessels represented by a count.

Sample

Given the size of the Angel assemblage, I had to make a number of compromises to complete this study in a timely fashion. A total of 22,383 sherds and vessels were analyzed in the course of this study, and 21,453 are described in the next three chapters. The sample represents slightly more than 1 percent of the more than 1.8 million pottery pieces that were recovered during excavations at Angel (Kellar 1967:463). The sample includes all known decorated or modified sherds; these are the pieces that are most frequently used to characterize a Mississippian assemblage and to create a pottery chronology. Counts of the "plain" sherds—which includes the fabric-impressed and cord-marked ones—can be obtained from the catalog and verified in most cases using the tabulation of the pottery assemblage begun by Black before his death (Kellar 1967:432).

Table 2.2 presents a summary tabulation of the total number of sherds recovered from each subdivision excavation and the number included in the sample. All areas of the site that have been excavated are represented. The majority of the sherds are from the 10.0 × 10.0 × 0.4 foot block levels, and the balance are from various kinds of features.

Data on basic vessel morphologies—shapes and sizes—are based on the characteristics of the decorated sherds, which include those that have handles, lugs, nodes, or other secondary attachments or modifications. Therefore, the data concerning shape and size are applicable directly only to the decorated or modified vessels. However, until the plain rim and body sherds are analyzed for the purpose of corroborating and amending this study, I am willing to assume that the vessels represented by the sample are representative of all vessel forms made, used, and discarded at the site. I realize, however, that the proportion of vessel forms described in this study is not representative of the different forms made, used, and discarded at the site. A number of forms, especially bowls, are probably underrepresented because they tend to be plain or have no attachments.

A unique *sherd number,* running sequentially from 1 to 22,383, permanently identifies each sherd in the sample. Observations made on each sherd are recorded in tables created within the Angel database. The entries have been checked for mistakes such as the occurrence of types or attributes that were known to not occur on certain vessel forms, pairs of attributes that should not co-occur, and measurements that seemed out of line. Also, a 1 percent sample of the sherds were selected at random, and the data entries were verified.

Classification

Each sherd is classified as completely as possible according to gross temper characteristics, vessel form, secondary modifications of the basic vessel form, and all decorations and attachments. The classification of the Angel pottery is based on earlier classifications of Mississippian pottery in the Ohio Valley and the Southeast (Clay 1963; Griffin 1949; Heimlich 1952; Lewis and Kneberg 1946; Lewis and Mackin 1984; Orr 1951; Peebles and Mann 1983; Phillips 1970; Phillips, Ford, and Griffin 1951; Steponaitis 1983; Vogel 1975; Williams 1954).

Each sherd was initially classed as having a smoothed surface and coarse particles of shell tempering, a well-smoothed to polished surface and fine particles of shell tempering, or another temper (usually grog or grit/sand or no discernable temper). The two shell-tempered categories correspond to the Mississippi and Bell wares discussed in the next chapter.

Next, each sherd was examined to determine whether it was possible to identify what kind of vessel was represented by the sherd. As appropriate, each sherd was identified as being part of a plate, bottle, bowl, or jar.

The final step in the classification process was to identify any modifications of the vessel form and any decorations. Examples of simple secondary modifi-

Table 2.2 Analytic Sample by Nature of Excavation and Subdivision		
Subdivision	Total Number in Subdivision[1]	Sample Total
EASTERN VILLAGE		
W-10-C	61,794	726
W-10-D	344,386	4315
W-11-A	345,069	3912
W-11-B	275,163	3101
X-10-C	50,248	840
X-11-A	4913	31
X-11-B	261,803	3752
X-11-C	232,119	2585
X-11-D	61,694	722
OTHER HABITATION AREAS		
N-13-D	5292	76
O-8-D	252	4
R-14-B	3257	33
S-11-D	38,758	406
U-11-D	3314	27
U-12-A	1342	19
V-11-A	8455	140
STOCKADES		
H-20-A	72	1
P-9-D	92	2

[1] This column does not sum to 1,822,583 because the subdivisions having no sherds in the sample are not included.

Q-8-D	375	10
Q-9-A	715	2
U-8-A	102	1
U-8-B	1648	3
U-9-A	655	9
V-8-C	8902	70
V-8-D	585	7
V-9-A	8882	168
V-9-B	4673	40
MOUND CONTEXTS		
Mound A	1110	21
Mound F	51,062	994
O-13-D (Md I)	9184	117
P-13-C (Md I)	2872	28
P-15-A (Md K)	6873	103
P-15-B (Md K)	13	1
R-11-D (Md A)	1072	7
R-12-A (Md A)	3004	27
OTHER CONTEXTS		
N-13-A (plaza)	152	1
T-13-C (terrace edge)	5586	51
X-7-D (third terrace)	2613	5
X-8-A (third terrace)	2659	3
Y-7-C (third terrace)	503	5
Y-8-B (third terrace)	7539	10
no information		8

cation of the basic vessel forms included scalloped lips, beaded lips, notched applique strips, and notched lips. More elaborate modifications included effigy features and closed and open handles. Decorations included incising, punctating, and painting; many of these have been given formal type names.

Most of the comparisons I make in this chapter and the next two are to other Mississippian assemblages in the lower Ohio Valley. These assemblages are stylistically the most similar to the Angel assemblage. The Kincaid assemblage is the most similar. This last conclusion is based on study of Kenneth Orr's (1951) descriptions and illustrations published in an appendix of the Kincaid report (Cole et al. 1951).

Angel Pottery Assemblage in the Lower Ohio Valley

Earlier in this chapter, I noted that because their pottery assemblages, among other things, were stylistically similar, the lower Ohio valley Mississippian towns of Kincaid, Wickliffe, Tolu, and Angel were grouped into the "Kincaid focus" (Cole et al. 1951:229). Furthermore, the stylistic similarities of the two artifact assemblages, the similar site plans, and the geographic proximity of the two large towns, Kincaid and Angel, led Muller (1986:179) to suggest that the two are the major settlements of a single polity. Whether this is the case or not (see discussion of this idea in Chapter 7), the similarities linking the two pottery assemblages are striking.

Archaeologists (Clay 1963, 1976, 1979; Riordan 1975) working in the lower Tennessee–Cumberland region, the area around and to the south of Kincaid, have divided the three- to four-century block of time represented by the "Angel phase" (*sensu* Honerkamp 1975, Power 1976) into three cultural-historical phases: Jonathan Creek (A.D. 1000/1100 to 1200), Angelly (A.D. 1200 to 1300), and Tinsley Hill (A.D. 1300 to 1450). Although the details, especially the absolute dating, have resulted in some interstate quibbling, the sequence has found general acceptance (Butler 1991, Muller 1986:180–185).

In pottery assemblages in the lower Tennessee–Cumberland, typically only 1 percent or less of the sherds are painted or incised. Painted types include Old Town Red, Angel Negative Painted, Kincaid Negative Painted, and Nashville Negative Painted. Incised types include Matthews Incised, Beckwith Incised, O'Byam Incised, and Mound Place Incised (Clay 1963:Tables 4, 7, 12, 15, 18, 21, 28; Kreisa 1991:111, Table 8-6; Pollack and Railey 1987: Tables 25 and 26; Riordan 1975:Appendix 1).

Archaeologists (Lewis and Mackin 1984; Wesler 1991a, 1991b, and 1991c) working in the Ohio-Mississippi confluence region have defined two parallel phase sequences. The Wickliffe phase sequence is defined in the same manner as the Kincaid-area phases and is used herein.

In pottery assemblages from the Wickliffe area, painted and incised sherds may represent as much as 3 to 4 percent of the total sherds (Lewis and Mackin 1984; Wesler 1991a, 1991b, and 1991c). Typical painted and incised types include those listed above for the lower Tennessee–Cumberland sites plus some incised, engraved, and painted types more typical of middle and lower Mississippi Valley pottery assemblages.

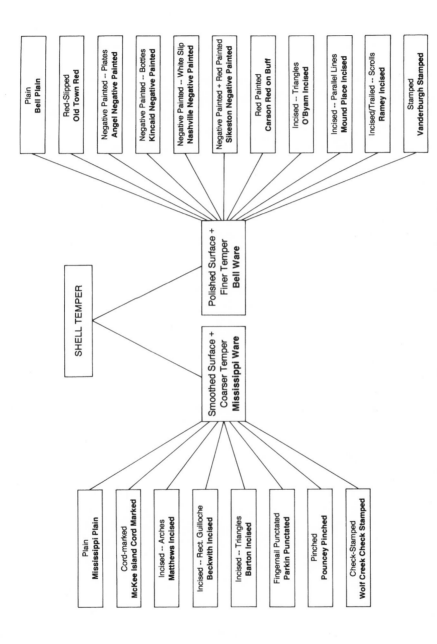

Figure 2.1. Dendritic sorting key for the defined pottery types in the Angel assemblage.

The Tolu site, the third "Kincaid focus" town, is located on a small tributary stream less than a mile from the Ohio River in Crittenden County, Kentucky (Webb and Funkhouser 1931). There has not been a formal description of pottery from Tolu, but a sketch may be drawn or constructed. Sherds of Matthews Incised, Barton Incised, and Mound Place Incised are shown in Webb and Funkhouser's excavation report (1931:Figures 62, 63, 64, 65, 67, 68, 76). Collections from Tolu at Western Kentucky University include sherds of Angel Negative Painted plates and Kincaid or Nashville Negative Painted bottles (Hilgeman 1985:Figures 4 and 6). Effigy bottle heads and bowl rim riders (Webb and Funkhouser 1931:Figure 75) and closed handles (Webb and Funkhouser 1931:Figure 76) are similar to those recovered at Kincaid (Orr 1951: Figures 5, 8, 11).

Angel, the fourth "Kincaid focus" town, has in its pottery assemblage many of the same decorative types as in the pottery assemblages of Wickliffe, Kincaid, and Tolu (Figure 2.1; Chapter 3). These include Old Town Red, Angel Negative Painted, Kincaid Negative Painted, and Nashville Negative Painted, Matthews Incised, Beckwith Incised, O'Byam Incised, and Mound Place Incised. In addition, the appearance of effigy bowl features and modifications of the closed handles (Kellar 1967:Figures 541 and 542) are similar to those from Kincaid (Orr 1951:Figures 5 and 11).

3 Decorated Plates, Bottles, Bowls, and Jars

Potters and cooks at Angel made and used five basic vessel forms—plates, bottles, bowls, jars, and pans. Mississippian plates are similar in shape to the dinner plates in the kitchen cabinets or china cupboards of many American homes. They have flattened, outflaring rims and wells. Late Prehistoric bowls also have modern counterparts and are usually hemispherical or cylindrical in shape. Plates and bowls are similar in that they provide unrestricted access to their contents. Plates are probably serving pieces, and bowls are multipurpose pots, fulfilling cooking, serving, and eating requirements.

Bottles have relatively large globular bodies and relatively narrow, tall necks. Given these proportions, pouring is the only way to access their contents. Jars also have globular bodies, but their necks are only slightly restricted when compared to the necks of bottles. As is the case with bowls, cooks can easily manipulate the contents of jars. Also like bowls, bottles and jars were probably multipurpose pots. Bottles could be storage, serving, and possibly drinking vessels, and jars could be storage, cooking, and serving vessels. Pans are extremely wide shallow bowls that could have been used for a myriad of food-preparation tasks.

The potters decorated some of the vessels they made. In the case of the pots made at Angel, they painted or incised the flat rims of plates or the exteriors of bottles with simple or elaborate designs. They also occasionally painted or incised bowls but more commonly decorated bowls with attachments to the lip area. More often, however, they embellished bowls and jars with no more than a pair of open or closed handles, but even these had decorative elements.

Over the years, archaeologists have used the presence and characteristics of such decorative elements to describe archaeological cultures, such as the "Kincaid focus" towns on the lower Ohio, and to construct pottery chronologies based on the systematic change in the decorations.

Angel potters, like many other Mississippian potters, made their pottery vessels from clay tempered with crushed mussel shell. Depending on the desired strength characteristics the potter wanted the finished vessel to exhibit, the potter ground the mussel shell into coarser or finer flakes. Archaeologists have found it useful to distinguish between the two wares—Bell and Mississippi—in both classificatory and functional studies of Mississippian pottery.

Bell And Mississippi Wares

Southeastern archaeologists divide shell-tempered pottery into coarsely and finely tempered wares: "An outstanding characteristic of shell-tempered plainware in many parts of the Southeast is that it can be separated into 'plain' and 'polished' categories that seem to be functionally significant. . . . On this basis we recognize two major types of shell-tempered plainware in the Lower Mississippi Valley, Mississippi Plain and Bell Plain. The statement has a charming simplicity and ignores the fact that sorting in specific instances is difficult if not impossible" (Phillips 1970:58–59).

The type Mississippi Plain is characterized by large particles of shell temper—generally greater than 1 to 2 millimeters in diameter—and undecorated vessel surfaces that are smoothed but not polished (Phillips 1970:130–135; see also Neeley's Ferry Plain in Phillips, Ford, and Griffin 1951:105–110). Bell Plain is characterized by small particles of shell temper—generally less than 1 millimeter in diameter—and undecorated vessel surfaces that are generally polished (Phillips 1970:58–61; see also Phillips Ford, and Griffin 1951:122–126).

It is useful to define two shell-tempered wares, Mississippi and Bell, in terms of these observed contrasts in surface finish and temper coarseness. The characterization of the wares is implicit in the descriptions of the Mississippi Plain and Bell Plain types and in the common practice among Southeastern archaeologists of describing the paste characteristics of many decorated Mississippian pottery types as resembling either a "Mississippi Plain paste" or a "Bell Plain paste" (see type descriptions in Phillips 1970). Therefore, use of the terms *Mississippi ware* for the combination of smooth surface finish and coarse shell temper and *Bell ware* for the combination of polished surface finish and fine shell temper seems merely to put appropriate labels on two existing concepts. In terms of the type-variety system, the concept of ware is a higher hierarchical level than type. Each ware—Mississippi ware or Bell ware—subsumes an undecorated type—Mississippi Plain or Bell Plain—and a number of decorated types (see again Figure 2.1).

The wares have functional significance. Plates, bottles, and some kinds of bowls tend to be made of Bell ware; jars, pans, and other kinds of bowls tend to be Mississippi ware. Steponaitis (1983:33–45) demonstrates that vessels made of Bell ware, primarily serving vessels, probably have greater resistance to breakage from mechanical stresses. Vessels made of Mississippi ware, which include many cooking vessels, have greater resistance to breakage from thermal stresses.

In his overview of the Angel pottery assemblage, Kellar (1967:468) describes two contrasting wares, and his description of them indicates that he is making a distinction between Mississippi and Bell wares. However, it is my impression, and the impression of visiting scholars (W. O. Autry, R. B. Clay, R. B. Lewis, and K. W. Wesler, personal communications), that the fine ware at Angel is typically coarser than Bell ware in the Ohio-Mississippi confluence area. Therefore, new varieties of Mississippi Plain and Bell Plain are set up here to reflect the local variation in the norm of the types. By extension, the characteristics of the new varieties define the local expression of Mississippi ware and Bell ware.

In the local variety of Bell Plain—Bell Plain, *variety Lilly*—temper particles are typically less than 2 millimeters and seem to average about 1 millimeter in diameter. Uniformly fine shell tempering, with the majority of the particles less than 0.5 millimeter in size, is rare. It is not, however, uncommon to see occasional pieces of temper greater than 2 millimeters. Vessel surfaces are well smoothed or polished.

Temper particles in the local variety of Mississippi Plain—Mississippi Plain, *variety Black*—are rarely less than 1 to 2 millimeters and are typically greater than 2 millimeters in diameter. Vessel surfaces are smoothed, but rough areas and scraping marks are common.

There is, however, considerable overlap in the local varieties of Mississippi Plain and Bell Plain, and as Phillips (1970) notes, there are often problems in sorting them consistently. In this classification, whenever there were conflicts in assigning a sherd to a particular ware because of nonagreement between surface finish and temper size, surface finish was given greater typological weight.

Table 3.1 presents a tabulation of sherds in the analytic sample assigned to each of the wares by type. Approximately three-quarters of the sherds in the sample are Bell ware, and one-quarter of the sherds in the sample are Mississippi ware.

The relative proportion of Bell ware to Mississippi ware in the analytic sample is not representative of the proportion of the two wares in the total Angel pottery assemblage. The proportion of Mississippi ware is vastly underrepresented in the sample because the majority of the decorated sherds are Bell ware. I estimate that at least 90 percent of the undecorated sherds are Mississippi ware.

Plates

Most of the decorated sherds, totaling 11,723 pieces, are from plates. The abundance of plate sherds in the sample does not correspond with the proportion of whole plates in the prehistoric household inventory. Plates were probably quite uncommon. Plates were relatively large vessels, with an average diameter of 32 centimeters. Large portions of the upper surface consisted of

Table 3.1 Summary Tabulation of Sherds in Analytic Sample by Ware and Type	
BELL WARE	
Bell Plain (includes 110 plate, 17 bottle, 1058 bowl, 107 jar, 279 effigy, 9 detached closed handle, and 637 detached open handle sherds)	2217
Old Town Red (includes 7245 plate, 1318 bottle, and 100 bowl sherds)	8663
Angel Negative Painted	3997
Carson Red on Buff (includes 81 plate and 10 bottle sherds)	91
O'Byam Incised	44
Vanderburgh Stamped	191
Kincaid Negative Painted (includes 502 bottle and 58 bowl sherds)	560
Nashville Negative Painted	3
Sikeston Negative Painted (includes 11 bottle and 2 bowl sherds)	13
Mound Place Incised	19
Ramey Incised	90
misc. incised bottle sherds	24

decorated rim. When a plate broke, it produced far more decorated, and therefore classifiable, sherds than did the typical plain jar or bowl of comparable size with one or two pairs of handles, lugs, or nodes.

Plates are similar to bowls in that both are flat, open vessels. However, a plate has a complex profile consisting of a flattened, outflaring rim and a distinct well (Figure 3.1), and a bowl has a simple curved or straight profile. When a plate is decorated, the decoration is generally restricted to the flat upper (interior) surface of the rim, beginning at the inner lip edge. Rarely is the well decorated. Because a plate tends to break along the unreinforced rim-well juncture, the more useful criterion for recognizing a sherd as a portion of a plate is the placement of the decoration.

Decorated plates are generally Bell ware; less than 1 percent are Mississippi

MISSISSIPPI WARE	

Mississippi Plain
    (includes 55 plate, 7 bottle, 226 bowl, 1941
    jar, 46 effigy, 683 detached closed handle,
    and 2134 detached open handle sherds)
	5092

McKee Island Cord Marked	5
Matthews Incised	32
Beckwith Incised	27
Barton Incised	16
Parkin Punctated	245
Pouncey Pinched	37
Wolf Creek Check Stamped	6
misc. incised jar sherds	24

ware (Table 3.1). The interior, decorated surfaces are generally polished to a soft luster. The temper of plates with a red slip tends to be somewhat coarse, varying from medium to fine, when compared with plates with an unslipped surface. It may be that this coarseness was not seen as detracting from the decoration because the red slip generally covered the temper particles on the decorated surfaces.

Plate Forms

Three plate forms, short rim plates, standard plates, and deep rim plates, occur in the Angel assemblage. These three terms are used relatively commonly in the Midsouth. Herein I am distinguishing them from each other on the bases of rim widths and vessel proportions.

SHORT RIM PLATE

Short rim plates are characterized by short, horizontal rims with a rim width (see Figure 3.2) of less than 28 millimeters. The well comprises more than two-thirds of the vessel height. In one variant (Figure 3.1, A) the rim forms a very obtuse angle with the upper wall of the well. In the other variant (Figure 3.1, B) the rim forms a sharper angle (between 130 and 90 degrees) with the upper well wall.

Other Southeastern archaeologists have considered this vessel form a bowl and refer to it as a flaring or flanged rim bowl. In this analysis, this vessel form is considered to be a plate because it represents a morphological precursor of the wider rimmed standard and deep rim plates. It also shares a number of

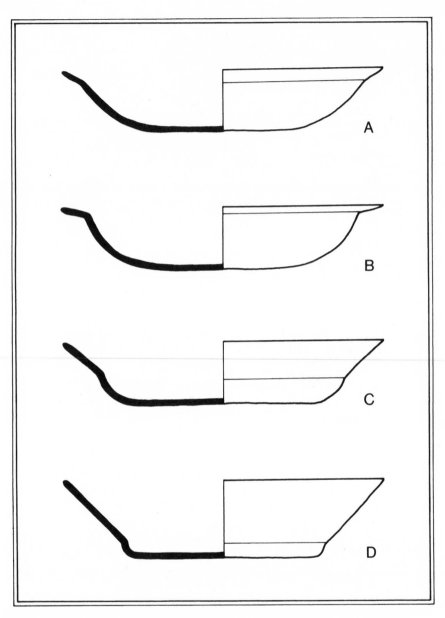

Figure 3.1. Plate forms. *A*, Short rim plate (obtusely angled variant), *B*, short rim plate (right-angled variant), *C*, standard plate, *D*, deep rim plate.

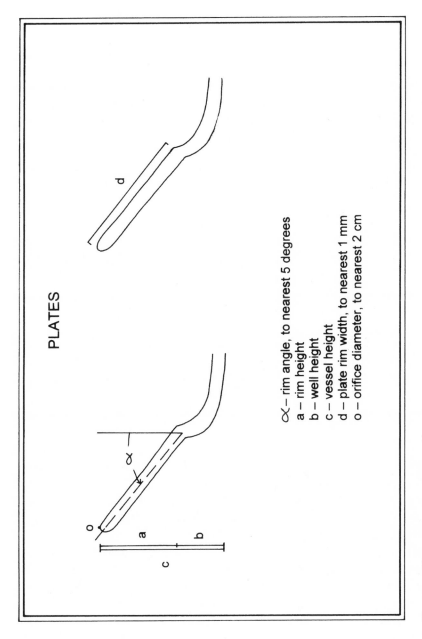

PLATES

α – rim angle, to nearest 5 degrees
a – rim height
b – well height
c – vessel height
d – plate rim width, to nearest 1 mm
o – orifice diameter, to nearest 2 cm

Figure 3.2. Plate measurement conventions.

decorative treatments with the other plate forms. The short rim plate appears to be equivalent to the *Bowl 34* category in the Kincaid assemblage (Orr 1951:Fig. 10, o).

There are 276 short rim plates in the analytic sample. Two hundred and ten are the obtusely angled variant, and sixty-six are the right-angled variant.

STANDARD PLATE

Standard plates are distinguishable from short rim plates because their vertical rim height typically comprises about half of the total vessel height (Figure 3.1, C). Standard plates have rim widths varying from 28 to 65 millimeters (Figure 3.3). The standard plates from Angel are similar to Orr's *Plate 42* (1951:Figure 9, p and q).

There are 115 standard plate rim sherds in the Angel decorated assemblage.

DEEP RIM PLATE

Deep rim plates have very wide rims and very shallow wells (Figure 3.1, D). The rim widths of deep rim plates vary from 66 to 122 millimeters (Figure 3.3), and the well height typically accounts for less than one-fourth of the total vessel height. Deep rim plates are similar to Orr's *Plate 41* and *Plate 42* (1951:Figure 9, p and q).

There are 264 deep rim plate sherds in the Angel decorated assemblage.

INDETERMINATE PLATE

The indeterminate plate category includes 11,068 plate sherds for which the specific form could not be determined with certainty. Most of these pieces are sufficiently large to indicate that they are fragments of either standard plates or deep rim plates.

DISCUSSION

It was possible to estimate the original vessel diameter, used here as a measure of vessel size, of 524 plate rim sherds by fitting the curve of the rim sherd chord to a standard diameter-measurement template (Joukowski 1980:423). The unimodal distribution of plate diameters (Figure 3.4) suggests that the prehistoric potters sought to make plates of a standard size.

The mean, standard deviation, and range of the plate diameter were calculated for the weakly angled short rim plates, right-angled short rim plates, standard plates, and deep rim plates. The mean vessel diameters by plate form are very similar (Table 3.2); the means of the most divergent classes—the obtusely and right-angled short rim plate variants—differ by less than a centimeter. The value of the Kruskal-Wallis H statistic ($H = 1.1872$) is not significant, indicating that none of the plate forms is significantly different from the others in terms of vessel size.

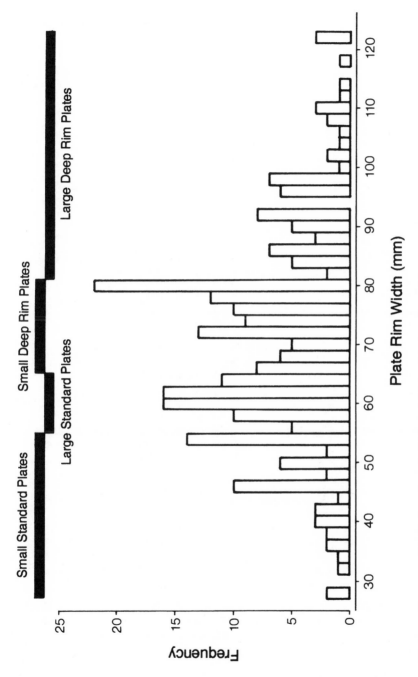

Figure 3.3. Frequency distribution of standard plate and deep rim plate rim widths.

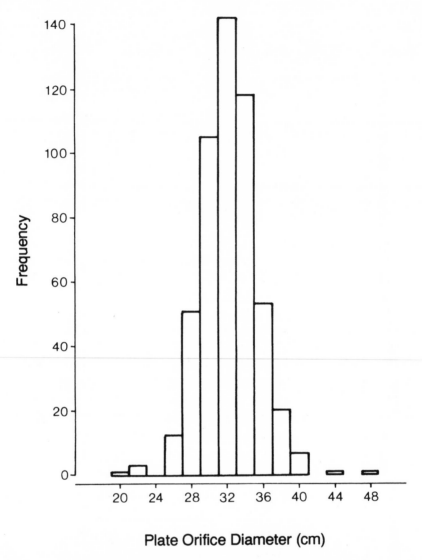

Figure 3.4. Frequency distribution of plate orifice diameters (all plate forms).

In his discussion of the Kincaid plates, Orr (1951:339) noted that the earlier plates tended to have shorter, more horizontal rims and the later plates tended to have wider, taller or more vertical rims. A similar temporal pattern of change in plate morphology, especially the increase in plate rim width, has been suggested for the adjacent lower Tennessee–Cumberland Valleys and the American Bottom–Illinois Valley (Clay 1976:47; Kelly 1984, 1991). As will be demonstrated in Chapter 6, the morphology of the Angel plates is also chronologically significant.

Table 3.2
Mean Plate Diameter by Plate Forms

PLATE FORM (count)	PLATE DIAMETER (mm)		
	mean	SD	range
obtusely-angled short rim plate (40)	31.7	6.4	16-48
right-angled short rim plate (25)	30.7	4.2	22-36
standard plate (92)	30.9	3.3	16-36
deep rim plate (127)	31.6	2.9	26-40

In order to evaluate whether the shorter standard plate rims are flatter (approaching 90 degrees) and the longer deep rim plate rims are more vertical, the standard plate and deep rim plate forms were subdivided by plate rim width (PRW) into small standard plates ($28 \leq$ PRW ≤ 55 mm), large standard plates ($56 \leq$ PRW ≤ 65 mm), small deep rim plates ($66 \leq$ PRW ≤ 81 mm), and large deep rim plates ($82 \leq$ PRW ≤ 122 mm). Means of plate rim angles for the four standard plate and deep rim plate categories are similar; the means of the most divergent classes—the small deep rim plates and the small standard plates—differ by less than 5 degrees (Table 3.3), which was the measurement interval. The value of the Kruskal-Wallis H statistic (H = 2.3463) is not significant, indicating that none of the standard plate and deep rim plate categories is significantly different from any of the other plate categories in terms of rim angle. Thus, there is no empirical support for Orr's observation concerning plate rim angles in the Angel plate assemblage.

Plate Types and Varieties

Sherds representative of five decorated types occur in the plate assemblage. There are three painted types, Old Town Red, Angel Negative Painted, and Carson Red on Buff; one incised type, O'Byam Incised; and one stamped type, Vanderburgh Stamped (Table 3.4).

OLD TOWN RED

There are at least two appropriate type names for shell-tempered, red-slipped pottery, Old Town Red and Varney Red. Phillips (1970:167) applies Varney Red exclusively to "all shell-tempered red filmed saltpan ware in the Lower Mississippi and perhaps beyond." He assigns all other shell-tempered, red-slipped pottery, regardless of whether the ware is Mississippi or Bell, to Old Town Red. In his discussion (Phillips 1970:145) of Old Town Red, he states that it is "impracticable to distinguish coarse and fine shell-tempered red filmed types

Table 3.3
Mean Plate Rim Angle
by Standard and Deep Rim Plate Categories

PLATE FORM (count)	PLATE RIM ANGLE		
	mean	SD	range
small standard plates (47) 28<=PRW<=55 mm	54.3	11.8	35-85
large standard plates (51) 56<=PRW<=65 mm	52.0	8.9	40-75
small deep rim plates (77) 66<=PRW<=81 mm	51.8	8.1	25-70
large deep rim plates (55) 82<=PRW<=122 mm	54.1	8.6	30.75

to correspond to Mississippi and Bell in the plainware category." Phillips (1970:145–147) maintains the distinction between the Mississippi and Bell wares in Old Town Red at the variety level.

Williams (1954:209), however, makes a distinction within the red-slipped category that is analogous to that between Bell Plain and Mississippi Plain. Old Town Red is restricted to pottery with a Bell Plain–like paste (Bell ware), and Varney Red includes all pottery with a Mississippi Plain–like paste (Mississippi ware).

Variety Knight. In spite of the precedent suggested by Williams, all of the red-slipped pottery from Angel is assigned to a single new, local variety of Old Town Red—Old Town Red, *variety Knight.* It includes red slipping or filming on a ware whose temper texture is medium to fine or from finer Mississippi to medium Bell ware. The slipped surface typically has been polished to a soft sheen. The slip is generally bright red or orangish red, but ranges from orange to a dark maroon or brownish red.

Red slipping is the most important decorative mode in the Angel pottery assemblage. There are 7,245 red-slipped plate sherds, primarily rim sherds and less frequently well sherds, assigned to Old Town Red, *variety Knight.* These include 17 short rim plate sherds, 23 standard plate sherds, and 107 deep rim plate sherds.

ANGEL NEGATIVE PAINTED

Negative painting is the second most important decorative mode in the Angel pottery assemblage. The "type collection" for Angel Negative Painted consists

Table 3.4
Summary Frequencies for the Decorated Plates

	Short Rim Plate (obtusely-angled)	Short Rim Plate (right-angled)	Standard Plate	Deep Rim Plate	Indeterminate Plate	Total
Types and Varieties						
Old Town Red, *var. Knight*	7	10	23	107	7098	7245
Angel Negative Painted, *var. Angel*	0	9	62	171	2690	2932
Angel Negative Painted, *var.Nurrenbern*	2	6	18	69	831	926
Angel Negative Painted, *var. Grimm*	0	0	1	28	110	139
Carson Red on Buff, *var. unsp.*	0	0	5	6	70	81
O'Byam Incised, all varieties	8	27	3	0	6	44
Vanderburgh Stamped, *var. Vand.*	182	9	0	0	0	191
Secondary Shape Features						
Symmetrical Scalloped Lip	7	6	2	3	10	28
Asymmetrical Scalloped Lip	6	1	0	3	4	14
Interior Thickening Strip	0	0	0	6	23	29
Pedestal	0	0	0	1	0	1
Modeled	0	0	0	0	2	2

of the 3,997 negative painted plate sherds from Angel. The definition of Angel Negative Painted used herein follows from Phillips, Ford, and Griffin's (1951:175–176; Table 10) characterization and is generally consistent with the definition of Kincaid Negative Painted (Cole et al. 1951:148). Chapter 5 includes a brief history of the negative painted terminology.

The designs are produced by applying a resist material, probably clay, to the inner rim surface of a red-slipped or unslipped plate. The decoration is usually restricted to the broad, flat rims; rarely are the wells decorated. Designs consist of line-filled, bounded triangular areas and Southeastern Ceremonial Complex motifs (see Chapter 5). Temper texture and surface polishing of the Angel Negative Painted plate sherds is the same as that of the Old Town Red plate sherds.

Phillips (1970:139–141) subsumed the Angel negative painted assemblage, regardless of vessel form, into Nashville Negative Painted, *variety Angel*. In this study, Phillips's *variety Angel* is restored to type status, and three new varieties are created to distinguish the presence, absence, and color of a slip.

Variety Angel. Sherds assigned to *variety Angel* have negative painted designs executed on red-slipped surfaces. This is the most common execution of the negative painted plates; there are 2,932 plate sherds, out of 3,997, that have this "black-on-red" color combination. These include 9 short rim plate sherds, 62 standard plate sherds, and 171 deep rim plate sherds.

Variety Nurrenbern. *Variety Nurrenbern* denotes all sherds that have negative painting on an unslipped or, less frequently, a white- to buff-slipped vessel surface. Nine hundred and twenty-six sherds exhibit this "black-on-buff" combination. They include 8 short rim plate sherds, 18 standard plate sherds, and 69 deep rim plate sherds.

Variety Grimm. This variety is characterized by "black-on-buff" negative painted designs that have portions of the designs highlighted by addition of red slip or paint. The red emphasis is usually added to the centers of suncircles and panels of the triangular line designs. One hundred and thirty-nine sherds exhibit this combination. These include one standard plate sherd and twenty-eight deep rim plate sherds.

CARSON RED ON BUFF, VARIETY UNSPECIFIED

In contrast to the all-over slipping of Old Town Red sherds, eighty-one sherds, including five standard plate sherds and six deep rim plate sherds, exhibit designs produced by direct painting, or applying a red paint in patterns on unslipped, polished plate rims (Figure 3.5, A to C). Design elements include solid circles and parallel line segments. For the present, these sherds are assigned to Carson Red on Buff, *variety unspecified* (Phillips 1970:62–63; Phillips, Ford, and Griffin 1951:132–133), although some or all of the sherds may represent Angel

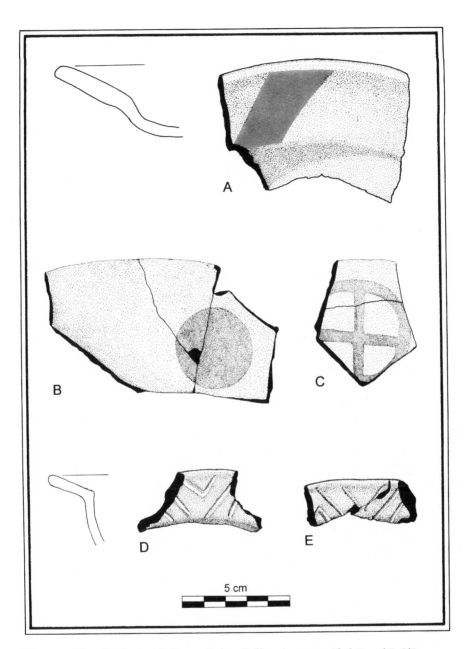

Figure 3.5. Plate sherds. *A to C,* Carson Red on Buff, *variety unspecified; D and E,* O'Byam Incised, *variety Adams.* (Catalog and sherd numbers for these and all subsequent artifacts that are illustrated are provided in Appendix D.)

Negative Painted, *variety Grimm* sherds from which the negative painted portion of the design has faded completely.

O'BYAM INCISED

O'Byam Incised is characterized by incised triangular designs on Bell ware plate rims. Forty-four sherds were sufficiently similar to the established description to warrant inclusion in the type (Figures 3.5, D and E; Figures 3.6, 3.7, and 3.8). There are pieces assignable to either of two of the defined varieties, *variety Adams* and *variety O'Byam* (Lewis and Mackin 1984:40–43; Phillips 1970:144; Williams 1954:222–23).

Variety Adams. Thirty-five short rim plate sherds have designs consisting of one or more incised or trailed line segments arranged in zigzags or chevrons (Figures 3.5, D and E; Figures 3.6, 3.7, 3.8, A and B). These are assigned to O'Byam Incised, *variety Adams.*

Variety O'Byam. Three incised standard plate sherds have incised designs consisting of line-filled triangles (Figure 3.8, C to E); these are assigned to O'Byam Incised, *variety O'Byam.*

Variety unspecified. Six incised plate rim sherds are small, and it is not possible to determine to which of the O'Byam varieties they belong.

VANDERBURGH STAMPED

This is a new type; it is created to set apart a collection of stamped short rim plates that form a chronologically important, albeit numerically minor, part of the decorated plate assemblage. The 191 Vanderburgh Stamped plates are Bell ware, but these sherds typically have finer temper textures and more carefully polished surfaces than do Old Town Red or Angel Negative Painted plate sherds. This type includes six regularly spaced stamped or notched patterns that occur on the rim surfaces of both short rim plate variants. For the present, all of this stamped material is placed in a single variety, *variety Vanderburgh.*

Variety Vanderburgh. Six different kinds of notching or stamping occur on the rims of short rim plates. The most common of these patterns consists of closely spaced, oblique cylindrical dowel impressions that begin at (Figure 3.9) or just inside the inner lip edge (Figure 3.10, A to C). The impressions that begin at the lip edge have a triangular plan, and the ones that begin inside the lip edge have a wedge-shaped plan. There are 117 sherds with cylindrical dowel impressions.

Numerically, the next most important set of impressions are a variety of cuts that are oriented vertically or obliquely to the lip line (Figure 3.11, A to G). Sixty-eight sherds have these cut patterns.

The most uncommon stamped pattern consists of subrectangular depressions produced by using a corrugated-textured stamp or stylus (Figure 3.10, D to F). Only six sherds exhibit this bar stamped pattern.

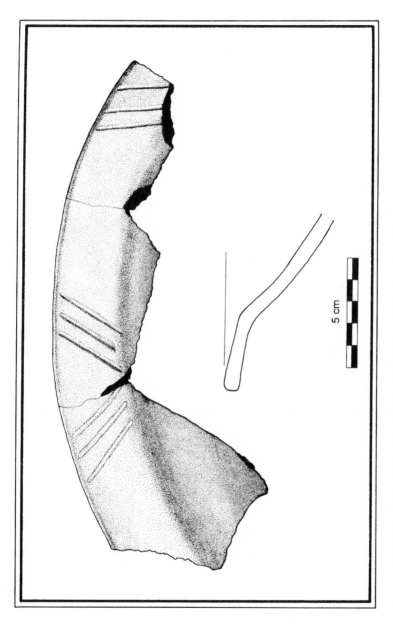

5 cm

Figure 3.6. Short rim plate (obtusely angled variant). O'Byam Incised, *variety Adams*.

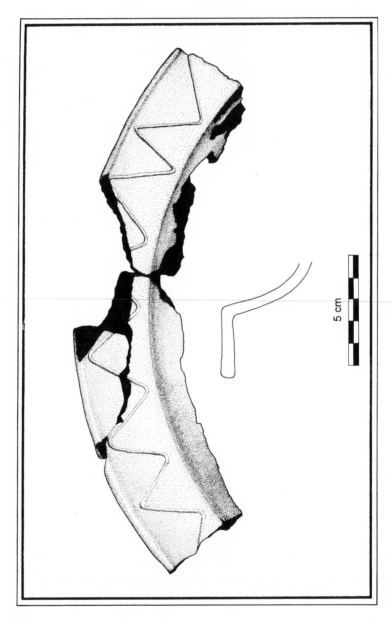

5 cm

Figure 3-7. Short rim plate (right-angled variant). O'Byam Incised, *variety Adams*.

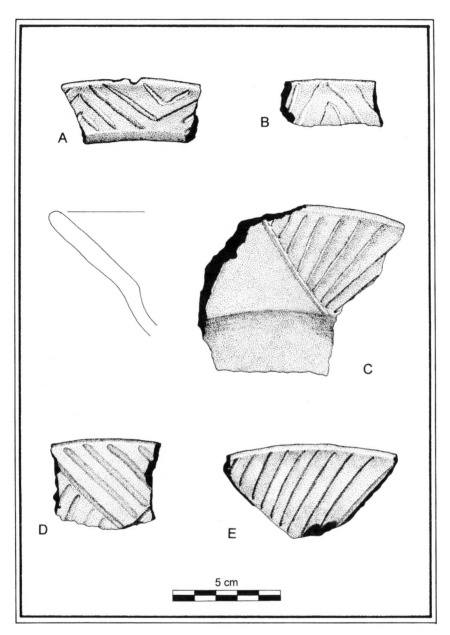

Figure 3.8. O'Byam Incised. *A and B, Variety Adams* (short rim plate); *C to E, variety O'Byam* (standard plate).

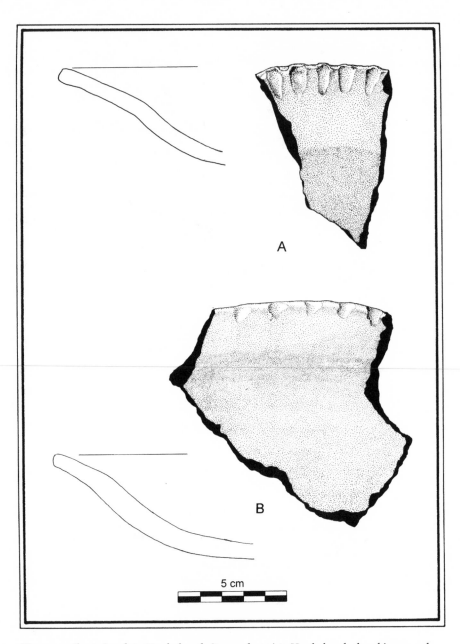

Figure 3.9. Short rim plate. Vanderburgh Stamped, *variety Vanderburgh*, dowel impressed.

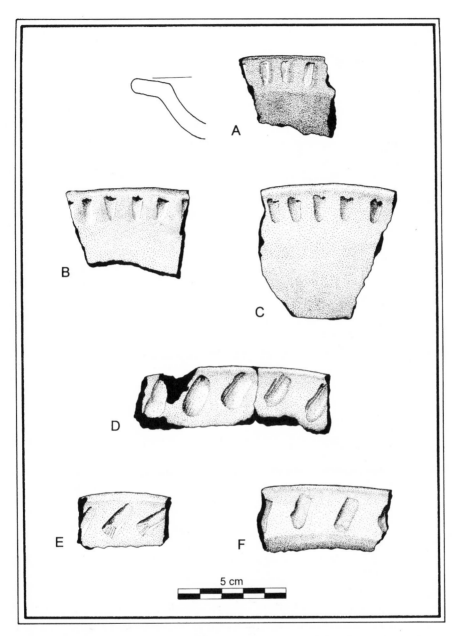

Figure 3.10. Short rim plate. Vanderburgh Stamped, *variety Vanderburgh*. *A to C*, Dowel impressed, *D to F*, rectilinear bar stamped.

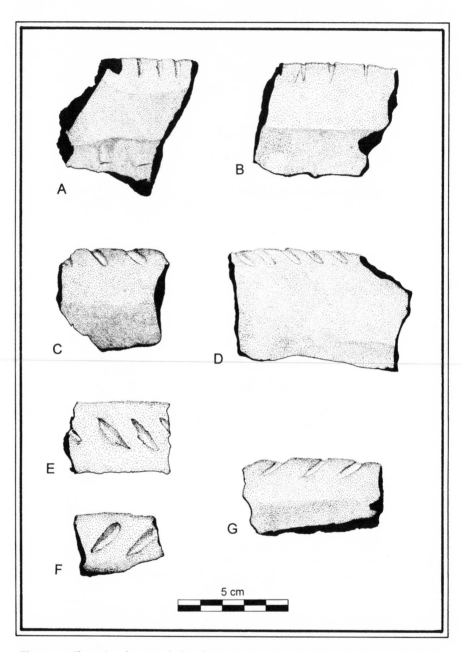

Figure 3.11. Short rim plate. Vanderburgh Stamped, *variety Vanderburgh*. *A and B*, Vertical cut; *C and D*, oblique cut; *E to G*, slashing cut.

Plate Secondary Shape Features

Five secondary shape features—symmetrical scalloped lips, asymmetrical scalloped lips, interior thickening strips, pedestal, and modeling—modify the basic plate morphology without radically altering it. All are rare (Table 3.4).

SYMMETRICAL SCALLOPED LIP

Symmetrical scallops of the plate lip have bilateral symmetry (Figure 3.12, A and B). This feature occurs on twenty-eight plate rim sherds, including thirteen short rim plate sherds, two standard plate sherds, and three deep rim plate sherds. Four sherds are red slipped, two are negative painted, and one is direct painted.

ASYMMETRICAL SCALLOPED LIP

These scallops have an asymmetrical "shark's fin" appearance (Figure 3.12, C and D). Fourteen plate rim sherds, including seven short rim plate sherds and three deep rim plate sherds, exhibit this modification. Four sherds are negative painted, and one is red slipped.

INTERIOR THICKENING STRIP

These strips consist of either a flattened clay coil or a thin wedge of clay appliqued to the interior or upper plate rim surface. The top or bulbous portion of the strip is occasionally notched with a fingernail or similarly sharp tool (Figures 3.13 and 3.14, A to C). Twenty-nine plate sherds are so modified; they include six deep rim plate sherds. Four also have a scalloped lip.

MODELED

Two indeterminate plate sherds have modeled cross-in-circle motifs (Figure 3.14, D and E).

PEDESTAL

One plate is unique; this is a plain deep rim plate set on a pedestal. Four equally spaced crosses are cut out of the walls of the pedestal (Figure 3.15).

Bottles

Bottles have relatively large, flattened globular bodies and relatively slender, cylindrical necks. Because of their small mouths and large capacities, bottles must be picked up and tipped over in order to extract their contents. Like the decorated plates, the decorated bottles are predominantly Bell ware (Table 3.1). However, when compared to the same plates, the surfaces of the bottles are generally more highly polished, and the temper particles are finer.

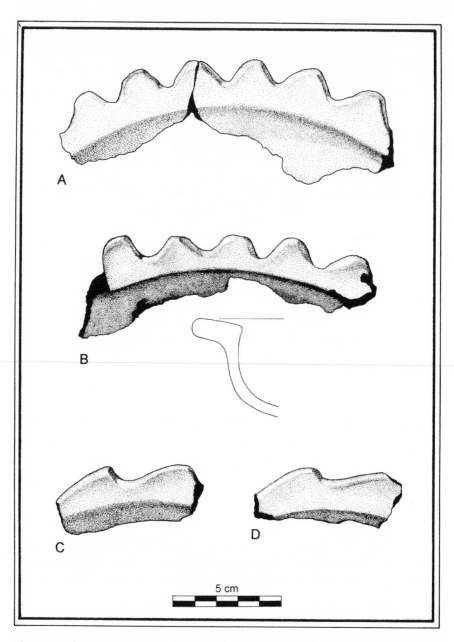

Figure 3.12. Plate secondary shape features. *A and B,* Symmetrical scalloped lips (short rim plates); *C and D,* asymmetrical scalloped lips (short rim plates).

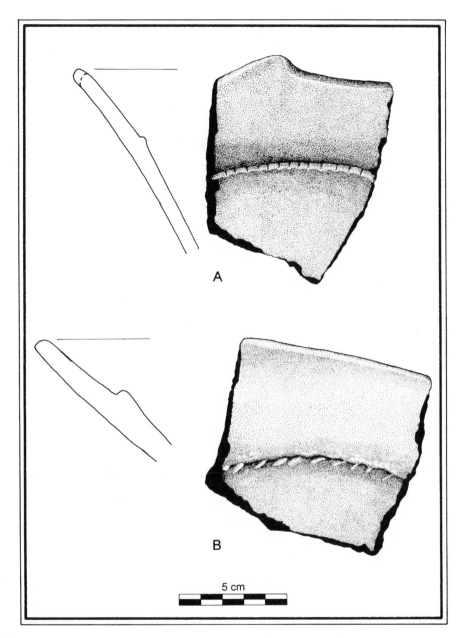

Figure 3.13. Plate secondary shape features. Interior thickening strips (deep rim plates).

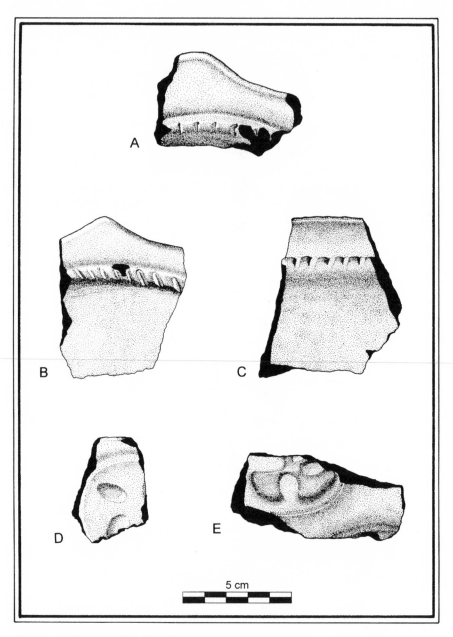

Figure 3.14. Plate secondary shape features. *A to C*, Interior thickening strips (deep rim plates); *D and E*, modeled cross-in-circle motifs.

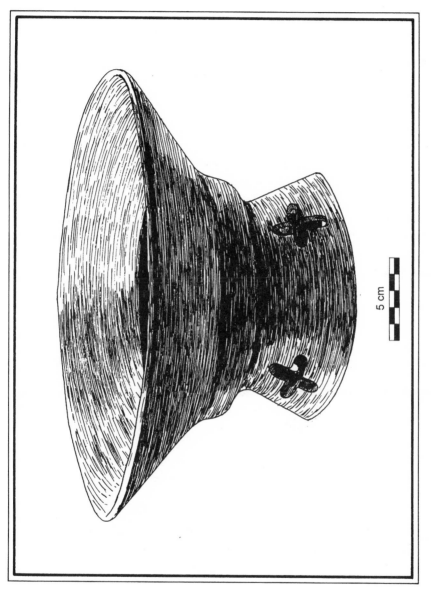

5 cm

Figure 3.15. Plate secondary shape feature. Deep rim pedestal plate. (Used by permission of the Glenn A. Black Laboratory of Archaeology, Indiana University, Bloomington.)

A few very well finished bottles may be tempered primarily with finely ground grog, which is previously fired clay. Thin-section analysis is necessary to determine whether the grog is shell-tempered.

Bottle Forms

Eight vessels, 98 rim sherds, and 1,786 body sherds (including some neck segments) are assigned to two bottle forms—narrow neck bottles and wide neck bottles—and one indeterminate category. The two identifiable forms are distinguished on the basis of neck proportions.

NARROW NECK BOTTLE

Narrow neck bottles are often referred to as "carafe-necked" bottles. This bottle form has a tall, narrow neck on a flattened, spherical body (Figure 3.16, top). The neck height comprises slightly less than one-half of the total vessel height. The neck has a slightly constricted, hourglass profile, and the lip flares upward and out. Narrow neck bottles have orifice diameters that vary from 4 to 8 centimeters, and the neck height is typically two or more times the orifice diameter (Figures 3.17 and 3.18; Table 3.5).

Three whole vessels (Figures 3.19, 3.20, 3.21) and thirty neck sherds are assigned to this bottle form. One of the whole bottles has a jar-form body, and the other two are negative painted. This bottle form is the same as Orr's *Cylindrical Necked Bottle 10* (1951:333; Figure 7).

WIDE NECK BOTTLE

These bottles have wide, short necks and large, flattened spherical bodies (Figure 3.16, bottom). The necks have straight-sided profiles, and the lips occasionally have slight flares. The bottle bodies generally comprise more than three-fourths of the total vessel height. Wide neck bottles have orifice diameters that vary from 6 to 14 centimeters, and the orifice is greater than the neck height (Figure 3.17, Table 3.5).

The wide neck bottle form is represented at Angel by four large reconstructed and partial vessels, four small whole vessels (Table 3.5), and forty-seven neck sherds. Wide neck bottles are equivalent to Orr's *Small-Mouth Jar 21* (1951:332–333; Figure 6, a and c). Similar forms from Mound Bottom in central Tennessee are called "shouldered jars" (O'Brien 1977:364–365).

INDETERMINATE BOTTLE

It was not possible to determine the form represented by the majority of the bottle sherds. Consequently, 1,804 neck and bottle body sherds are assigned to the indeterminate category. This category also includes a female effigy bottle (Figure 3.22), a red-slipped owl effigy bottle (Figure 3.23), and two modeled sherds that may be from effigy bottles.

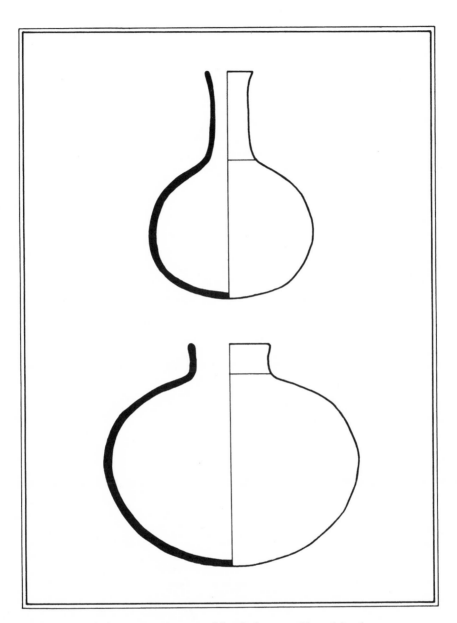

Figure 3.16. Bottle forms. *Top,* Narrow neck bottle; *bottom,* wide neck bottle.

Bottle Types and Varieties

Six decorated types are represented in the Angel bottle assemblage. In addition, there is a group of indeterminate trailed, incised, and engraved bottle sherds that do not conform to any defined type (Table 3.6).

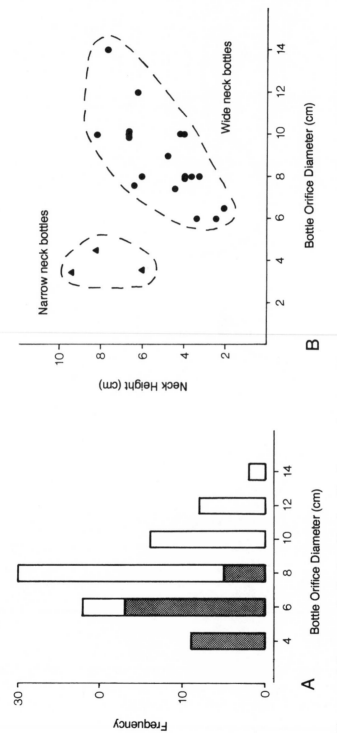

Figure 3.17. A, Frequency distribution of bottle orifice diameters (narrow neck bottles are shaded); B, scatterplot of bottle neck height by orifice diameters (triangles are narrow neck bottles).

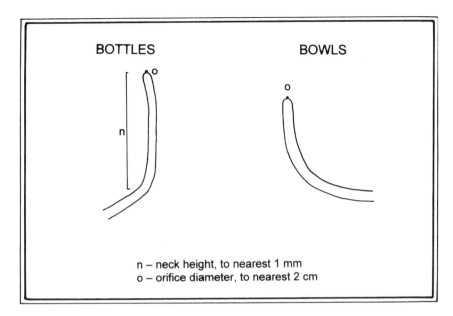

BOTTLES BOWLS

n – neck height, to nearest 1 mm
o – orifice diameter, to nearest 2 cm

Figure 3.18. Bottle and bowl measurement conventions.

OLD TOWN RED, *VARIETY KNIGHT*

The most frequently occurring bottle decoration is red slipping. An owl effigy bottle (Figure 3.23) and 1,317 bottle sherds, including 23 narrow neck and 33 wide neck bottle sherds, are red slipped. They are assigned to Old Town Red, *variety Knight.*

KINCAID NEGATIVE PAINTED

The original descriptions of Kincaid Negative Painted (Cole et al. 1951:148) or Nashville Negative Painted, *variety Kincaid* (Phillips 1970:140–141) includes negative painted designs on unslipped or red-slipped Bell ware bottles and plates. In my plate discussion, I used Angel Negative Painted exclusively for the negative painted plate sherds. Therefore, I am using Kincaid Negative Painted for the negative painted bottles, the vessel form that is common in the Kincaid negative painted assemblage. Two complete bottles and five hundred sherds are assigned to two proposed varieties of Kincaid Negative Painted. Designs are similar in content to those of the negative painted plates and include suncircle and cross-in-circle motifs and line-filled triangular areas.

Variety Kincaid. This is a new local variety proposed to denote negative painting executed on a red-slipped bottle surface (Figure 3.24, A to C). Three hundred and two sherds, including five narrow neck and six wide neck bottle sherds, are assigned to *variety Kincaid.*

Variety Massac. This a second new variety proposed to denote negative

Decorated Vessel Forms 63

Table 3.5 Dimensions of Narrow and Wide Neck Bottles				
VESSEL ID (sherdno)	ORIFICE DIAMETER (mm)	NECK HEIGHT (mm)	TOTAL VESSEL HEIGHT (cm)	MAXIMUM BODY DIAMETER (cm)
NARROW NECK BOTTLES				
X-11-C/1512 (22410)	34	94	19.2	13.7
X-11-C/1472 (22538)[1]	35	60	15.0	13.0
Y-07-C/14 (22497)[2]	45	82	22.6	16.2
LARGE WIDE NECK BOTTLES				
W-11-A/5157 (22470)	100	42	26.8	32.7
W-10-D/4958 (22464)[3]	100	40	-	-
W-10-D/14983 (22468)[3]	140	77	-	-
W-11-A/11353 (22472)[3]	90	48	-	-
SMALL WIDE NECK BOTTLES				
X-11-B/1705 (22528)	74	23	12.2	13.0
X-11-B/4857 (22489)	74	45	14.7	15.4
W-10-D/6815 (22415)	73	33	11.1	12.2
W-11-A/11350 (22427)	65	21	11.6	13.5

[1] Bottle cannot be located; measurements and observations based on full-sized drawings and photographs.

[2] Jar-form body.

[3] Neck and shoulders only.

Figure 3.19. Narrow neck bottle. Kincaid Negative Painted, *variety Massac*. (From *Angel Site: An Archaeological, Historical, and Ethnological Study* by Glenn A. Black, Figure 532, copyright 1967 by the Indiana Historical Society, Indianapolis. Used by permission.)

Figure 3.20. Narrow neck bottle. Kincaid Negative Painted, *variety Massac*. (From *Angel Site: An Archaeological, Historical, and Ethnological Study* by Glenn A. Black, Figure 544, copyright 1967 by the Indiana Historical Society, Indianapolis. Used by permission.)

painting on an unslipped or white-slipped surface. The two complete negative painted narrow neck bottles (Figures 3.19, 3.20) and 198 sherds, including an additional narrow neck bottle sherd and three wide neck bottle sherds (Figure 3.24, D; Figure 3.25) are assigned to *variety Massac*.

NASHVILLE NEGATIVE PAINTED, *VARIETY UNSPECIFIED*

The female effigy bottle is decorated with negative painted designs, now faded, on a well-polished white-slipped surface (Figure 3.22). The effigy vessel form and negative painting on a white-slipped surface are defining characteristics of Nashville Negative Painted, defined narrowly (Phillips 1970:139–141; Phillips,

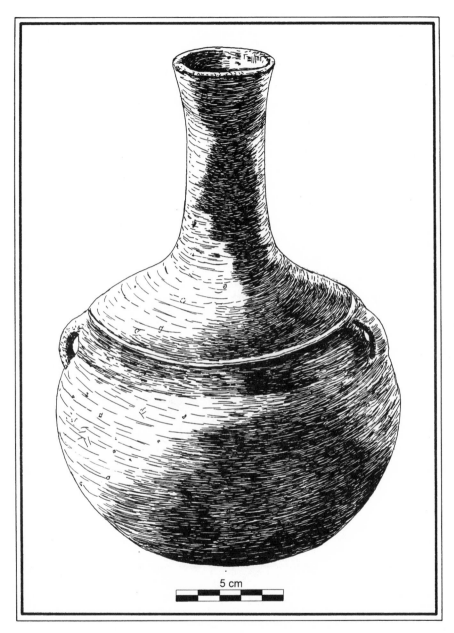

Figure 3.21. Narrow neck bottle with jar-form body. (Used by permission of the Glenn A. Black Laboratory of Archaeology, Indiana University, Bloomington.)

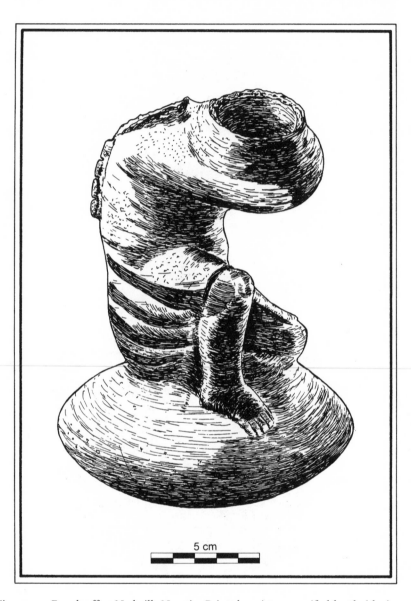

Figure 3.22. Female effigy Nashville Negative Painted, *variety unspecified,* bottle (she is holding a pot). (Used by permission of the Glenn A. Black Laboratory of Archaeology, Indiana University, Bloomington.)

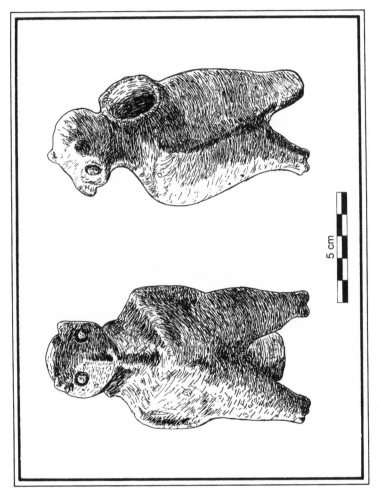

5 cm

Figure 3.23. Owl effigy Old Town Red, *variety Knight*, bottle (front and side views). (Used by permission of the Glenn A. Black Laboratory of Archaeology, Indiana University, Bloomington.)

Table 3.6 **Summary Frequencies for the Decorated Bottles**				
	Narrow Neck Bottle	Wide Neck Bottle	Indet. Bottle	Total
Types and Varieties				
Old Town Red, *var. Knight*	23	33	1262	1318
Kincaid Negative Painted, *var. Kincaid*	5	6	291	302
Kincaid Negative Painted, *var. Massac*	3	3	194	200
Nashville Negative Painted, *var. unsp.*	0	0	3	3
Sikeston Negative Painted, *var. unsp.*	0	3	8	11
Carson Red on Buff, *var. unsp.*	0	2	8	10
trailed, incised, engraved	1	2	21	24

Ford, and Griffin 1951:174–175). The effigy bottle and two modeled bottle sherds are assigned to Nashville Negative Painted, *variety unspecified.*

SIKESTON NEGATIVE PAINTED, *VARIETY UNSPECIFIED*

The combination of direct and negative painting is the defining characteristic of Sikeston Negative Painted (Phillips 1970:141; Phillips, Ford, and Griffin 1951:176–177; Williams 1954:212). Eleven sherds, including three wide neck bottles, exhibit a combination of black-on-buff negative painting and direct red painting (Figure 3.24, E and F), and these pieces are assigned to Sikeston Negative Painted, *variety unspecified.* Design elements include fragmentary suncircles and line segments.

CARSON RED ON BUFF, *VARIETY UNSPECIFIED*

Ten sherds, including two wide neck bottle sherds, have designs rendered in direct red painting on an unslipped surface (Figure 3.24, G and H). These are provisionally assigned to Carson Red on Buff, *variety unspecified* (Phillips 1970:62–63; Phillips, Ford, and Griffin 1951:132–133). As is the case with the plate sherds assigned to this type, these bottle sherds may represent Sikeston Negative Painted sherds from which the negative portions of the design have faded completely.

TRAILED, INCISED, ENGRAVED

Five bottle sherds are trailed, five are incised, and fourteen are engraved. None could be assigned to a defined type, although eight engraved sherds (Figure

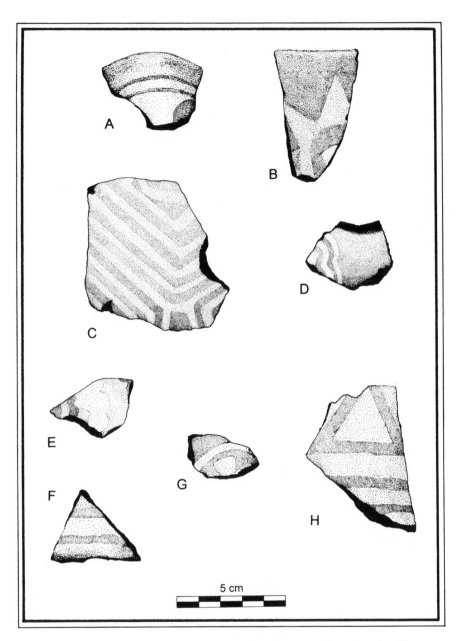

Figure 3.24. Painted bottle sherds. *A to C*, Kincaid Negative Painted, *variety Kincaid; D*, Kincaid Negative Painted, *variety Massac; E and F*, Sikeston Negative Painted, *variety unspecified; G and H*, Carson Red on Buff, *variety unspecified*.

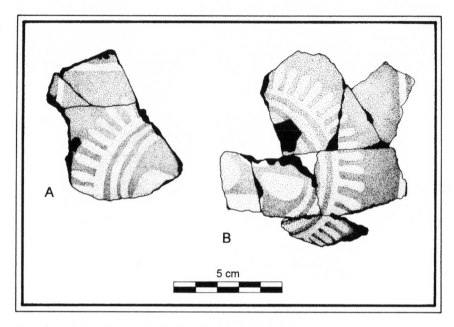

Figure 3.25. Painted bottle sherds. Kincaid Negative Painted, *variety Massac*.

3.26, E to K) have been described as Walls Engraved-like (Kellar 1967:470). Only one engraved sherd has a recognizable design element: a large (> 16 cm long) bilobed arrow on the shoulder of a wide neck bottle.

Bottle Secondary Shape Features

Three secondary shape features—stirrups, shoulders, and modeling—occur in the Angel bottle assemblage. All are extremely rare (Table 3.6).

STIRRUP

A stirrup is a semicircular clay tube that is attached at both ends to the shoulder of a bottle to form a loop. A single vertical neck is joined onto the tube at its apex. Fragments of four stirrups are recognizable. The body forms cannot be determined with certainty, but the narrow diameters of the stirrups indicate that these are probably fragments of narrow neck bottles.

SHOULDERED

Seven negative painted bottle body sherds, possibly from a single vessel, exhibit sharply angled shoulders. It is not possible to determine whether the body sherds are from a wide neck or narrow neck bottle, but the body sherds are very similar to two wide neck bottle neck sherds.

MODELED

This is a catch-all category for twelve sherds that cannot be described more precisely. Nine sherds exhibit line work consisting of narrow to broad grooves that may have been formed by drawing a finger or dowel across a still-pliable vessel wall. Two of the sherds with broad grooves are Nashville Negative Painted. In addition to the grooved sherds, there are two sherds that have strips of clay added to the exterior surfaces, and one sherd that has a thumb-sized oval dimple. The latter sherd may be from a bottle similar to one from Kincaid (Orr 1951:Figure 7, h) that has a circle of dimples around the base of the bottle neck. Some of these sherds may be fragments of effigy bottles.

Bottle Effigy Features

Two forms of effigy bottles occur in the Angel assemblage. The first includes vessels in which the whole vessel is modeled in the likeness of the subject; these are naturalistic effigy bottles. The second includes vessels in which only the neck and orifice are altered; these are the hooded or blank-face bottles. Effigy bottles of either form are extremely rare at Angel.

NATURALISTIC EFFIGY BOTTLE

Three naturalistic effigy bottles are known. One is the Nashville Negative Painted bottle depicting a human female holding a pot (Figure 3.22). The second is a Bell Plain sherd depicting the torso of a human male with hands splayed across the stomach (Figure 3.26, C). The third is an Old Town Red bottle in the form of an owl (Figure 3.23).

HOODED/BLANK-FACE EFFIGY BOTTLE

The hooded or blank-face bottle has a spherical "head" or hood with an orifice at a right angle to the vertical axis of the bottle. Portions of eight hoods occur (Figure 3.26, A and B). The otherwise featureless hoods have two cones projecting from their tops, producing a silhouette that suggests a horned or eared owl (Peterson 1980:172–173). The interior of one of the hoods is red slipped.

Bowls

Bowls are open vessels that are generally wider than they are tall. Approximately 85 percent of the decorated bowl sherds are Bell ware. This figure is deceptive because a majority of the bowls are plain, and many of the plain ones are Mississippi ware.

Bowls are morphologically similar to plates; both provide unrestricted access to their contents. However, decorated bowls tend to be smaller vessels. The

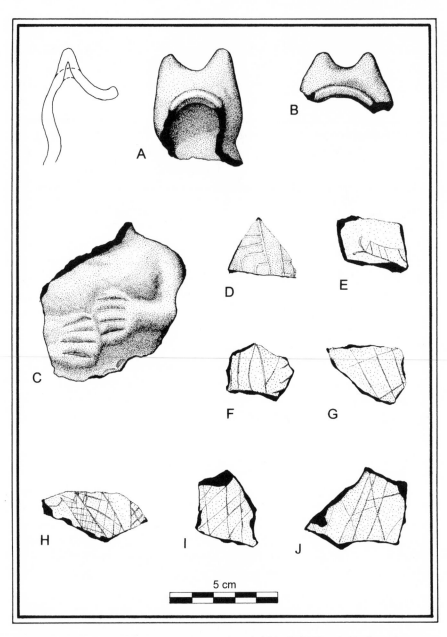

Figure 3.26. Decorated bottle sherds. *A and B,* Hooded/blank-face bottle heads; *C,* human effigy bottle torso; *D to J,* Walls Engraved-like.

mean of the orifice diameters of the complete bowls and 353 larger rim sherds is 20.4 centimeters with a standard deviation of 6.4 centimeters. Comparison of the distribution of bowl diameters (Figure 3.27; see also Figure 3.18) with the distribution of plate diameters (Figure 3.4) shows that, although the size distributions of the two vessel forms overlap, bowls and plates are distinct in terms of their typical size ranges.

Bowl Forms

Nineteen complete and reconstructed vessels, 1,174 rim sherds, 270 body sherds, and 325 effigy features are assigned to seven bowl forms and one indeterminate category.

SIMPLE BOWL

Simple bowls are those whose shape represents a segment of up to one-half of a flattened sphere (Figure 3.28, A). This is the most numerous bowl form in the sample. Ten complete vessels and 452 sherds are assigned to this category. The form is the same as Orr's (1951:344; Fig. 10b) *Hemispherical Bowl 31*.

RESTRICTED BOWL

In contrast to the simple bowl, the restricted bowl represents a segment of more than one-half of a flattened sphere (Figure 3.28, B); thus, the orifice diameter is less than the maximum vessel (body) diameter. Two complete vessels and 157 sherds are classified as restricted bowls. This form is equivalent to Orr's (1951:344; Fig. 10f) *Spheroidal Bowl 37*.

COLANDER

For the purposes of this study, the colander is considered to be a special case of the restricted bowl. It could just as easily be considered a separate vessel form. Colanders are small—about the size of a small orange—flattened spherical vessels with two equidistant 1-centimeter orifices. The body exhibits closely spaced perforations that are less than 2 millimeters in diameter (Figure 3.28, C; Figure 3.29). They appear to be the prehistoric equivalent of the modern tea infuser. Two partial vessel and 159 sherds occur in the Angel assemblage.

The colander sherds from Angel are superficially similar to Fox Farm (Fort Ancient Tradition) colander sherds (Griffin 1966:349; Plate CXVI), but the paste of the Angel sherds is much finer (Bell ware), and the surfaces are generally polished and frequently black filmed (smudged).

CYLINDRICAL BOWL

The cylindrical bowl has relatively straight, vertical walls and a rounded or flattened base. As is the case with the simple and restricted bowls, cylindrical bowls are wider than they are tall (Figure 3.28, D). Two complete vessels and fifteen

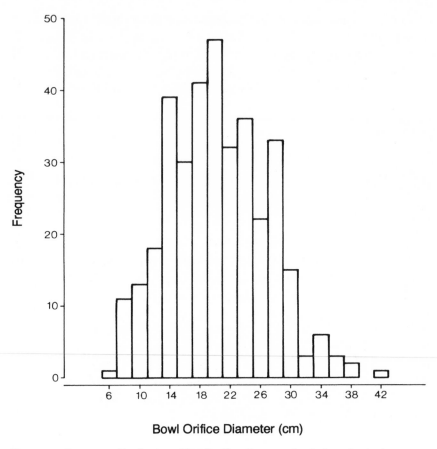

Figure 3.27. Frequency distribution of bowl orifice diameters (excludes colanders).

sherds are included in the cylindrical bowl category. This bowl form is the same as Orr's (1951:344; Fig. 10e) *Cylindrical Bowl 31b*.

BEAKER (OR BEAN POT)

The beaker is a special case of the cylindrical bowl. Beakers are typically at least as tall as they are wide and have distinctive cigar-shaped open handles (Figure 3.28, E). The form was initially recognized in the Cahokia–American Bottom area and is often referred to as a "bean pot" (Griffin 1949:57–58; Vogel 1975:106, Figures 68 and 69). Four sherds appear to be from beakers. Eighteen detached beaker handles are described in Chapter 4.

SHORT NECK BOWL

Short neck bowls have the appearance of standard jars, with constricted necks and short, outflaring rims. However, their globular bodies are very short, re-

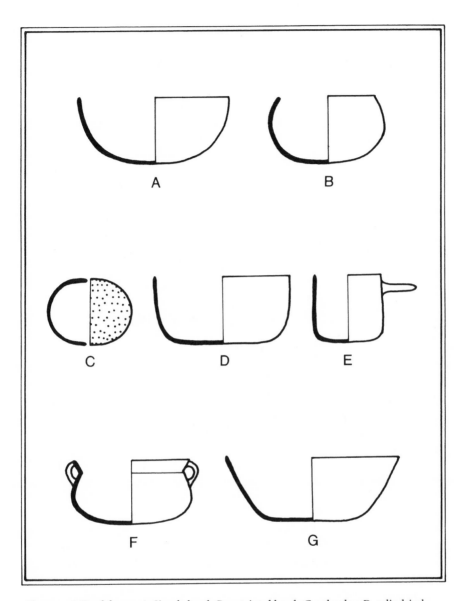

Figure 3.28. Bowl forms. *A*, Simple bowl; *B*, restricted bowl; *C*, colander; *D*, cylindrical bowl; *E*, beaker (bean pot); *F*, short neck bowl; *G*, outflaring bowl.

sulting in vessel height-to-width proportions similar to the other bowl forms (Figure 3.28, F). Two complete vessels and five sherds are included in this category. This total probably underestimates the number of short neck bowls in the sample because sherds with minimal shoulder segments would have been classed as standard jars rather than short neck bowls.

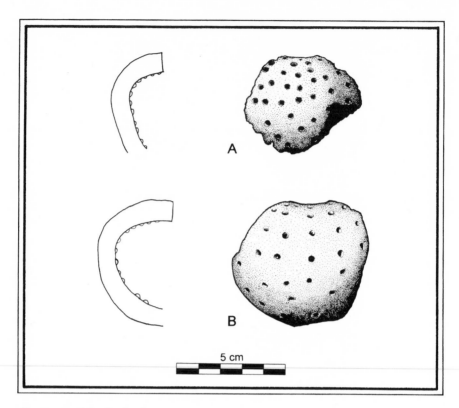

Figure 3.29. Colander sherds.

OUTFLARING BOWL

An outflaring bowl has relatively straight, outslanting, or outflaring walls (Figure 3.28, G). A sherd from an outflaring bowl resembles a sherd from a deep rim plate. An outflaring bowl is distinguished from a deep rim plate by the absence of a demarcated well and by having decorations and attachments on the lip or exterior. In the case of sherds, the placement of the decorations is the more important criterion for recognition. Two complete vessels and 230 sherds are from outflaring bowls.

INDETERMINATE BOWL

It was not possible to determine the specific bowl form represented by 421 sherds.

Bowl Types and Varieties

Four types—Old Town Red, Kincaid Negative Painted, Sikeston Negative Painted, and Mound Place Incised—are represented in the Angel bowl assemblage (Table 3.7). All are Bell ware.

Table 3.7
Summary Frequencies for the Decorated Bowls

	Simple Bowl	Restricted Bowl	Cylindrical Bowl	Beaker	Short Neck Bowl	Outflaring Bowl	Indet. Bowl	Total
Types and Varieties								
Old Town Red, *var. Knight*	11	30	4	1	0	8	46	100
Kincaid Negative Painted, *var. Kincaid*	1	13	1	1	0	0	17	33
Kincaid Negative Painted, *var. Massac*	9	4	0	0	0	0	12	25
Sikeston Negative Painted, *var. unsp.*	1	1	0	0	0	0	0	2
Mound Place Incised, *var. Mound Place*	11	0	0	0	0	0	5	16
Mound Place Incised, *var. Chickasawba*	1	0	0	0	0	1	1	3
Secondary Shape Features								
Beaded Rim	58	13	2	0	0	21	7	101
Notched Applique Strip	5	7	0	0	0	0	23	35
Scalloped Lip	17	0	0	0	0	47	16	80
Asymmetrical Knobbed Lip	0	0	0	0	0	11	0	11
Notched Lip	78	8	3	0	1	60	142	292

OLD TOWN RED, *VARIETY KNIGHT*

As is the case with the plates and bottles, red slipping is the most common bowl decoration. One hundred red-slipped bowl sherds are assigned to Old Town Red, *variety Knight*. This total includes eleven simple bowl sherds, thirty restricted bowl sherds, four cylindrical bowl sherds, one beaker sherd, eight outflaring bowl sherds, and forty-six indeterminate bowl sherds.

KINCAID NEGATIVE PAINTED

Fifty-eight bowl sherds are negative painted (Figure 3.30, B to D; Figure 3.31). They form a minor part of the negative painted assemblage at Angel. However, they represent a significant portion of the decorated bowl assemblage. Negative painted bowls are not unique to the Angel assemblage; they also occur in assemblages from the Nashville Basin, another center of negative painting.

The negative painted bowl sherds conform to the definition of Kincaid Negative Painted (Cole et al. 1951:148; Phillips 1970:140–141) with the exception of the vessel form. Because the layouts and content of the bowl designs resemble those of the bottles more than they do plates, I favor assigning the sherds to the two Kincaid Negative Painted varieties created for this analysis.

Variety Kincaid. Thirty-three bowl sherds are black-on-red negative painted. They are similar to the *variety Kincaid* bottle sherds and are assigned to that variety. The total includes thirteen restricted bowls, one simple bowl, one cylindrical bowl, one beaker, and seventeen indeterminate bowls. One restricted bowl rim sherd has attached to it the tail of a lug-and-rim beaver(?) tail effigy bowl (Figure 3.31).

Variety Massac. Twenty-five negative painted bowl sherds are black-on-buff. They are assigned to Kincaid Negative Painted, *variety Massac*. These include nine simple bowls, four restricted bowls, and twelve indeterminate bowls. Both surfaces of seven sherds are negative painted, and two sherds have red-slipped interiors.

SIKESTON NEGATIVE PAINTED, *VARIETY UNSPECIFIED*

Two negative painted bowl sherds have decorations that are black-on-buff with areas highlighted by a red paint. They are similar to the Sikeston Negative Painted bottle sherds in the collection and thus are assigned to that type. One sherd is from a simple bowl, and one is from a restricted bowl (Figure 3.30, A).

MOUND PLACE INCISED

Nineteen bowl rim sherds have two or more incised lines parallel to each other and the vessel lip. They conform to the type description of Mound Place Incised (Phillips 1970:135–136) (Figures 3.32, 3.33). There are twelve simple bowl rim sherds, one outflaring bowl, and six indeterminate bowl rim sherds.

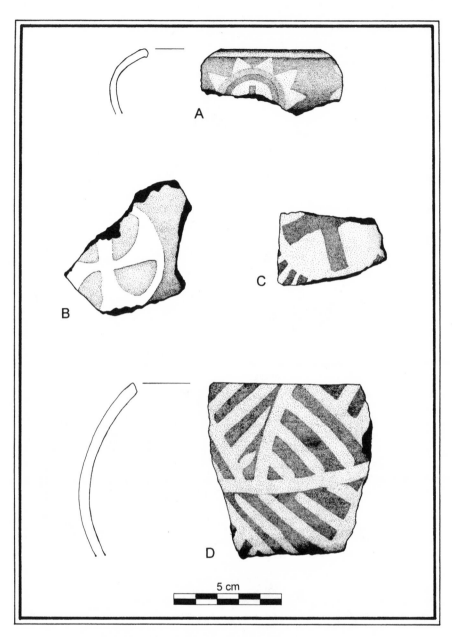

Figure 3.30. Negative painted bowl sherds. *A*, Sikeston Negative Painted, *variety unspecified; B to D*, Kincaid Negative Painted.

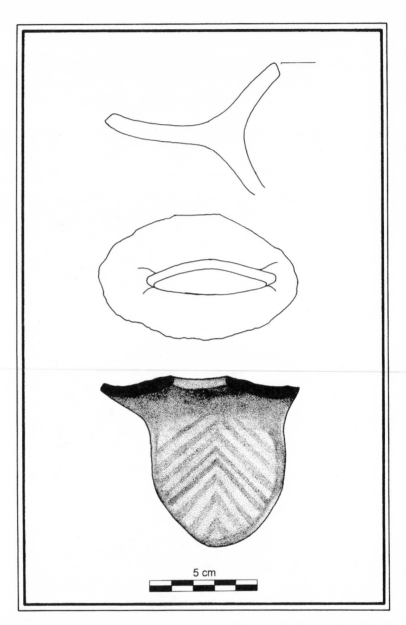

Figure 3.31. Kincaid Negative Painted, *variety Kincaid* beaver tail effigy restricted bowl.

Variety Mound Place. This variety includes all Mound Place Incised sherds that conform strictly to the type definition (Phillips 1970:135–136). Sixteen bowl sherds, which have two or more parallel incised lines, are assigned to this variety. There are eleven simple bowl rim sherds and five indeterminate bowl rim sherds.

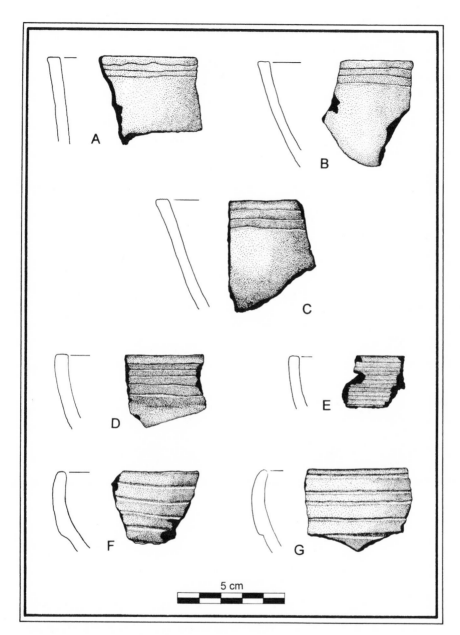

Figure 3.32. Mound Place Incised, *variety Mound Place.*

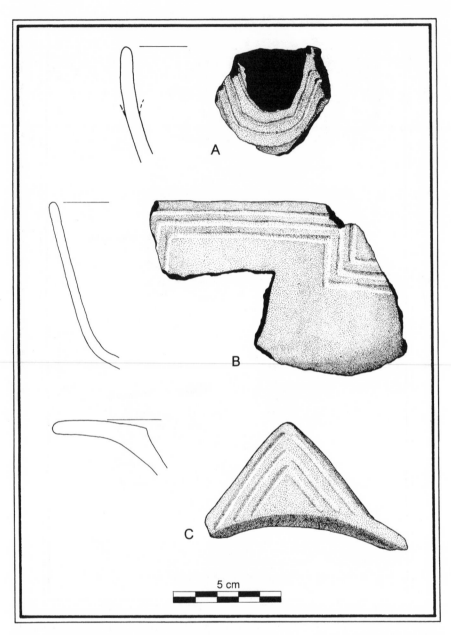

Figure 3.33. Mound Place Incised, *variety Chickasawba*.

There is, however, considerable variation in the number of lines present and in their execution. A lot of seven sherds, probably representing three vessels, has smoothed to poorly polished exterior surfaces and three sloppily incised lines (Figure 3.32, A–C). A second lot of nine sherds, representing at least five vessels, differs from the first in both surface finish and line execution. The surfaces are polished to a dull sheen, and the line work is more neatly executed, relatively deeper and wider, and more numerous than in the first group. Only one sherd in this second lot has three lines; another has a minimum of eleven (Figure 3.32, D–G).

Variety Chickasawba. Variety Chickasawba includes all Mound Place Incised sherds that have the parallel incised lines forming rectilinear or semicircular "festoons" (Phillips 1970:135–136). These festoons often encircle the base of rim-rider effigies. Three sherds in the Angel assemblage are assigned to this variety.

The three sherds are similar in surface and execution to the more poorly finished *variety Mound Place* sherds. Two sherds, a simple bowl sherd with a detached rim rider and an indeterminate bowl sherd with a rim rider, have three or four incised lines that form a semicircular festoon around the base of the rim riders (Figure 3.33, A). The third sherd is a partial outflaring bowl. Three trailed lines form rectilinear festoons on the side of the bowl. The three lines are repeated on the margins of the attached triangular lug (Figure 3.33, B and C).

Bowl Secondary Shape Features

Five secondary shape features occur on bowls—beaded rims, notched applique strips, scalloped lips, asymmetrical knobbed lips, and notched lips—and are described in this section (Table 3.7). Closed and open handles are discussed in Chapter 4.

BEADED RIM

A beaded rim consists of a continuous horizontal band of closely spaced nodes, or a strip of clay modeled into such a series, placed on the bowl exterior just below the lip (Figure 3.34). On smaller sherds, distinguishing between a beaded rim and a set of nodes (an open handle) is arbitrary; herein, most are considered sets of nodes. One hundred and one bowl sherds have beaded rims. Fifty-eight occur on simple bowls, thirteen on restricted bowls, two on cylindrical bowls, twenty-one on outflaring bowls, and seven on indeterminate bowls.

NOTCHED APPLIQUE STRIP

A notched applique strip is a strip of clay, usually triangular or semicircular in cross-section, applied to the bowl exterior just below the lip. The strip is notched with a sharp, wedge-shaped instrument (Figure 3.35, A). Thirty-five

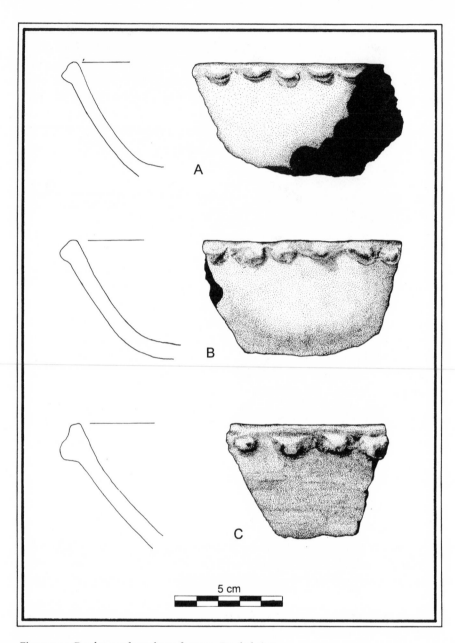

Figure 3.34. Bowl secondary shape features. Beaded rims.

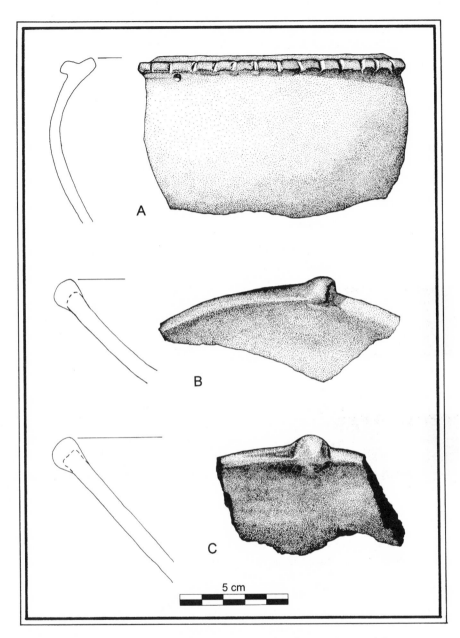

Figure 3.35. Bowl secondary shape features. *A*, Notched applique strip; *B and C*, asymmetrical knobbed lip.

rim sherds have notched applique strips. Seven occur on restricted bowls, five on simple bowls, and twenty-three on indeterminate bowls.

SCALLOPED LIP

A scalloped lip may take a number of forms. Scallops vary from triangular to semicircular in plan. The larger scallops appear to have been produced by cutting away portions of the rim, whereas the thicker scallops appear to have been formed by applying luglike additions vertically to the bowl lip. They grade into tabs, an open handle form (see Chapter 4). Eighty rim sherds have scalloped lips. Seventeen occur on simple bowls, forty-seven on outflaring bowls, and sixteen on indeterminate bowls.

ASYMMETRICAL KNOBBED LIP

This unusual lip modification consists of a node or a knob applied to the lip of a bowl. The knobs are asymmetrical in plan; one side of the knob is tapered to the line of the bowl lip, and the other is abruptly truncated (Figure 3.35, B and C). No extant pieces are sufficiently large to determine whether these knobs are part of larger structures, for example, a deeply notched lip lug or scallop. Eleven examples of asymmetrical knobbed lips are known; all occur on outflaring bowls.

NOTCHED LIP

Lip notching varies from wide pie-crust modeling to very fine notching made with a fingernail, chert flake, mussel shell, or an equally sharp edge. Finer notching is the more common condition. Two hundred and ninety-two sherds exhibit notched lips; these include 78 simple bowls, 8 restricted bowls, 1 short neck bowl, 60 outflaring bowls, 3 cylindrical bowls, and 142 indeterminate bowls.

Bowl Effigy Features

The majority of the effigy vessels and sherds recovered at Angel were portions or modifications of bowl forms. Steponaitis (1983:74–75) describes two classes of effigy bowls: the lug-and-rim effigy bowl and the structural effigy bowl. Both occur in the Angel assemblage.

The lug-and-rim form is a bowl minimally modified by the addition of two complementary appendages, usually representing the head and tail or limbs of a human or other animal, to opposite sides of the bowl. The appendages are often referred to as rim riders because their bases are welded around the bowl's lip and the appendage projects vertically or horizontally from the rim. One hundred and ninety-seven bowl sherds and detached features are assigned to this effigy class. The majority of these are heads; the plainer tails and appendages are probably included in the lugs (open handles, see Chapter 4).

The structural class form involves some modification of the vessel's walls to suggest the animal being depicted in addition to the application of modeled features. Two hundred and sixty-eight bowl sherds and detached features are assigned to this category.

Whenever possible, the animal effigy features are assigned to the general categories of human, mammal, bird, amphibian, fish, or conch/gourd. No reptilian effigies are known in the Angel effigy bowl assemblage. All of these identifications are based on similarly identified examples in drawings and photographs in many books showing prehistoric Southeastern pottery vessels. Given the variety of identifications suggested to me by friends and colleagues, they should be considered suggestions only.

HUMAN

Twenty-seven pieces are considered human effigies (Figures 3.36, 3.37). Eighteen are heads or portions of faces; the remainder appear to be arms and hands. Many heads appear to be rim riders. Approximately half of these are "rattle heads"; they are hollow and enclose small ceramic beads. Three heads still rattle. The features may be finely modeled, or they may be minimally indicated by crudely modeled noses and ears and incisions for eyes and mouths.

MAMMAL

Thirty-four pieces are considered mammals (Figures 3.31, 3.38, 3.39). Suggested identifications include dogs, deer, bears, otters, and beavers. Two-thirds seem to be rim riders, and the remainder have the heads modeled within the bowl walls.

BIRD

One hundred and fifteen effigy features appear to represent different kinds of birds. All but two are rim riders. One of the latter is a simple bowl with modeled and incised wings. Some heads are recognizable as owls and perhaps hawks (or some other raptor) (Figure 3.40), ducks (Figure 3.41), and possibly woodpeckers. However, the majority could represent any of a number of common Eastern Woodlands birds (Figures 3.42, 3.43).

Steponaitis (1983:75–76) notes that in the Moundville assemblage there are two variants of the bird head rim riders. One is a conventionalized, two-dimensional head with a "cookie-cutter" appearance, and the other has a more naturalistic appearance. At Moundville, the flat head is chronologically early, and the naturalistic head is late. Orr notes the presence of both of the variants in the Kincaid assemblage (Orr 1951:345–348; Figure 11, r to dd; Plate XXIV, A), but the temporal trend is reversed in the Kincaid assemblage.

Both the cookie-cutter and naturalistic forms are common in the Angel assemblage. The contrast is not great, however, because there are a large number of "intermediate" forms. The contrast in the Moundville and Kincaid as-

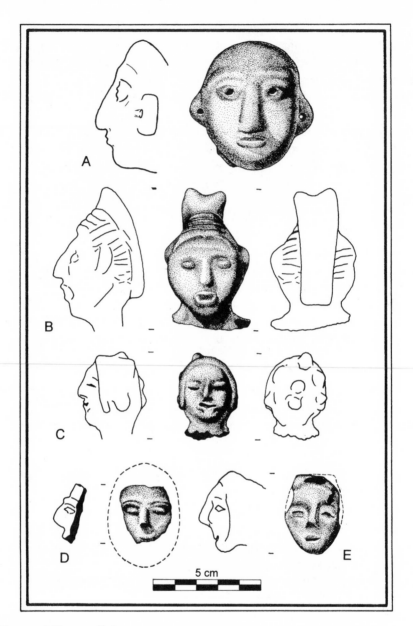

Figure 3.36. Human effigies.

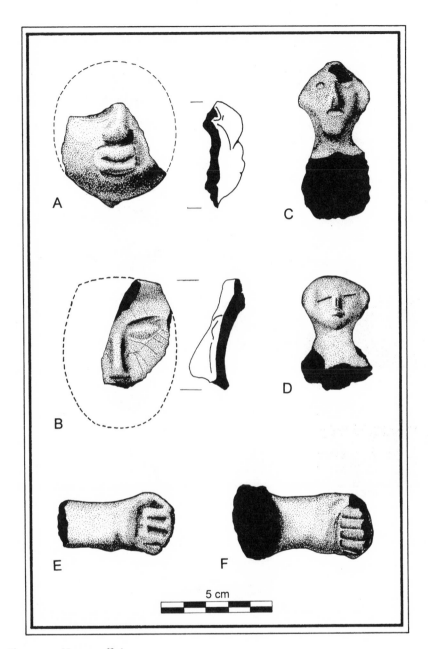

Figure 3.37. Human effigies.

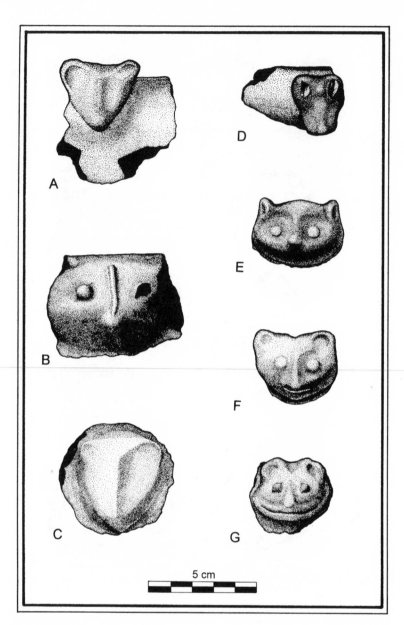

Figure 3.38. Mammal effigies.

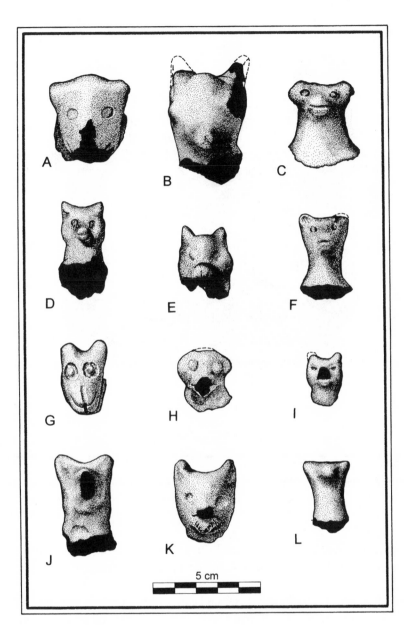

Figure 3.39. Mammal effigies.

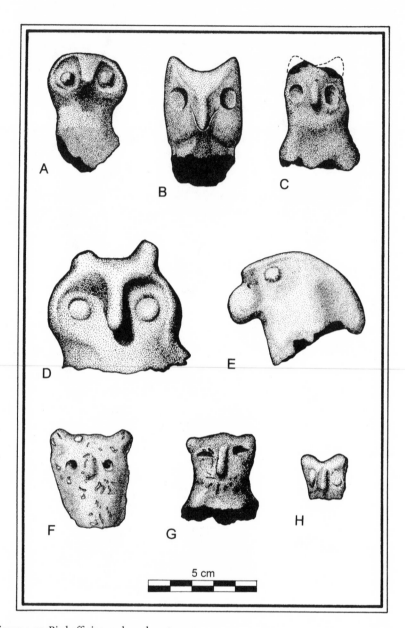

Figure 3.40. Bird effigies: owls and raptors.

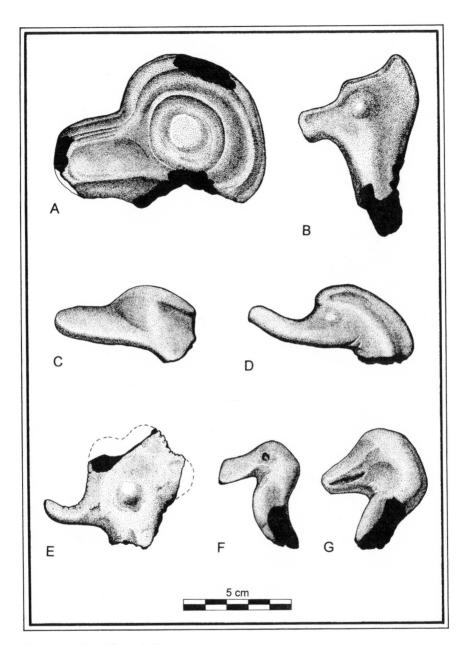

Figure 3.41. Bird effigies: ducks.

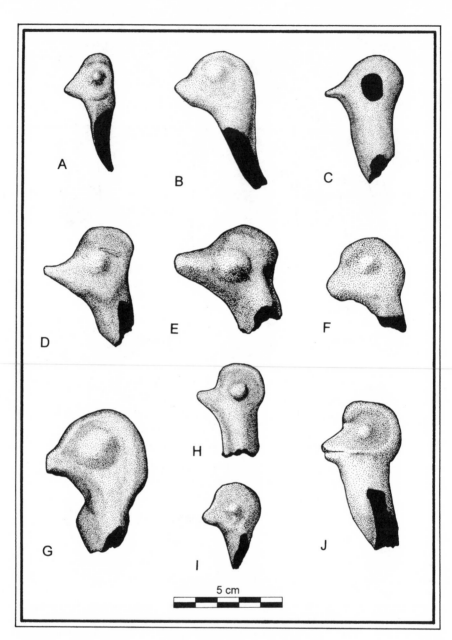

Figure 3.42. Bird effigies.

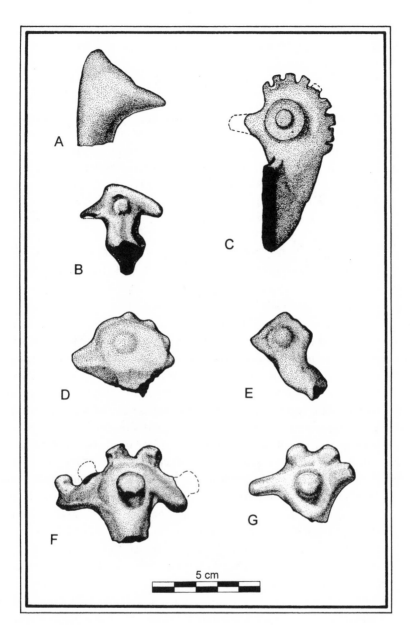

Figure 3.43. Bird effigies.

semblages may be due in large part to the smaller number of examples from each site.

AMPHIBIAN (FROG)

Six effigy features seem to represent frogs (Figure 3.44). These include two smaller heads that may be rim riders, one larger rim-rider head, one structural head, and two bowl wall segments with appliqued legs.

FISH

Two complete vessels and sixty-three effigy features represent fish effigies (Figures 3.45, 3.46). The features include eleven heads, nine tails, twelve (ventral?) fin pairs, and thirty-one single (dorsal?) fins made by incising or notching a long thin lug. The heads and tails demonstrate that fish effigy bowls grade from structural to lug-and-rim effigy forms. The larger, more elaborately modeled heads are structural forms.

CONCH/GOURD

A conch or gourd effigy bowl grades from a lug-and-rimlike form to a structural effigy form. It minimally consists of a circular arrangement of nodes, usually seven, on one side of a simple or restricted bowl. The nodes represent the shell's spire or the gourd's stem, and a spout on the opposite side represents the tip or root. Four sherds and partial vessels are relatively complete and show that the bowl walls have been modeled to suggest the shape of a conch shell cup or dipper (Figures 3.47, 3.48). The two complete vessels are both small, simple bowls and could represent either shells or gourds (Figure 3.49, A and B). Twenty-one sherds preserve the characteristic node arrangement (Figure 3.49, C and D), and eight are recognizable tip or root segments.

INDETERMINATE EFFIGY

This category includes 181 pieces that represent fragments of effigies and possible effigies.

Jars

Jars are pottery vessels that have spherical to slightly flattened spherical bodies and constricted necks. The complete and reconstructed vessels conform to Steponaitis's (1983:69) characterization that "the neck is typically less than one third of the height of the body, and the minimum diameter of the neck is no less than three-fourths of the maximum diameter of the body." About 90 percent of the jar sherds in the sample are Mississippi ware.

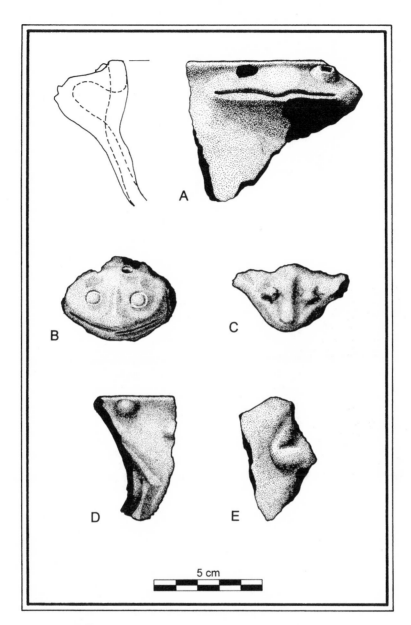

Figure 3.44. Frog effigies.

Jar Forms

Twenty-six complete or reconstructed vessels, 1,925 rim sherds, and 656 body sherds are assigned to two jar forms—standard jars and neckless jars—and one indeterminate category.

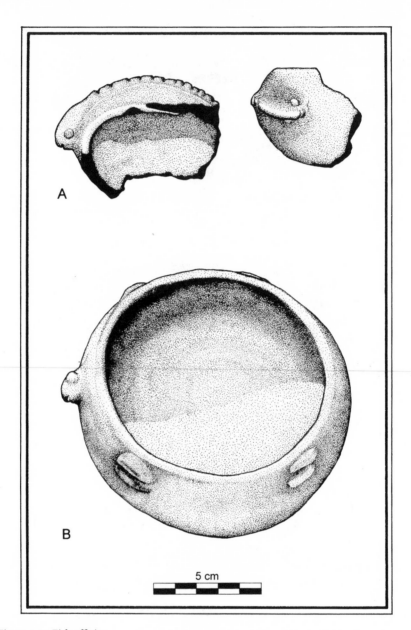

Figure 3.45. Fish effigies.

STANDARD JAR

The more common jar form in the Angel assemblage (Figure 3.50, top) is often referred to as the "standard Mississippian jar" (Phillips, Ford, and Griffin 1951:105). Above the constricted neck the rim segment is vertical or outslanting.

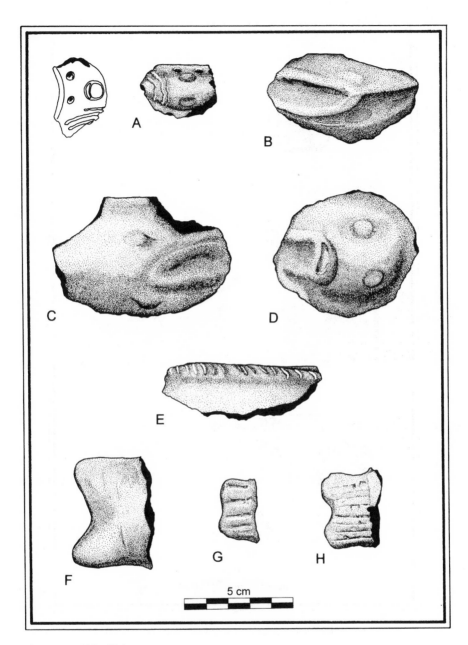

Figure 3.46. Fish effigies.

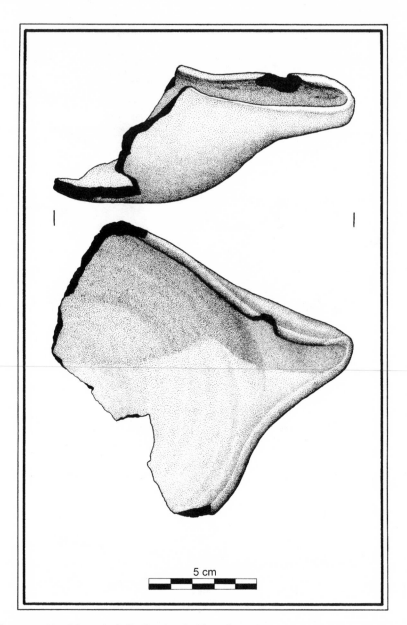

Figure 3.47. Partial conch shell effigy bowl, side and top view.

Rim angles vary from 0 (vertical) to 80 degrees with a mean of 18.3 degrees and standard deviation of 10.8 degrees (Figure 3.51; see also Figure 3.52). Twenty-six whole and reconstructed vessels, 1,559 rim sherds, and 19 body sherds are standard jars. This total represents more than 97 percent of the jar sherds for which it was possible to determine the specific form.

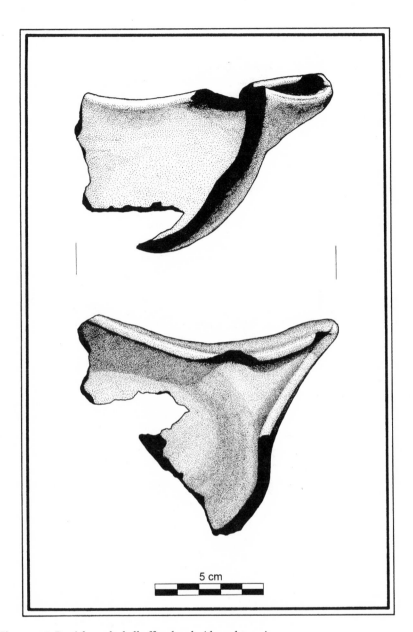

5 cm

Figure 3.48. Partial conch shell effigy bowl, side and top view.

NECKLESS JAR

Neckless jars differ from standard jars in that the maximum orifice constriction occurs at the lip (Figure 3.50, bottom). There is no neck, and the "rim" segment never reaches a point of vertical tangency. Rim angles vary from 355

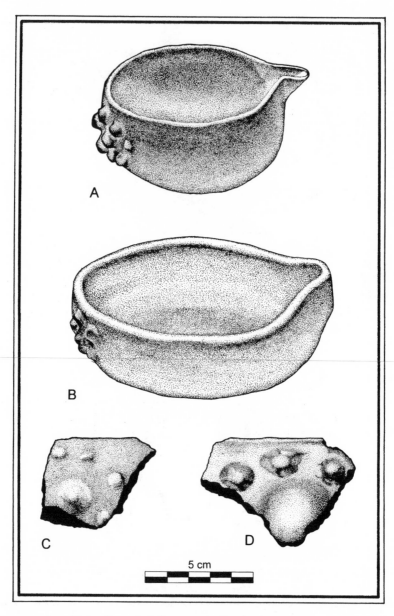

Figure 3.49. *A and B,* Small conch shell or gourd effigy bowls; *C and D,* conch shell or gourd effigy spire or tip ends.

to 340 degrees (Figure 3.51), with a mean of 352.5 degrees and standard deviation of 3.7 degrees. This jar form is rare in the Angel assemblage; forty-one rim sherds are neckless jars.

INDETERMINATE JAR

Three hundred and twenty-five rim sherds and 637 body sherds are classed as indeterminate jars.

DISCUSSION

Herein effective jar orifice diameter is used as a surrogate for jar size. In the case of the standard jar the greatest constriction occurs at the plane of the neck, and in the case of the neckless jar it occurs at the plane of the lip. Effective jar orifice diameter is measured across the most constricted part of a vessel and is calculated for standard jars by taking the sine of the jar rim angle times the rim length times 2 subtracted from the jar orifice diameter as measured at the vessel lip. The smallest jar had an effective jar orifice diameter of 6 centimeters and the largest 42 centimeters.

The distribution of effective jar orifice diameters may be partitioned into three jar size categories: small (8 to 18 cm), large (20 to 30 cm), and very large (32 to 42 cm) jars (Figure 3.53). There are 242 small jars, 221 large jars, and 64 very large jars. Hally (1986) suggests that very large jars may have been used for long-term storage, large jars used for preparing large quantities of foodstuffs, and small jars used for cooking or heating small quantities of food.

There are many jar rim sherds in the Angel assemblage that preserve too little of the arc of the orifice to estimate the original orifice size. These sherds generally contribute little to a characterization of the size distribution of a jar assemblage. However, in the case of the Angel jars, the sample of sherds for which it was possible to measure both vessel diameter and jar rim length (Figure 3.54) was large enough to demonstrate that jar rim length is a reasonably good estimator of orifice diameter.

A regression curve of jar rim length with effective jar orifice diameter (Figure 3.55) indicates a positive, though somewhat weak, relationship (r = 0.70) between these two morphological variables. The relationship is probably not strong enough to assign a specific jar rim length to a specific orifice diameter range, but appears to be sufficiently strong to assign rim sherds to small, large, and very large categories based on increasing rim lengths.

Jar Types and Varieties

Five hundred and fifty-nine jar rim and body sherds are assigned to nine decorated types, two categories, and one miscellaneous incised lot. All are shell-tempered Mississippi or Bell ware (Table 3.1), except the Yankeetown decorated

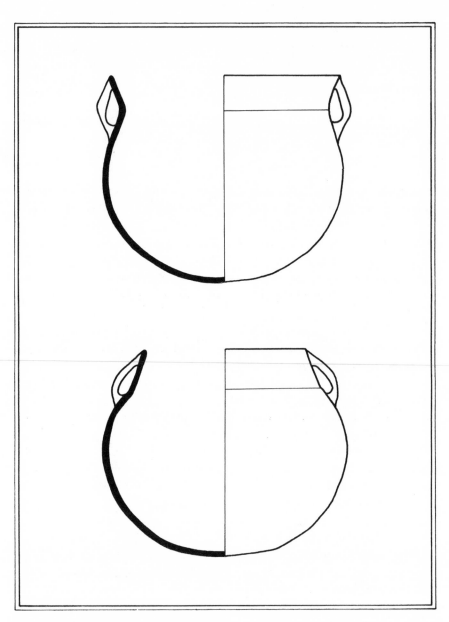

Figure 3.50. Jar forms. *Top*, Standard jar; *bottom*, neckless jar.

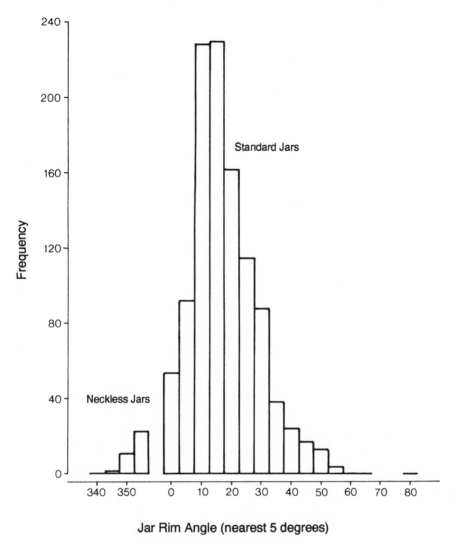

Figure 3.51. Frequency distribution of jar rim angles.

sherds, which are grog tempered, and the Cobb Island Complicated Stamped
sherds, which are sand or grit tempered.

RAMEY INCISED

Ninety rim and body sherds preserved sections of trailed curvilinear "scroll"
patterns (Figure 3.56). The ware of these jar sherds is Bell, and the two rim
sherds indicate that the trailed designs occur on the shoulders of short-
rimmed, angled-shouldered jars (Figure 3.56, A and B), similar to Morehead
phase (A.D. 1200–1275, Hall 1991:9, Figure 1.3) Powell jars (Holley 1989). These

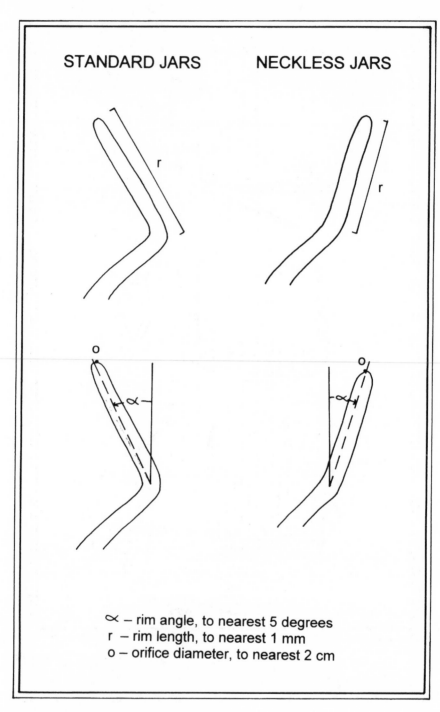

STANDARD JARS   NECKLESS JARS

∝ – rim angle, to nearest 5 degrees
r – rim length, to nearest 1 mm
o – orifice diameter, to nearest 2 cm

Figure 3.52. Jar measurement conventions.

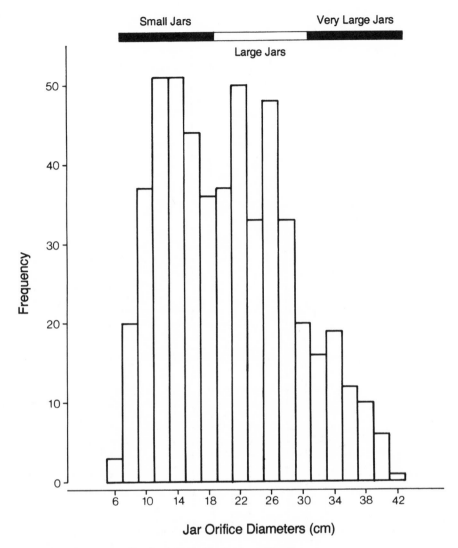

Figure 3.53. Frequency distribution of effective jar orifice diameters.

sherds are similar to Ramey Incised (Griffin 1949:51; Griffith 1981; O'Brien 1972; Vogel 1975:95–96). The sherds from Angel are placed in a new variety, *variety Green River,* to indicate a local variation of the type.

Variety Green River. The consensus of three American Bottom archaeologists—John Kelly, George Holley, and George Milner (1988, personal communication)—is that, as a group, the Ramey Incised sherds from Angel do not "fit" within the American Bottom norm. They are not as well finished as Ramey Incised sherds from the Cahokia area. Much the same comment can be made, however, relative to the corpus of Angel jars; the Ramey jar sherds do not "fit"

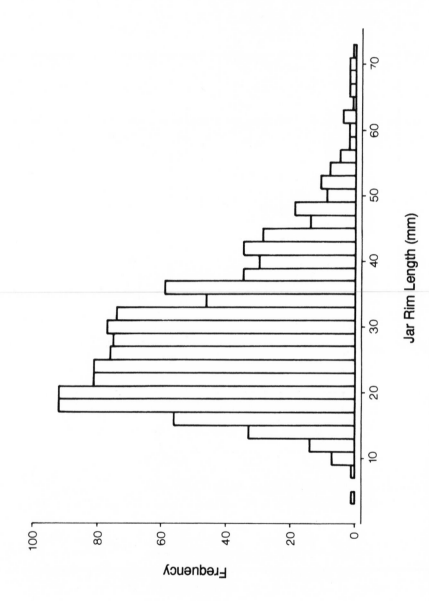

Figure 3.54. Frequency distribution of jar rim lengths.

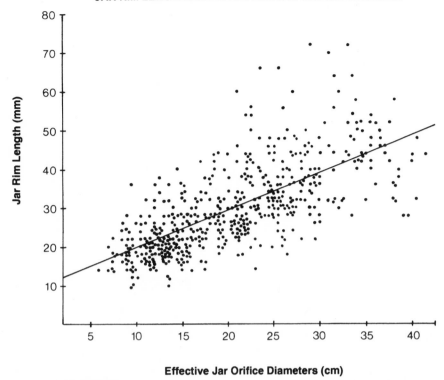

JAR RIM LENGTH AND EFFECTIVE JAR ORIFICE DIAMETER

Effective Jar Orifice Diameters (cm)

Figure 3.55. Regression of jar rim length on effective jar orifice diameters. Total of 525 cases plotted. Regression statistics: Correlation 0.69887, R Squared 0.48842, SE of Est 8.13947, 2-tailed Sig. 0.0000, Intercept (SE) 9.35931 (0.97449), Slope (SE) 0.09800 (0.00439).

at Angel either. The morphology of the Ramey Incised jars is different from the typical Mississippi ware jar from Angel, the paste is usually finer, and the surface is more smoothed and polished. Thus, they may represent local copies of classic Ramey Incised jars from Cahokia. A local variety of Ramey Incised, *variety Green River*, is created herein to include the Ramey Incised sherds from Angel.

MATTHEWS INCISED

Thirty-two rim and body sherds have decorations consisting of concentric incised or incised-and-punctated lines forming series of running arches or semicircles on the upper shoulders of jars (Figure 3.57, A to D; Figure 3.58). These sherds are assigned to *variety Matthews* and *variety Manly* of Matthews Incised (Phillips 1970:127–128).

Matthews Incised, Beckwith Incised, and Manly Punctated were originally

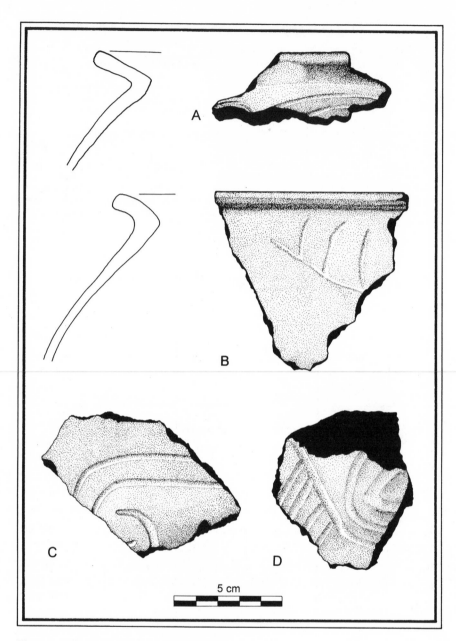

Figure 3.56. Ramey Incised, *variety Green River.*

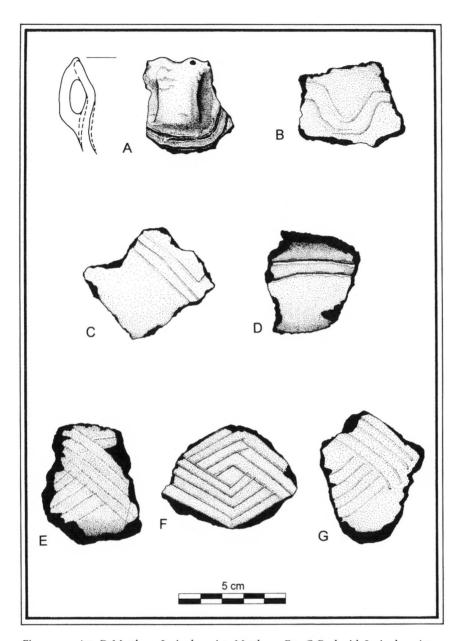

Figure 3.57. *A to D,* Matthews Incised, *variety Matthews; E to G,* Beckwith Incised, *variety unspecified.*

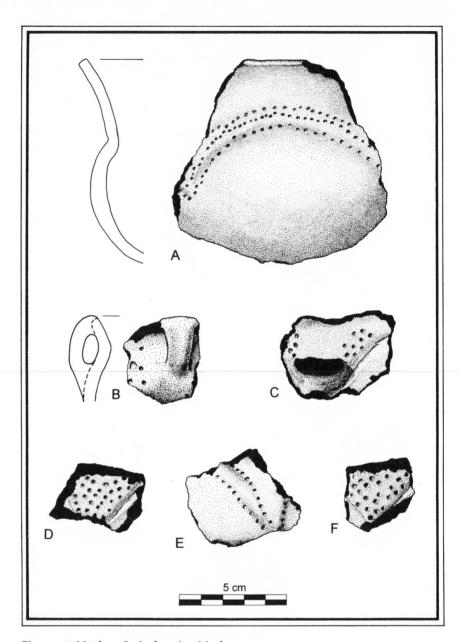

Figure 3.58. Matthews Incised, *variety Manly.*

defined as separate types in the 1940s and 1950s (Phillips, Ford, and Griffin 1951:147; Walker and Adams 1946:91, Plate XV; Williams 1954:223–224). Phillips (1970:127–128) collapsed the three types into varieties of Matthews Incised, citing the similar "continuous undulating motifs running around the vessel" on Mississippi ware jar neck and shoulder sherds.

Although the single type and three varieties construct is usually adhered to in the lower Ohio and Ohio-Mississippi confluence region (Lewis and Mackin 1984:35; Wesler 1988), it does not represent a consensus. In the lower Mississippi Valley, Brain (1988:375–376) includes *variety Manly* within Owens Punctated, and Smith (1990:136) groups Matthews, Carthage, and Moundville Incised together. Clay (1990, personal communication) notes that *variety Matthews* and *variety Manly* can be accommodated within the same type because they share the running arch motif; *variety Beckwith,* with its rectilinear guilloche motif, remains the stylistic outlier. In this classification, I am retaining *variety Matthews* and *variety Manly* within Matthews Incised and am restoring type status to Beckwith Incised.

Variety Matthews. The fourteen sherds assigned to *variety Matthews* have two or three concentric incised curved lines forming a series of running arches on the upper shoulders of smaller jars (Figure 3.57, A–D). The line work was incised with a sharp tool, and the cross-sections of the lines are v-shaped. The vessel surfaces were not yet leather-hard when the incising was done.

Variety Manly. The eighteen sherds of *variety Manly* have the running arch motif produced by two or three lines of small, circular punctations with or without a concentric incised line, in the manner of *variety Matthews,* on the shoulders of smaller jars. The points of the arches are occasionally filled with additional punctations (Figure 3.58).

BECKWITH INCISED, *VARIETY UNSPECIFIED*

The incised decorations on twenty-seven sherds consist of rectilinear guilloche motifs executed on the rims or upper shoulders of jars (Figure 3.57, E–G). The line work was incised with a sharp tool on vessel surfaces that were not yet leather hard. The characteristics of these sherds are consistent with the type descriptions of Beckwith Incised (Phillips 1970:127–128; Williams 1954:223–224). Because of the up-and-down typological history of the Beckwith Incised type, no varieties have ever been designated.

BARTON INCISED, *VARIETY BARTON*

The decorations on sixteen incised sherds consist of a band of line-filled triangles (Figure 3.59, A–D); the band is located on the rim or upper shoulders of jars. The line work is similar to that of the Matthews Incised and Beckwith Incised sherds. The sherds are sufficiently similar to the description of Barton

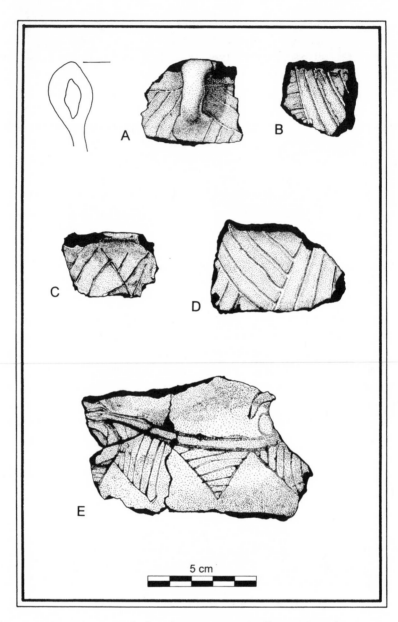

Figure 3.59. *A to D*, Barton Incised, *variety Barton; E*, miscellaneous incised.

Incised, *variety Barton* (Phillips 1970:43–44) to warrant inclusion in that type and variety.

MISCELLANEOUS INCISED

This is a catchall category for twenty-four shell-tempered sherds too fragmentary or ambiguous to assign to a particular type (Figure 3.59, E). The incising on the majority of the sherds is generally similar to that of the Barton Incised, Matthews Incised, and Beckwith Incised sherds.

PARKIN PUNCTATED, *VARIETY PARKIN*

The most common form of jar decoration that occurs in the Angel assemblage, after cord marking, consists of crescent punctations, produced with a fingernail or a curved stylus, as an overall body treatment on Mississippi ware jars (Figure 3.60; Figure 3.61, A). The punctations do not seem to extend onto the necks of the jars. One complete jar and 244 sherds are decorated in this manner. These sherds are assigned to Parkin Punctated, *variety Parkin* (Phillips 1970:150–151).

POUNCEY PINCHED

The surfaces of thirty-seven shell-tempered sherds are "decorated" with tightly packed arrays of crude nodes (Figure 3.61, C and D) that are formed by pinching up the surface clay. The arrangement of the arrays is generally random, but in a few cases ridges occur (Figure 3.61, B). One larger sherd preserves the neck region of medium-sized jar; on this sherd, the nodes do not extend above the base of the neck.

These sherds are similar to the type Pouncey Pinched as defined by Williams and Brain (1983:200). Their description is a modification of the original type description of Pouncey Ridge Pinched (Phillips 1970:154–155). In his original description, Phillips noted that the nodes or corrugations often are arranged in rows. By means of a modified type description and name, Williams and Brain (1983:200) wished "to allow the technique of pinching alone as the defining characteristic."

Variety Newburgh. There are no previously defined varieties of Pouncey Pinched for sherds that customarily do not exhibit the ridge pinching. Therefore, the pieces from Angel are assigned to a new local variety, *variety Newburgh*. *Variety Newburgh* includes all Pouncey Pinched sherds that most often have randomly arranged, pinched nodes as an all-over jar body surface treatment, but includes the occasional sherd with the ridge pinching.

WOLF CREEK CHECK STAMPED, *VARIETY UNSPECIFIED*

Six shell-tempered sherds have a waffle grid of small subrectangular depressions as an all-over body surface treatment (Figure 3.62, D to F). The depres-

Figure 3.60. Parkin Punctated, *variety Parkin* standard jar. (From *Angel Site: An Archae-ological, Historical, and Ethnological Study* by Glenn A. Black, Figure 544, copyright 1967 by the Indiana Historical Society, Indianapolis. Used by permission.)

sions were probably produced by striking the vessel surface with a carved paddle. These check-stamped sherds are comparable to Wolf Creek Check Stamped as defined by Hanson (1960:17–18; 1970:42) for material from east-central Kentucky. No varieties have been defined, and I will not define any here on the basis of six sherds. Kreisa (1991:80) notes that "check-stamping is a more common surface treatment during the Mississippian period further to the southeast in eastern Tennessee."

MCKEE ISLAND CORD MARKED, *VARIETY UNSPECIFIED*

Clay (1963:247) uses the type McKee Island Cord Marked, originally defined by Heimlich (1952:27ff) in the Tennessee Valley in northern Alabama, as a catch-all for Mississippi ware, cord-marked jar sherds from the lower Tennessee–

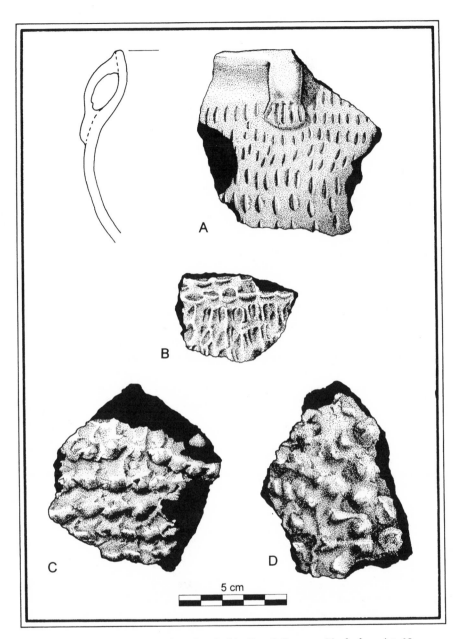

Figure 3.61. *A*, Parkin Punctated, *variety Parkin; B to D*, Pouncey Pinched, *variety New-burgh.*

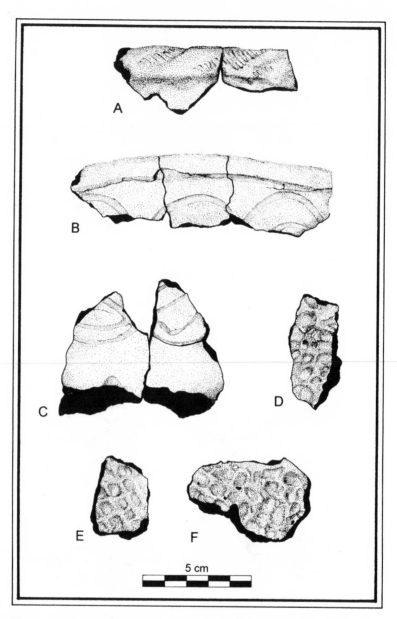

Figure 3.62. *A to C*, Oliver decorated; *D to F*, Wolf Creek Check Stamped, *variety unspecified.*

Cumberland region. A synonymous type designation in the central Mississippi Valley is Crosno Cord Marked (Lewis and Mackin 1984:113; Wesler 1988; Williams 1954:98–100).

As noted earlier, the cord-marked sherds from Angel are not systematically included in this analysis. However, five sherds with handles are cord marked (Figure 3.63, A). Kellar (1967:468) notes that cord marking is probably the most common jar surface treatment after plain surfaces; he estimates that about 0.2 percent of the Angel sherds are cord marked.

COBB ISLAND COMPLICATED STAMPED, *VARIETY UNSPECIFIED*

Kellar (1967:480, 484, Figure 192) assigned forty-five sand- or fine grit-tempered rim and body sherds (Figure 3.63, B and C), possibly representing a single vessel, to the type Cobb Island Complicated Stamped (Polhemus and Polhemus 1966). A synonym is Pisgah Complicated Stamped (Dickens 1976:171–198). The collared rims have castellations and decorative herringbone patterns formed by deep linear punctations. The castellations have vertical, luglike projections. The deeply impressed, rectilinear complicated stamped body pattern may be the result of paddling the exterior with a complexly woven cord-wrapped stamp or paddle. Autry (1991, personal communication) notes that these sherds are more finely finished than the Appalachian materials.

OLIVER DECORATED

This is a catch-all category for all material that is similar to central and southern Indiana Oliver phase (Fort Ancient Tradition) pottery (Dorwin 1971; Griffin 1966; Helman 1950; McCullough 1991; Redmond 1991). Recent investigations indicate that the Oliver phase is contemporaneous with the Middle Mississippian occupation of Angel (Redmond 1991).

Five rim sherds and three body sherds occur in the Angel assemblage (Figure 3.62, A to C). All are shell tempered and appear to be from globular jars with outflaring rims. Four rims are thickened with an added band or strip. One of these bands has obliquely placed, cord-wrapped dowel impressions (Figure 3.62, A). The one beveled rim has plain dowel impressions. Five sherds have trailed or incised curvilinear guilloche designs on the neck that are vaguely similar to Beckwith Incised designs (Figure 3.62, B and C); in one case, the guilloche design is superimposed on cord marking. One sherd has an incised line-filled triangular design similar to that of Barton Incised.

YANKEETOWN DECORATED

Yankeetown decorated is a second catch-all category created for this analysis to include all of the distinctively decorated, grog-tempered pottery of the local Emergent Mississippian Yankeetown phase (Blasingham 1953:32–48; Redmond 1990:50–158). Twenty-four sherds of Yankeetown pottery are known from An-

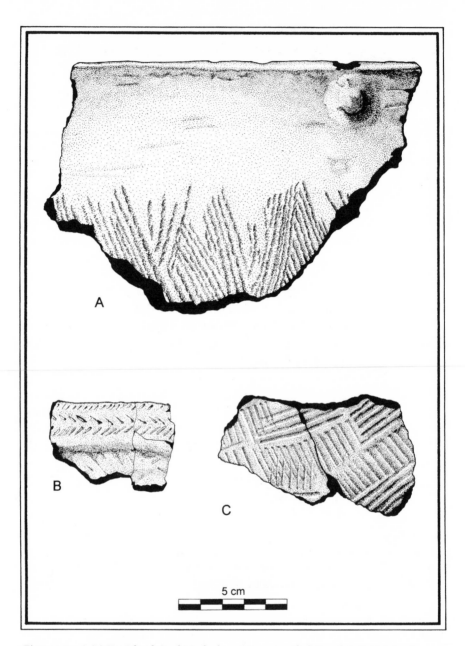

Figure 3.63. *A*, McKee Island Cord Marked, *variety unspecified*; *B and C*, Cobb Island Complicated Stamped, *variety unspecified*.

gel. These include fourteen body sherds of Yankeetown Incised (Figure 3.64, D to G), five body sherds of Yankeetown Fillet (Figure 3.64, A and B), one sherd of pseudo-fillet (a rare variant of Yankeetown Incised that gives the same decorative effect as Yankeetown Fillet (Redmond 1990:58)) (Figure 3.64, C), one red-slipped body sherd, and three bar-stamped or punctated rim sherds. All of the sherds appear to be from the Yankeetown version of the standard Mississippian jar (Redmond 1990:Figures 3-3a and 3-35).

Jar Secondary Shape and Effigy Features

Three kinds of secondary shape or effigy features occur on eight jar sherds.

DIMPLED SHOULDER

One reconstructed jar (Figure 3.65) and two sherds (Figure 3.64, H) have a series of thumb-sized depressions or dimples on the upper shoulders.

LOBED BODY

Four jar sherds have bodies that are lobed. Two of these are plain, and two have a double row of small circular punctations—Matthews Incised, *variety Manly*—outlining the top of the lobes (Figure 3.58, A). None of the sherds is sufficiently large to determine the number of lobes on the vessel, but the typical number for Mississippian vessels seems to be four. The visual effect of a dimpled shoulder or lobed body is a squash-shaped jar body. Thus, they may be effigy vessels.

FROG(?) EFFIGY

One jar sherd has an appliqued curvilinear strip on the upper body (Figure 3.64, I). The appearance is reminiscent of a frog effigy bowl, and the vessel is tentatively considered a frog effigy jar.

Summary

A total of 18,010 sherds were described in the classification presented in this chapter. Within each vessel form, they have been described in terms of paste characteristics (shell-tempered Mississippi or Bell wares, sand- or grit-tempered ware, or grog-tempered ware), defined pottery types, and other secondary modifications and decorations.

The Angel pottery assemblage is often described as plain, in that the relative frequency of decorated sherds in the Angel assemblage is lower than the frequency in contemporary Mississippian pottery assemblages in the Midsouth. The occurrence of decorated sherds in the Angel assemblage is summarized in Table 3.8. This is a similar range of decorative types as that tabulated for the assemblages in the region, and the percentages should therefore be comparable.

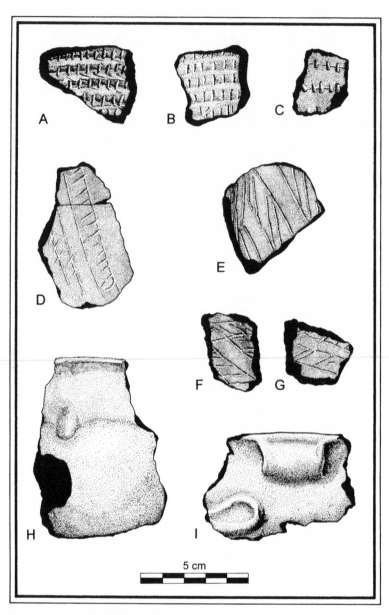

Figure 3.64. *A and B,* Yankeetown Fillet; *C,* Yankeetown Pseudo-fillet; *D to G,* Yankeetown Incised; *H,* dimpled shoulder, *I,* frog(?) effigy jar sherd.

Figure 3.65. Standard jar with dimpled shoulder. (From *Angel Site: An Archaeological, Historical, and Ethnological Study* by Glenn A. Black, Figure 544, copyright 1967 by the Indiana Historical Society, Indianapolis. Used by permission.)

The Angel pottery assemblage consists of more than 1.8 million sherds; about 0.8 percent of these sherds, the specimens described in this chapter, are decorated.

The extreme plainness of the Angel pottery assemblage contrasts with Mississippian assemblages to the southwest of Angel. In assemblages from the Mississippi counties of extreme western Kentucky (Ohio-Mississippi confluence area), painted and incised sherds—including sherds assigned to Matthews Incised, O'Byam Incised, Mound Place Incised, Barton Incised, Old Town Red, and Nashville Negative Painted—may represent as much as 3 to 4 percent of the pottery sherds (Lewis and Mackin 1984; Wesler 1991b, 1991c). In the Tennessee-Cumberland region, 1 percent or less of the typical Middle Mississippian pottery assemblage is painted and incised (Clay 1963:Tables 4, 7, 12, 15, 18, 21, 28;

Table 3.8
**Decorated Sherds
in the Angel Pottery Assemblage**

	count	% all sherds[1]
Old Town Red[2]	9208	0.50
negative painted[3]	4664	0.26
other decorated[4]	749	0.04

---

[1] 1,822,583 sherds

[2] Includes 545 sherds of indeterminate vessel form not included in the analysis.

[3] Includes all four negative painted types: Angel Negative Painted, Kincaid Negative Painted, Nashville Negative Painted, and Sikeston Negative Painted; and Carson Red on Buff, assuming they are faded negative painted sherds.

[4] Includes all incised types, all miscellaneous incised, trailed, and engraved sherds, Parkin Punctated, Pouncey Pinched, and Vanderburgh Stamped.

Kreisa 1991:111, Table 8-6; Pollack and Railey 1987:Tables 25 and 26; Riordan 1975:Appendix 1). The low percentage of decorated sherds in the Angel assemblage is similar to percentages in the lower Tennessee–Cumberland assemblages and far less than percentages in the Ohio-Mississippi confluence area assemblages.

The composition of the Angel decorated pottery assemblage also contrasts with the assemblages to the southwest of Angel. Incised sherds represent less than 4 percent of the decorated sherds. Red-slipped sherds (Old Town Red, *variety Knight*) represent about 64 percent of the decorated sherds, and negative painted sherds (all four types) represent 32 percent of the decorated sherds. Thus, painted sherds represent an impressive 96 percent of the decorated sherds. Painted sherds are between twenty-three and twenty-four times more common than incised sherds. In contrast, in Mississippian assemblages from the Ohio-Mississippi confluence area and from the Tennessee-Cumberland area, incised sherds are two or more times more common than painted sherds. The Angel pottery assemblage is very distinctive in the Midsouth because of the dominance of the painted pottery decoration.

4 Closed and Open Handles

The lip area of Mississippian bowls and jars often bears handles that aid in covering and moving the vessels. A closed handle, like the handle on a coffee cup, is a cylindrical or flattened clay loop attached to the vessel at both the top and bottom of the loop. Open handles are attached to the vessel at one end or point; they are much like the tabs on modern baking dishes.

The morphology and decoration of the closed and open handles represent a major form of stylistic variability in the Angel pottery assemblage. In addition, previous studies have indicated that the morphologies of both closed and open handles may have temporal significance. Many scholars (Clay 1963, 1976; Orr 1951:331; Phillips, Ford, and Griffin 1951:152; Smith 1969; Williams 1954:114) note that, in the Midsouth, closed handles tend to have a round cross-section earlier in time and a flattened cross-section later in time. Orr (1951:331) also notes that earlier lugs, a form of open handle, tend to be thicker than later lugs at Kincaid.

Closed handles almost always occur on jars in the Angel pottery assemblage. There are only two examples of closed handles on other vessel forms. One is the bottle with the jar-form body, and the second is a short neck bowl. In contrast, open handles are common on both bowls and jars. Of sherds for which vessel form was determinable, approximately one-fifth of those with nodes are bowl sherds; about one-third with lugs are bowl sherds.

Closed Handles

A total of 1,514 closed handles and fragments of closed handles were studied. The vast majority of sherds with closed handles are Mississippi ware; only about 1 percent of the closed handle sherds are Bell ware. Six measurements—total number of handles on the vessel, top width, middle width, bottom width, middle thickness, and handle height—were recorded whenever possible (Figure 4.1). In addition, nineteen modifications of the simple handle morphology were noted. These measurements are similar to those used by Mann (1983:23–29) to characterize the Lubbub Creek Mississippian assemblage.

Closed Handle Size and Shape

When at least one-fourth of the circumference of the vessel rim is intact, it is possible, assuming symmetry, to estimate the total number of handles on a

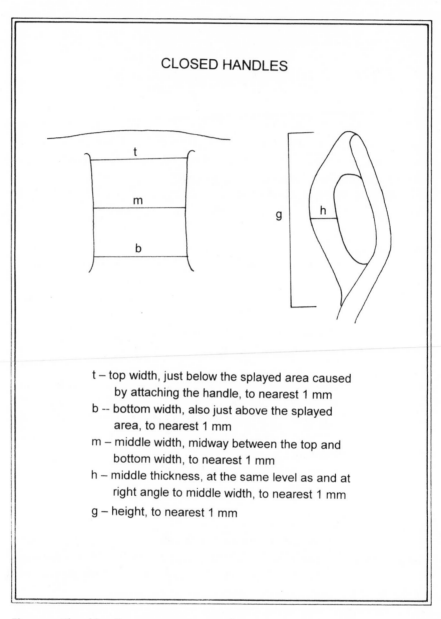

CLOSED HANDLES

t – top width, just below the splayed area caused
   by attaching the handle, to nearest 1 mm
b -- bottom width, also just above the splayed
   area, to nearest 1 mm
m – middle width, midway between the top and
   bottom width, to nearest 1 mm
h – middle thickness, at the same level as and at
   right angle to middle width, to nearest 1 mm
g – height, to nearest 1 mm

Figure 4.1. Closed handle measurement conventions.

vessel. Only nineteen sherds are large enough to make this estimate. In no case
is there evidence that more than one pair of closed handles, located on opposite
sides, occurred on a jar.

Handles are generally rectangular in plan (top width ≅ middle width ≅ bottom width) rather than triangular in plan (top width > middle width > bottom

width). The mean of the bottom width to top width ratio is 0.96, with a standard deviation of 0.10 and a range from 0.47 to 1.40 (Figure 4.2). Handles with a ratio of approximately 0.80 to 1.20 appear rectangular in plan. Of the 609 handles for which this ratio is calculable, only 33 (or about 5 percent) had a ratio less than 0.80 or more than 1.20.

Closed handles are often described as "loop" or "strap" handles in the Mid-southern archaeological literature. The ratio of middle thickness to middle width (Figure 4.3) is used in this study to quantify this aspect of handle shape. A total of 1,041 closed handles are complete enough for both measurements to be taken. Handles with a ratio of 0.1 are ten times as wide as they are thick, and those with a ratio of 1.0 are as thick as they are wide. The former are the most extreme cases of strap handles, and the latter are true loop handles.

The distribution shown in Figure 4.3 can be divided into four segments. Loop handles have ratios of more than 1.0 to 0.75, and strap handles have ratios of 0.38 to 0.10. The intermediate group is divided into two categories, from 0.74 to 0.57 and from 0.56 to 0.39. The former group, the narrow-intermediate handles, is more similar to the loop handles, and the latter, the wide-intermediate handles, is more similar to the straps. There are 581 strap handles, 228 wide-intermediate handles, 134 narrow-intermediate handles, and 103 loop handles (Figures 4.4–4.12). Assuming there was never more than one pair of closed handles per jar, for every jar made with loop handles, almost six jars had strap handles.

Handle height, which ranges from 9 millimeters to 79 millimeters (Figure 4.13), is positively related to jar rim length (r = 0.70; Figure 4.14) and effective jar orifice diameter (r = 0.62; Figure 4.15). Thus, smaller handles are applied to smaller jars, and larger handles are applied to larger jars. This is a rather commonsense finding, but it does have practical applications. In the absence of sufficiently large rim sherds, handles are acceptable estimators of jar size.

Furthermore, the wider handles are attached to a wider range of jar sizes (Table 4.1). Jars with loop handles have a mean jar rim length of 22.1 millimeters, with a standard deviation of 6.6 and a range of 12 to 40 millimeters. Jars with strap handles have a mean jar rim length of 28.6 millimeters, with a standard deviation of 9.7 and a range of 11 to 63 millimeters. The statistics of jars with intermediate handles lie between these two extremes. These figures do suggest that the wider handles are attached to a larger range of jar sizes.

Certain handles shapes, however, are better indicators of jar size than others. The chi-square statistic ($X^2 = 37.0$; Table 4.2), calculated for the four handle forms and six categories of jar rim lengths, is significant and indicates that the occurrence of certain handle shapes is nonrandom with respect to jar size. Yet, the means, standard deviations, and ranges of handle heights do not vary a great deal across the handle forms (Table 4.3). The chi-square statistic ($X^2 = 15.5$; Table 4.4), calculated for the four handle forms and six categories of han-

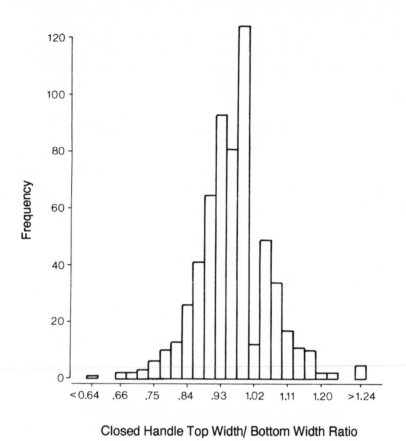

Figure 4.2. Frequency distribution of closed handle top width/bottom width ratios.

dle height, is not significant and indicates that the same range of handle heights characterize each of the handle forms. Taken together, these findings suggest that, in terms of size, the wider handle forms are in better proportion with the jars to which they were attached and thus may be used as relatively accurate estimators of jar size. The relationship between the heights of the narrower handle forms and jar sizes is poorer, and these handles are not as good estimators of jar size.

Closed Handle Attachment

Whenever it was observable, the mode of handle attachment was recorded. It was usually possible to observe the attachment only when the handle top or base was broken in such a way that the joint was exposed or when the joint, especially a rivet, was poorly finished or had begun to fail.

Riveting involved cutting a hole in the vessel wall or a notch in the lip. The

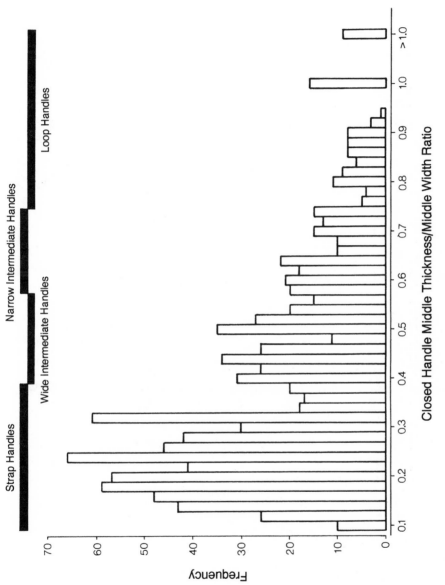

Figure 4.3. Frequency of closed handle middle thickness/middle width ratios.

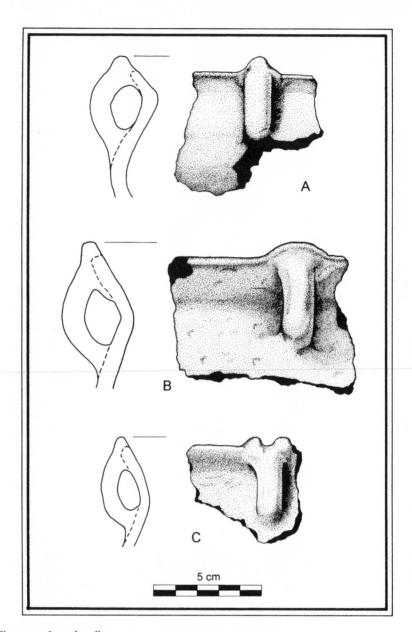

Figure 4.4. Loop handles.

handle end was then placed in the opening, and the excess clay was smoothed out to obliterate evidence of the breach. A strip of clay was frequently added to the inner, acutely angled attachment area; it reinforced the attachments and filled the inner corner. In the case of a *luted* handle, the handle fabric was welded onto the vessel lip and wall without greatly modifying either.

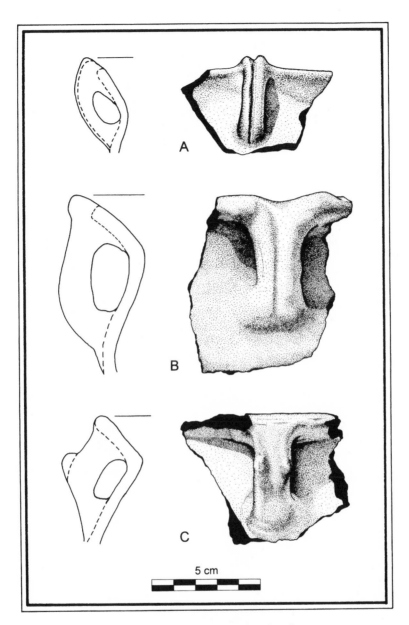

Figure 4.5. *A and B*, Loop handles; *C*, narrow intermediate handle.

Presumably, handles are useful pieces of fired clay, and their decorative aspects are secondary. Therefore, the attachment of the handle to the jar must be strong, or else there would be little reason for the handle. When the relative frequencies (Table 4.5) of methods of attaching tops and bottoms are compared, an interesting pattern emerges. About 94 percent (380 of 403) of the

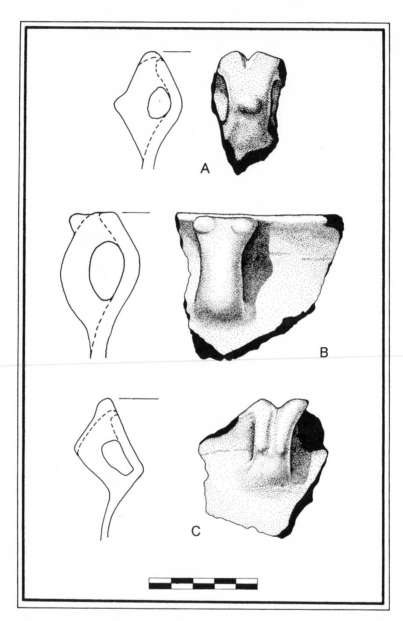

Figure 4.6. Narrow intermediate handles.

handle tops are attached by luting. Furthermore, the handle tops are lap luted, by which I mean that the clay of the handle top was folded over the vessel lip. This method gives the handle a good "grip" on the vessel, resulting in a more firmly attached handle top. In about 68 percent (392 of 577) of the cases, the base of the handle is attached to the vessel wall by riveting. The result of this

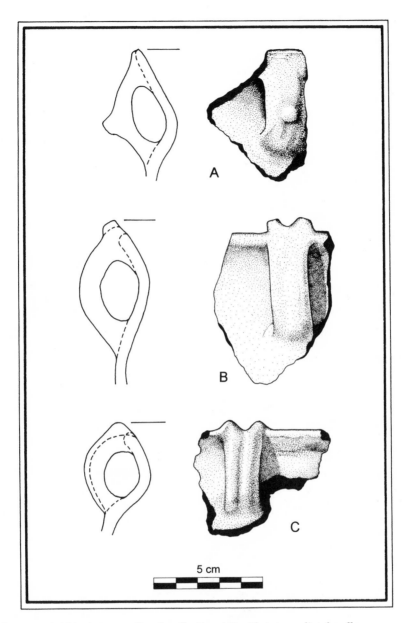

Figure 4.7. *A,* Narrow intermediate handle; *B and C,* wide intermediate handles.

combination, a lap-luted top and riveted bottom (Figure 4.16, A), is a well-attached handle.

The strength of the lap-luted top and riveted bottom combination has seemingly profound effects on the use-life of the jar. If a top- and bottom-luted handle breaks away from the jar, it is more likely to leave a relatively intact,

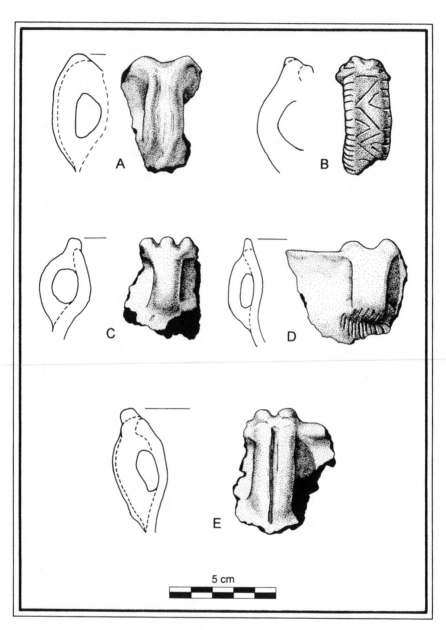

Figure 4.8. Wide intermediate handles.

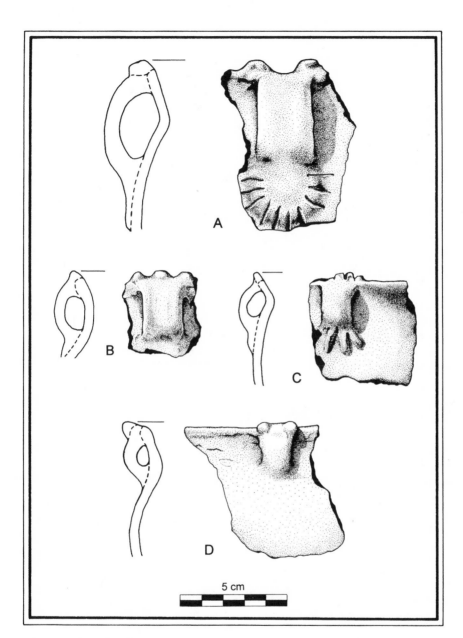

Figure 4.9. Strap handles.

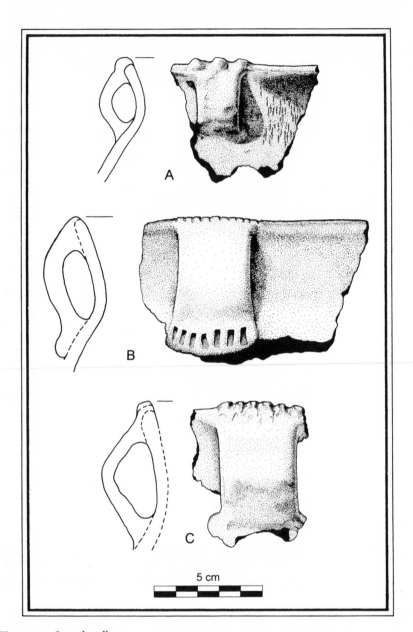

Figure 4.10. Strap handles.

usable jar. The handle is more likely to detach cleanly and less likely to take a piece of the rim with it. The more common pattern of attachment at Angel, a lap-luted top and a riveted bottom, means that when the handle detaches, it often takes along with it a piece of the jar at least as big as the handle itself. The increased handle strength conferred by the lap-luted top and riveted bot-

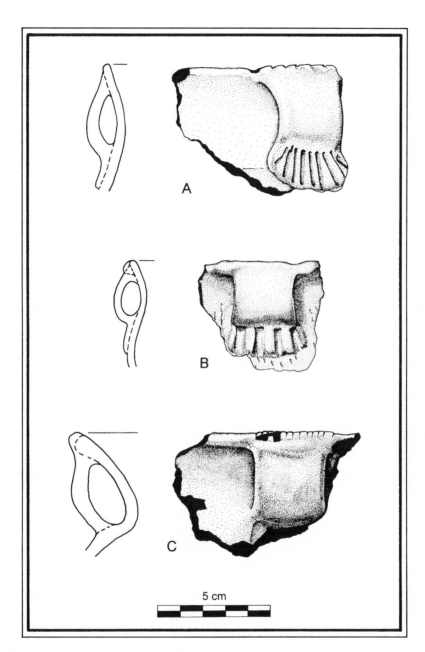

Figure 4.11. Strap handles.

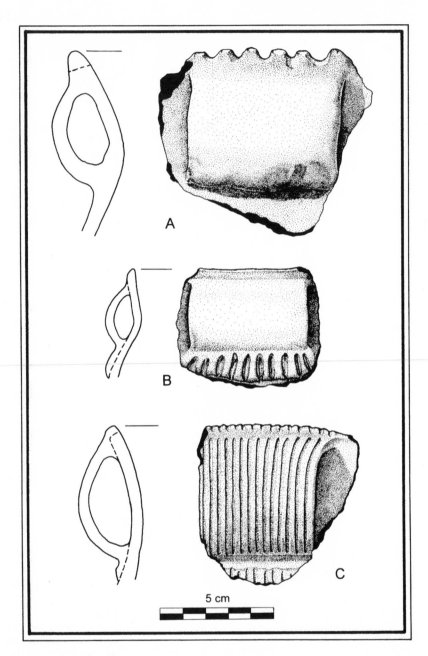

Figure 4.12. Strap handles.

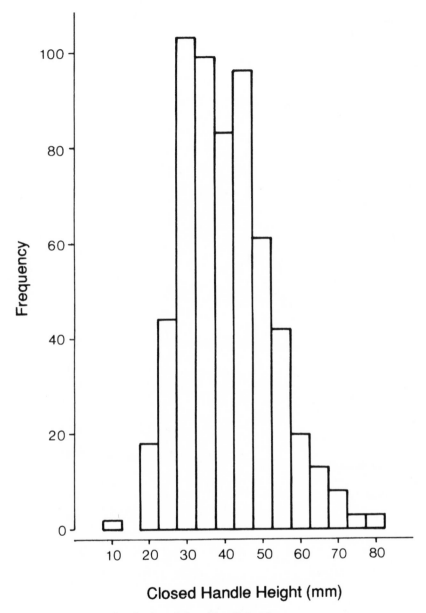

Figure 4.13. Frequency distribution of closed handle heights.

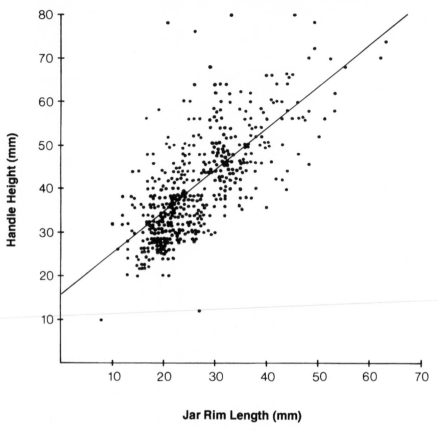

HANDLE HEIGHT AND JAR RIM LENGTH

Jar Rim Length (mm)

Figure 4.14. Regression of closed handle height on jar rim length. Total of 455 cases plotted. Regression statistics: Correlation 0.70444, R Squared 0.49624, SE of Est 8.51764, 2-tailed Sig. 0.0000, Intercept (SE) 15.53321 (1.25597), Slope (SE) 0.93317 (0.04418).

tom must have offset—in the judgment of the potter—the inevitably catastrophic vessel failure.

Closed Handle Top Secondary Shape Features

Of the 894 closed handles for which the top was preserved, 409 have plain tops, and the other 54 percent have the tops modified in some way (Figure 4.17; Table 4.5). Seven modifications of the handle top occur. Certain handle-top modifications occur on handles of a particular shape, such as loop or strap handles (Figure 4.18). A unique treatment consists of a loop handle depending from a triangular, luglike projection (Figure 4.16, B).

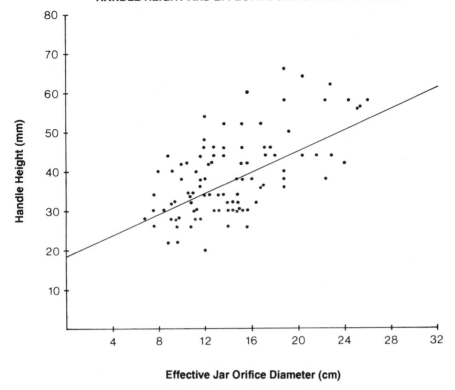

HANDLE HEIGHT AND EFFECTIVE JAR ORIFICE DIAMETER

Figure 4.15. Regression of closed handle height on effective jar orifice diameter. Total of 96 cases plotted. Regression statistics: Correlation 0.61632, R Squared 0.37985, SE of Est 8.04893, 2-tailed Sig. 0.0000, Intercept (SE) 18.57175 (2.73344), Slope (SE) 0.13862 (0.01827).

SINGLE HORN

The single horn consists of a conical projection on the handle top (Figure 4.4, A). It is an uncommon modification, and only thirty-one handles have single horned tops. This top tends to occur on loop and narrow-intermediate handles. This is the same as Orr's (1951:Fig. 5K) *Single Horn G5b.*

DOUBLE HORN

In the case of the double-horn modification, the clay of the top of the handle is modeled onto a pair of conical projections (Figures 4.4, C; 4.5, A and B; 4.6, A–C; 4.7, B and C; 4.8, A, D, and E; 4.9, A and D; 4.11, B). This is the most common handle top modification. A total of 167 (or about 19 percent) of the handles have double-horned tops. It occurs more frequently on the loop and intermediate handles. This treatment is equivalent to Orr's (1951:51) *Double Horn G5a.*

Table 4.1
Mean Jar Rim Lengths by Closed Handle Forms

HANDLE FORM (count)	JAR RIM LENGTH (mm)		
	mean	SD	range
loop handles (35)	22.1	6.6	12-40
narrow intermediate handles (48)	24.3	7.6	8-44
wide intermediate handles (87)	25.1	7.1	10-46
strap handles (264)	28.6	9.7	11-63

Table 4.2
Cross-Tabulation of Jar Rim Lengths by Closed Handle Forms

JAR RIM LENGTH	HANDLE FORM count (expected value)				
	strap	wide-intermediate	narrow-intermediate	loop	Row Total
<=17 mm	23 (30.4)	11 (10.0)	6 (5.5)	10 (4.0)	50 11.5%
18-21 mm	52 (54.7)	16 (18.0)	14 (10.0)	8 (7.3)	90 20.7%
22-25 mm	40 (48.1)	22 (15.8)	9 (8.7)	8 (6.4)	79 18.2%
26-33 mm	77 (77.9)	30 (25.7)	14 (14.2)	7 (10.3)	128 29.5%
34-41 mm	45 (33.5)	5 (11.0)	3 (6.1)	2 (4.4)	55 12.7%
>=42 mm	27 (19.5)	3 (6.4)	2 (3.5)	0 (2.6)	32 7.4%
Column Total	264 60.8%	87 20.0%	48 11.1%	35 8.1%	434 100.0%

SINGLE SCALLOP

The single scallop may be a wide variation of the single-horn handle top modification (Figure 4.4, B), better suited to the width of a strap handle. This is another handle top treatment that occurs infrequently. Only thirty-six handles have single-scalloped tops.

Table 4.3
Mean Handle Height by Closed Handle Form

HANDLE FORM (count)	HANDLE HEIGHT (mm)		
	mean	SD	range
loop handles (57)	39.1	9.0	21-68
narrow intermediate handles (68)	41.9	11.9	9-79
wide intermediate handles (110)	41.8	11.9	21-79
strap handles (325)	39.8	12.0	12-78

Table 4.4
Cross-Tabulation of Handle Height by Closed Handle Forms

HANDLE HEIGHT	HANDLE FORM count (expected value)				
	strap	wide-intermediate	narrow-intermediate	loop	Row Total
<= 27 mm	41 (35.4)	12 (12.0)	4 (7.4)	4 (6.2)	61 10.9%
28-37 mm	120 (111.4)	29 (37.7)	21 (23.3)	22 (19.5)	192 34.3%
38-47 mm	81 (94.6)	36 (32.0)	24 (19.8)	22 (16.6)	163 29.1%
48-57 mm	59 (58.0)	22 (19.6)	12 (12.1)	7 (10.2)	100 17.9%
>=58 mm	24 (25.5)	11 (8.6)	7 (5.3)	2 (4.5)	44 7.9%
Column Total	325 58.0%	110 19.6%	68 12.1%	57 10.2%	560 100.0%

DOUBLE SCALLOP

The double scallop may be a wide variation of the double horn. The paired scallops tend to be centered at the edges of the handle. Eighty-one handles have double-scalloped tops. More than half of these are strap handles.

FINELY NOTCHED SINGLE SCALLOP

This variation of the single-scalloped top is produced by notching the edge of a single scallop with a thin, sharp tool (Figures 4.10, B; 4.11, A and C; 4.12, C).

Table 4.5
Summary Frequencies of Handle Attributes by Handle Shape

	HANDLE FORM (count)				
	loops (103)	narrow intermediate (134)	wide intermediate (228)	straps (581)	others (468)
ATTACHMENT					
luted top	19	33	57	164	107
riveted top	3	3	4	7	6
luted bottom	15	14	22	69	65
riveted bottom	38	45	76	142	91
HANDLE TOP					
plain	27	40	74	197	71
single horn	14	12	2	0	3
double horn	15	29	38	63	22
single scallop	1	2	8	17	8
double scallop	3	2	7	45	24
finely notched sing. scal.	1	0	6	20	15
coarsely notched sing. scal.	0	1	4	20	37
small scallops or horns	0	2	3	30	31
not preserved	42	46	86	189	257
HANDLE BODY					
plain	89	97	185	558	161
cross	1	2	2	0	2
single groove	9	26	32	10	4
multiple grooves or incised	0	2	3	7	4
single horn	1	4	2	0	0
double horn	1	4	1	2	0
elbow	2	0	5	3	0
not preserved	0	1	2	1	296

HANDLE BASE					
plain	75	92	143	347	170
slashed or notched	0	1	1	22	55
hand- or paw-like	1	0	1	8	16
not preserved	27	41	83	204	227

Forty-two handles have finely notched single-scalloped tops; about one-half of these are strap handles.

COARSELY NOTCHED SINGLE SCALLOP

The coarse notches on the single scallops are produced with a thicker-edged tool (Figures 4.9, C; 4.10, C) than is the case with the finely notched single-scalloped tops. Sixty-two handles have coarsely notched single scallop tops. About one-third of these are strap handles.

SMALL SCALLOPS OR HORNS

This is yet a third variation on the single-scalloped handle top. The handle top is modeled into a series of horns or small scallops (Figures 4.8, C; 4.9, B; 4.10, A; 4.12, A). Sixty-six handles bear this top modification. About one-half of these are strap handles.

Closed Handle Body Secondary Shape Features

Handle bodies are much less frequently modified than are the tops. Ninety percent (1,090 of 1,214) of the intact handle bodies are plain (Table 4.5). The remaining 10 percent are modified in one or more ways.

SINGLE GROOVE

A single-grooved handle body consists of a narrow V-shaped to wide U-shaped incised line or groove extending down the length of the handle (Figures 4.5, A and B; 4.6, C; 4.7, C; 4.8, A and E). When the handle top has a double horn, as it frequently does, the groove is a downward continuation of the trough between the horns. Eighty-one handles have single-grooved bodies.

MULTIPLE GROOVES

This body modification includes all examples of two or more vertical parallel lines or grooves on the handle body (Figure 4.12, C). Sixteen handle bodies are grooved or incised in this way.

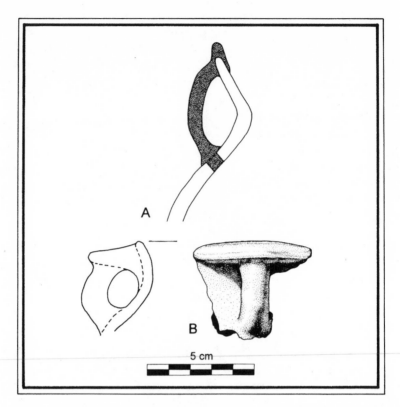

Figure 4.16. *A,* Typical closed handle attachment pattern (shaded area indicates handle body); *B,* loop handle depending from a triangular lug.

ELBOW PROFILE

Ten handles have nearly right-angled profiles (Figure 4.6, C) rather than the typical flat to slightly curved profile. Orr (1951: Fig. 5, n, o, p) illustrated a similar treatment of handle bodies in the Kincaid assemblage.

DOUBLE HORN

A double-horned handle body consists of a pair of nodes placed side by side near the middle of the handle body (Figures 4.5, C; 4.6, C). Eight handles are modified in this way. In three cases, the horns were placed on either side of a single groove. Orr (1951:Fig 5p) notes a similar treatment of the Kincaid handle bodies.

UNIQUE TREATMENTS

Seven handles have single horns (nodes) placed near the middle of the handle body (Figures 4.6, A; 4.7, A). Seven handles have cross-shaped handle bodies (Figure 4.19). Four handle bodies are incised; three have chevron patterns (Fig-

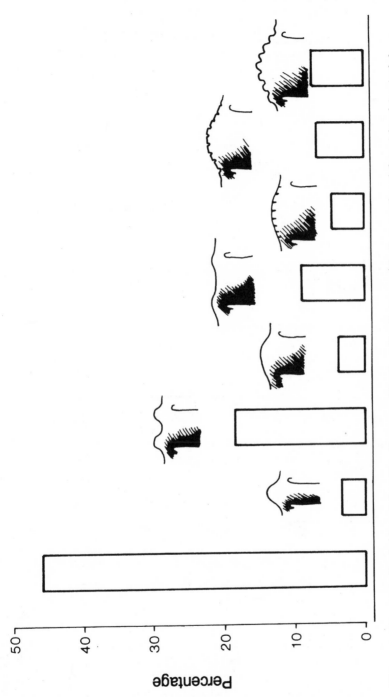

Figure 4.17. Percentage distribution of closed handle top modifications. Handle top modifications are, from left to right, plain, single horn, double horn, single scallop, double scallop, finely notched single scallop, coarsely notched single scallop, and small scallops or horns.

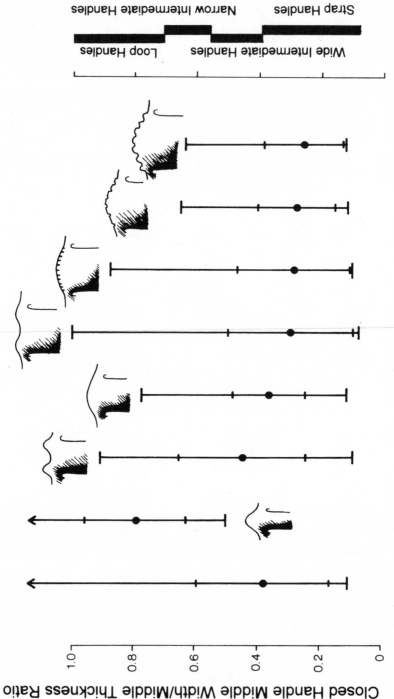

Figure 4.18. Closed handle shape (middle thickness/middle width ratio) by handle top modifications (*dot*, mean; *short bars*, one standard deviation; *long bars*, range).

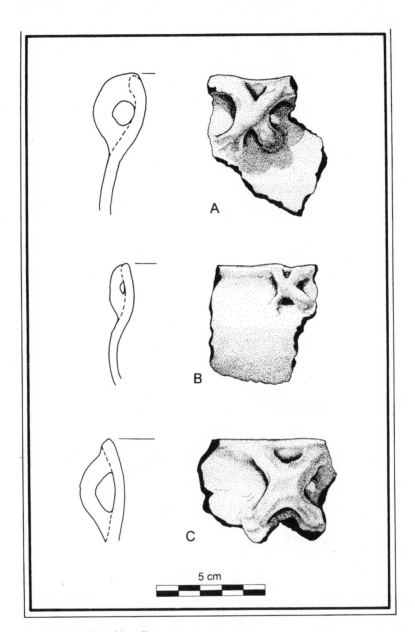

Figure 4.19. Cross-shaped handles.

ure 4.8, B), and one bears a fragmentary curvilinear pattern. Two handles are perforated (Figure 4.20, A and C). On one specimen the perforations are an all-over treatment; on the other, the perforations are limited to two larger holes at the top of the handle body. One handle is modeled into an animal effigy (Figure 4.20, B), and one is braided (Figure 4.20, D).

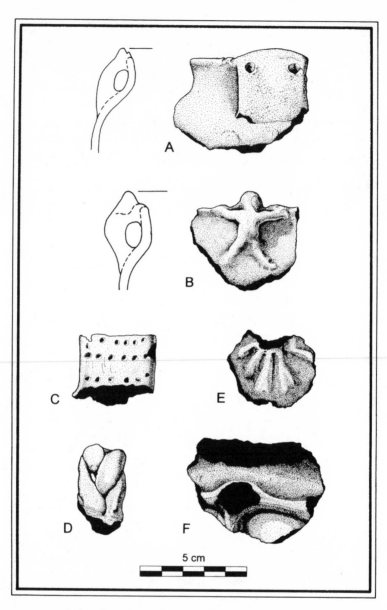

Figure 4.20. *A and C*, Perforated strap handles; *B*, animal effigy handle; *D*, braided handle; *E and F*, pawlike handle bases.

Closed Handle Base Secondary Shape Features

As is the case with the bodies, handle bases are typically plain; 89 percent (827 of 932) are unmodified (Table 4.5). Two forms of handle base alterations—slashed or notched bases and handlike or pawlike bases—are known.

SLASHED OR NOTCHED

A group of parallel vertical or oblique slashes or notches is the more common decorative treatment of a handle base. The slashes or notches begin on the base and usually extend out onto the vessel wall (Figures 4.8, D; 4.9, A; 4.10, B; 4.11, A and B; 4.12, B and C). Seventy-nine handle bases are modified in this way.

HANDLIKE OR PAWLIKE

Twenty-six handle bases are modified by slashes, notches, or occasionally modeling to resemble human hands or animal paws (Figures 4.9, C; 4.20, E and F; 4.21). The hands or paws appear to be holding the jar. The more common slashed or notched base may be a simplification of this idea.

Open Handles

Open handles are those that are attached to a jar or bowl at a single point or along a single line at or just below the lip of a vessel. Four kinds of open handles—beanpot handles, tabs, nodes, and lugs—occur in the Angel pottery assemblage. Approximately three-fourths of the open handle sherds are Mississippi ware.

Beaker Handles

A beaker handle is a thick, cigar-shaped cylinder of clay. One end of the cylinder is attached to a vessel, and the other end is tapered to a rounded point (Figure 4.22, A and B). In the Cahokia area, this distinctive form of open handle occurs on beakers or beanpots, hence the name (Griffin 1949:57–58; Vogel 1975:106, Fig. 68 and 69). The eighteen examples from Angel are all detached; however, I assume that they were once attached to such bowls. Thirteen of the beaker handles are Bell ware.

Tabs

Tabs are scallop-like open handles that occur on bowls and jars. Tabs, however, appear to be separate pieces of clay attached to the vessel lip (Figure 4.22, C), whereas scallops are cut from or pulled up from the lip. Unfortunately, it is not always clear which technique was used, so the distinction is at times arbitrary. Orr (1951:Fig. 10, l) illustrates the same or similar attachments; he calls them "lip lugs".

Figure 4.21. Standard jar with handlike handle bases. (From *Angel Site: An Archaeological, Historical, and Ethnological Study* by Glenn A. Black, Figure 531, copyright 1967 by the Indiana Historical Society, Indianapolis. Used by permission.)

Sixty-nine tabs are known; seven occur on jars, and eighteen occur on bowls. About 60 percent of the tabs are Bell ware.

Nodes

A node is ideally a clay hemisphere that is about as thick as it is wide. More often, however, a node is somewhat elongated parallel to the vessel lip. Nodes rarely occur singly; sets of two, three, or more nodes are the rule (Figure 4.23). One complete bowl has one pair of two nodes and one pair of three nodes. They grade into lugs as their width increases. On bowls, they also grade into beaded rims.

There are 2,457 sherds with nodes and detached nodes. A total of 1,982 (or about 81 percent) are Mississippi ware, and 473 are Bell ware. The vessel form is identifiable for 981 sherds; 790 (or about 80 percent) are jar sherds, and 191 are bowl sherds.

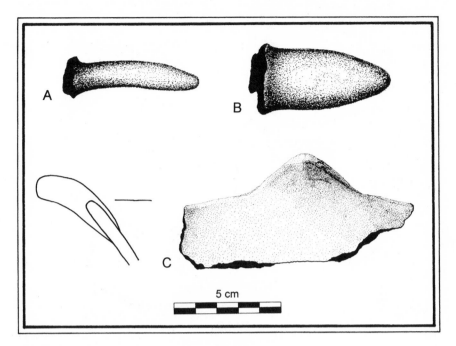

Figure 4.22. *A and B*, Beaker handles; *C*, tab handle.

Lugs

A lug is distinguished from a node on the basis of proportions. Its horizontal width is greater than one and one-half times its vertical thickness. Lugs also tend to occur singly. A total of 1,914 sherds with lugs and detached lugs occur in the Angel assemblage. Two hundred and thirty-four pieces are bowl sherds, and 464 are jar sherds.

The distribution of the ratio of vertical thickness to horizontal width (Figure 4.24), a measure of relative thickness or thinness, of lugs is unimodal, not bimodal as expected (Figure 4.25). Therefore, there is no reason to divide the lugs from Angel into thick and thin categories to parallel Orr's (1951:331) characterization of the Kincaid lugs.

LUG FORMS

Lugs have four simple plans: round to oval, rectanguloid, trianguloid, and crenelated. Approximately 4 percent of the known lugs have an indeterminate shape. Some lugs, especially those of finer Mississippi ware or Bell ware, may be the tails and appendages from lug-and-rim effigy bowls.

Round to oval. The round-to-oval lug shape (Figures 4.26, A; 4.27, A–C) occurs most commonly. A total of 1,634 (or about 85 percent) lugs have this shape. Approximately 80 percent of the round-to-oval lugs are Mississippi ware. Four

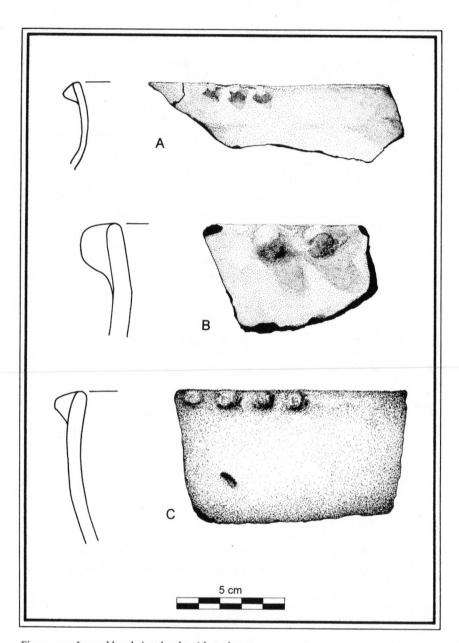

Figure 4.23. Jar and bowl rim sherds with nodes.

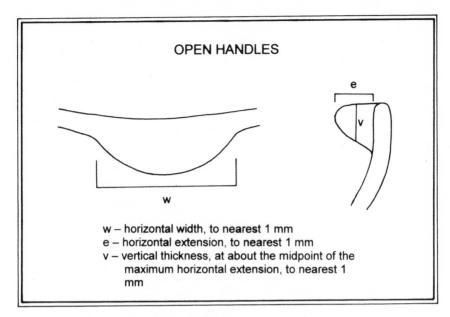

OPEN HANDLES

w – horizontal width, to nearest 1 mm
e – horizontal extension, to nearest 1 mm
v – vertical thickness, at about the midpoint of the
maximum horizontal extension, to nearest 1
mm

Figure 4.24. Lug (open handle) measurement conventions.

hundred and twenty-two of these lugs occur on jar sherds, and 169 occur on bowl sherds.

Rectanguloid. One hundred and thirty-five lugs are rectanguloid in plan (Figure 4.28, A). About 80 percent of these are Bell ware. Forty-one occur on bowls, and only four are known to occur on jars.

Trianguloid. Seventy-two lugs are trianguloid in plan (Figures 4.27, E; 4.28, B and C). Thirty-seven are Mississippi ware, and thirty-five are Bell ware. Thirteen occur on jars, and twelve occur on bowls.

Crenelated. Five lugs have stair-step edges (Figure 4.27, D); "crenelated" is Orr's (1951:Figure 5i) term for such a shape. Three crenelated lugs are Bell ware, and two are Mississippi ware. Three occur on bowls, and two occur on jars.

MODIFICATIONS OF BASIC LUG SHAPE

There are five known modifications of the basic lug shapes just described: bifurcated, notched, perforated, incised, and red painted. Approximately 22 percent of the lugs are so modified.

Bifurcated. Bifurcated lugs have a single, centered, deep notch that divides the lug into lobes (Figure 4.26, B). Each of the lobes may by strongly asymmetrical, or they may be further modeled into the appearance of a pair of lugs or nodes. Two hundred and seventy lugs are bifurcated. All but two are round to oval in plan.

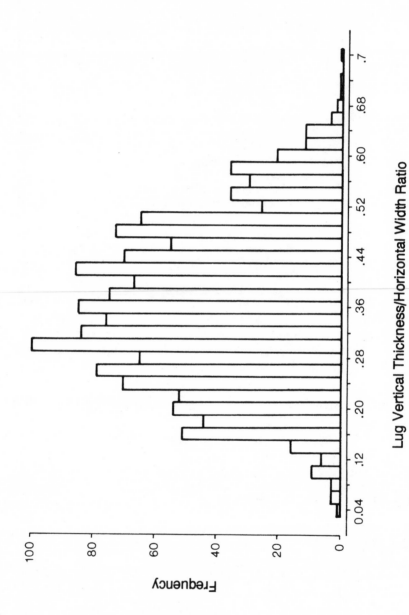

Figure 4.25. Frequency distribution of lug vertical thickness/horizontal width ratios.

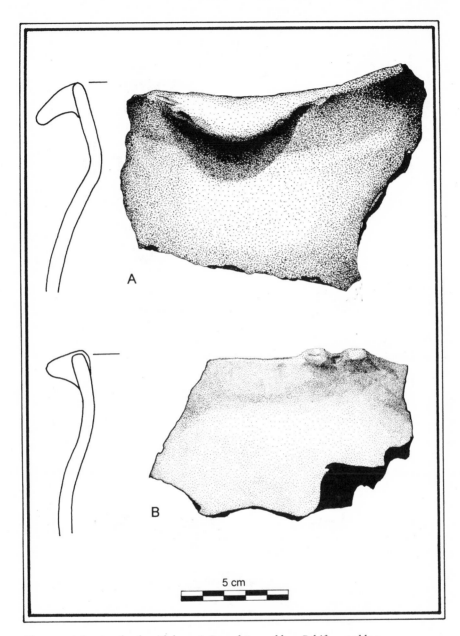

Figure 4.26. Jar rim sherds with lugs. *A*, Round-to-oval lug; *B*, bifurcated lug.

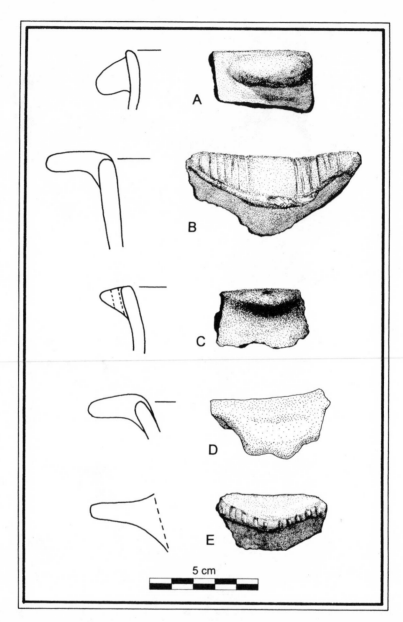

Figure 4.27. *A to C*, Round-to-oval lugs; *D*, crenelated lug; *E*, notched trianguloid lug.

Notching on edge. One hundred and thirty-four lugs have notched edges (Figure 4.27, E). All but six have a round-to-oval plan.

Perforated. Nineteen lugs are pierced with one or two holes (Figure 4.27, C); all are round-to-oval lugs. Presumably, these perforations were for suspending the vessel or tying on a cover.

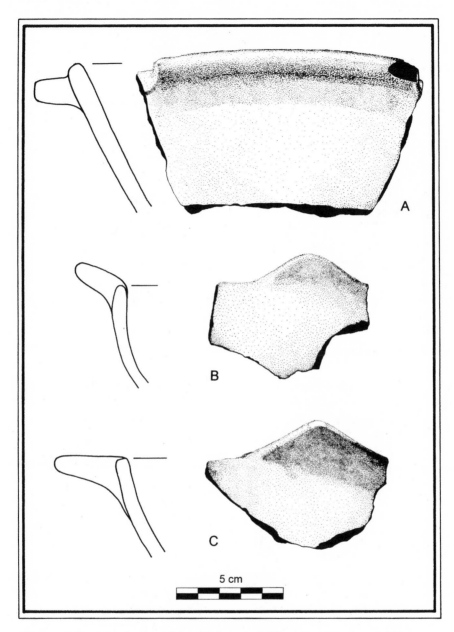

Figure 4.28. Bowl rim sherds with lugs. *A*, Rectanguloid lug; *B and C*, trianguloid lugs.

HANDLE FORM (count)	EFFECTIVE JAR ORIFICE DIAMETER (cm)		
	mean	SD	range
closed handles (101)	14.4	4.6	7.0-26.0
lugs (160)	22.6	8.2	8.4-40.7
nodes (262)	21.9	8.1	6.9-41.7
open handles (lugs+nodes) (422)	22.1	8.1	6.9-41.7

Table 4.6
Mean Jar Orifice Diameters
by Closed or Open Handle Forms

Incising on top. Twelve lugs are decorated with incised lines (Figure 4.27, B). Nine are round to oval, two are trianguloid, and one is rectanguloid in plan.

Red painted. One round-to-oval and one rectanguloid lug are painted with a red pigment. The vessel walls are unpainted.

Jar Size and Handle Function

Closed and open handles probably aided in covering and moving pottery vessels. Therefore, I want to conclude this chapter with a brief functional consideration of the handles with respect to the sizes of the jars to which they were attached.

Closed and open handles do not occur on the same range of jar sizes (Tables 4.6, 4.7). Closed handles occur on smaller jars, with effective jar orifice diameters ranging from 7 to 26 centimeters. Both smaller and larger jars bear lugs and nodes. The effective orifice diameters of jars with open handles vary from 7 to 42 centimeters. The chi-square statistic ($X^2 = 78.7$) for the three handle categories, closed handles, lugs, and nodes, using the three jar size classes described in Chapter 3, is significant and indicates that the occurrence of different handle types on differently sized jars is clearly nonrandom. Open handles occur on a wider range of jar sizes than do closed handles.

Lewis noted a similar pattern in the handles from the Callahan-Thompson and Hess sites in southeast Missouri and suggested a reasonable explanation: "These differences may have a functional rather than a stylistic basis. One could, for example, handle a large vessel that has firmly attached carrying points with greater ease than a vessel which has only straps luted to the side of the rim" (Lewis 1982:23).

Larger jars were more likely used for storage or for long, slow cooking (Hally 1986). Closed handles on such jars were probably of little use because such ves-

Table 4.7
Cross-Tabulation of Jar Sizes by Closed or Open Handle Forms

JAR SIZE (effective jar orifice diameter)	HANDLE FORM count (expected value)			
	closed handle	lug	node	Row Total
small jars (8-18 cm)	85 (46.5)	58 (73.7)	98 (120.7)	241 46.1%
large jars (20-30 cm)	16 (41.9)	71 (66.4)	130 (108.7)	217 41.5%
very large jars (32-42 cm)	0 (12.6)	31 (19.9)	34 (32.6)	65 12.4%
Column Total	101 19.3%	160 30.6%	262 50.1%	523 100.0%

sels were not moved very often or over great distances. Furthermore, closed handles were likely to break because of the weight of the jar and the contents, if used to move the vessel when it was only partially full. The breakage of a closed handle would also probably result in a large, handle-sized gap and numerous cracks in the jar's rim and neck area. A large jar used for storage did need a cover, and one or two pairs of lugs or node sets were probably sufficient to tie a flexible cover in place.

Smaller jars were more likely used as general-purpose cooking and serving vessels. They were moved more frequently, and the closed handles were probably useful, and sufficiently strong, to move the smaller jars short distances.

5   Angel Negative Painted Plates

In their discussion "Negative Painting in the Eastern United States," Phillips, Ford, and Griffin (1951:173–177) made the following observation: "Whether this term [Angel Negative Painted] will actually be used by Glenn A. Black in his description of the predominant painted ware at the Angel Site in southwestern Indiana is not known, but certainly there is present at that site a phenomenally large number of examples of negative painting on the inner rim of plates" (Phillips, Ford, and Griffin 1951:175).

The term "negative painting" actually refers to the appearance of the finished pottery vessel rather than the method of achieving that appearance. Shepard (1956:206) distinguished between a negative style and resist painting. A negative style is "the effect of ratio of dark and light in painting." Darker colors predominate in a negative style; portions of the design that are normally light are dark and vice versa. The style may be produced by painting in the background with a darker colored paint, by painting the design in a light-colored paint on a dark background, or by resist painting (Shepard 1956:206–207, Fig. 17).

Resist painting produces a design by (1) painting the elements on the surface of an already fired vessel with a temporary protective material, the "resist"; (2) applying a wash of a darker paint over the surface; and (3) removing the resist. The design is rendered in the lighter color of the original vessel surface against the darker color of the applied pigment (Shepard 1956:206).

As enumerated in Chapter 3, the negative painted assemblage from Angel consists of 3,997 plate sherds (assigned to the type Angel Negative Painted), 512 bottles and bottle sherds (assigned to Kincaid, Nashville, or Sikeston Negative Painted), and 60 bowl sherds (also assigned to Kincaid, Nashville, or Sikeston Negative Painted). Negative painting is the second most common decorative technique for pottery at Angel; red slipping (Old Town Red) is about two times more common. It is the relative importance of the red-slipped and negative painted pottery, especially the negative painted plates, that makes the Angel pottery assemblage so distinctive.

In this chapter, the Angel Negative Painted plate sherds are considered from several perspectives. First, they are placed within the corpus of negative painted and other decorated pottery from the Midsouth. Second, the negative (resist) painting technique is examined. Third, the structure of the negative painted designs is described. Finally, the significance of the design structure is considered by reference to a group of ethnohistorically known harvest ceremonies.

History of Negative Painted Type Designations

In 1951 Fay-Cooper Cole defined Kincaid Negative Painted: "This type is characterized by the presence of designs of negative painting on the exterior of bottles and interior of plates. The positive element of the design is dark gray to black, closely resembling carbon smudging resulting in firing. . . . The designs are confined to the body of bottles (usually all-over, including base); to the rims of plates. Typical design elements include circled swastika and nested diamonds and chevrons arranged in recurring motifs within encompassing bands" (Cole et al. 1951:148).

In the same year, Phillips, Ford, and Griffin (1951:173–177) defined the other three negative painted pottery types—Nashville, Sikeston, and Angel—primarily on the basis of geographical distribution and to a lesser degree on vessel form and presence or absence of a slip (Hilgeman 1985:196–197). Nashville Negative Painted refers to vessels primarily from the Cumberland River valley in central Tennessee. Typical vessel forms include lobed-bodied, carafe-necked bottles and human and owl effigy bottles. "Nashville Negative Painted may be divided into two groups, depending on whether or not a slip has been applied to the paste," but "negative painting on a white slip [was] evidently the definitive decorated pottery for the Cumberland" (Phillips, Ford, and Griffin 1951:174). Sikeston Negative Painted (see also Williams 1954:212) refers to specimens (generally) from the Cairo Lowland region of southeast Missouri that are either negative painted alone or that have direct painting in combination with negative painting. Vessel forms are primarily carafe-necked bottles and human, animal, or fish effigy bottles. Vessel surfaces are typically unslipped. Angel Negative Painted refers to the combination of the plate vessel form and the rectilinear or curvilinear and Southeastern Ceremonial Complex motifs (Ford and Willey 1941:358; Waring and Holder 1945) that occurs in relatively large numbers at Angel. Vessel surfaces are both unslipped and red slipped. Angel Negative Painted also includes the negative painted pottery from the Kincaid site.

In a more recent discussion, Phillips (1970:139–141) collapsed the Nashville, Angel, and Sikeston types into *varieties* of the type Nashville Negative Painted and added a description of *variety Kincaid*. He referred to Cole et al.'s (1951) earlier definition of Kincaid Negative Painted, commenting that although *variety Kincaid* was "said to be very similar to Angel Negative Painted (or Nashville Negative Painted, *variety Angel*, as I would call it here) . . . from what one can tell from the published descriptions . . . , there are sufficient differences to warrant separation on the variety level" (Phillips 1970:140). *Variety Sikeston* is more specifically identified with the combination of negative painting and direct painting (Phillips 1970:141).

In a recent article (Hilgeman 1985), I reverted to the type-level designations Angel Negative Painted, Kincaid Negative Painted, Nashville Negative Painted, and Sikeston Negative Painted, as opposed to four varieties of a single type. Regional differences in typical vessel forms and the presence, absence, and color of a slip distinguish the four negative painted types. The differences in vessel forms imply that differences also exist in design content and structure.

In addition to the technological and morphological differences, Angel Negative Painted is distinguishable from Nashville Negative Painted and Sikeston Negative Painted (and many other elaborately painted or decorated Mississippian pottery) by archaeological context (Hilgeman 1991:4). The Nashville and Sikeston Negative Painted bottles were almost exclusively employed as burial furniture (Williams 1954; William O. Autry 1989, personal communication).

The negative painted pottery vessels from Angel—plates and bottles—were not deliberate burial inclusions. In spite of the fact that the designs indicate that the vessel are ceremonial pieces, they are disposed of in the same manner as other pottery debris. Negative painted sherds represent a rather consistent, albeit small, proportion of the sherds from all kinds of contexts, both feature and midden (Table 5.1). Also, there is little evidence that any one kind of context contained a disproportionally large assemblage of negative painted sherds. The primary exception to this statement is Mound F. The primary mound surface of Mound F does have a higher percentage of negative painted sherds (0.57 percent) when compared with the typical range (0.10 to 0.25 percent) elsewhere in the site. A large rectangular pit in the primary mound surface (F12/Mound F) contained the single example of a negative painted vessel, a black-on-red plate decorated with owl heads and striped or spotted poles, which was recovered from a specific "ceremonial" context.

The archaeological context of the negative painted material from Kincaid, which seems to represent approximately equal proportions of plate and bottle sherds, appears to be similar to the context of the material from Angel (Orr 1951:296–298).

Angel Negative Painted and Other Decorated Plates

Not only is Angel Negative Painted one of a group of four types of negative painted pottery, but with O'Byam Incised and Wells Incised, it forms a group of three decorated pottery types linked by the same vessel form—the plate—and a similar line-filled triangular design (Clay 1976:41–45; Hilgeman 1991:6). At Angel, the design is rendered by negative painting; incised plates are extremely rare (see Chapter 3; Hilgeman 1985:197). Elsewhere in the lower Ohio and middle Mississippi Valleys the incised version is common; negative painted examples are rare or absent except at Kincaid.

The incised plates from Kincaid and elsewhere are generally assignable to the types O'Byam Incised or Wells Incised (Clay 1963, 1976; Griffin 1949:56, Plate III; Kelly 1984, 1991; Lewis and Mackin 1984:193; Phillips 1970:144; Vogel 1975:104–106; Williams 1954:220–223). Each type had designated varieties with temporal significance.

In western Kentucky assemblages, O'Byam Incised, *variety Adams,* a short rim plate with incised chevron patterns on the rim, predates O'Byam Incised, *variety O'Byam,* a standard plate with incised line-filled triangular patterns on the rim (Lewis and Mackin 1984:194). A late, deep rim plate with engraved line work in this area is O'Byam Incised, *variety Stewart* (Clay 1963:271–275; 1976:46–50).

In the American Bottom and Illinois Valley, a similar morphological and temporal series occurs, consisting of, from early to late, Wells Incised, *variety Broad Trailed* (short rim plate), Wells Incised, *variety Fine Incised* (standard plate), and Crable Deep Rimmed Plates (Conrad 1991; Kelly 1984; Vogel 1975:104). Both series span the A.D. 1200 to 1450 time period (Clay 1976; Conrad 1991; Kelly 1984, 1991; Lewis and Mackin 1984). The red-slipped and negative painted plate forms from Angel have a similar chronological significance (Chapter 6).

Why did the potters from Angel choose to negative paint the designs that potters elsewhere in the Midsouth incised? One explanation for such stylistic variation—and one that I favor—is that the variation signals group membership (Wobst 1977). The designs could not vary; they indicated for what the plates were used. Nonetheless, the method of execution could—and did—vary. Thus, the negative painted plates signaled to the residents of Angel, as well as to any visitors, their group identity. The message spread to people who had never visited Angel when a plate was given to a visitor and the visitor carried it to his home community.

The archaeological context of Well Incised plates may be similar to that of the negative painted plates at Angel in that they are also not mortuary furniture. Kelly (1984) noted that Wells Incised plates are generally absent at mortuary sites. The majority of the Wells Incised plates from the Orendorf site (Settlement C, thirteenth century A.D.) in the Illinois Valley were recovered from around the plaza (Kelly 1984, 1991). The significance of the plates may have changed in the Illinois Valley because Crable Deep Rimmed plates do occur with burials on some late, post-A.D. 1300 sites.

Replicating the Resist Painting Technique

In order to generate information about negative painted pottery, a limited number of replication experiments were designed to explore the additional

	PLATES		BOTTLES & BOWLS	
SUBDIVISION	features	midden	features	midden
EASTERN VILLAGE				
W-10-C	1	99	0	14
W-10-D	75	636	11	93
W-11-A	53	613	22	75
W-11-B	29	139	2	11
X-10-C	40	158	2	21
X-11-A	1	3	0	1
X-11-B	234	786	47	109
X-11-C	51	519	2	96
X-11-D	18	105	2	23
OTHER HABITATION AREAS				
N-13-D	2	9	0	0
O-8-D	0	0	2	0
R-14-B	0	1	0	0
S-11-D	0	5	0	0
V-11-A	2	9	0	0
STOCKADES				
Q-8-D	0	1	0	0
Q-9-A	0	1	0	0
V-8-C	13	0	0	1
V-8-D	0	1	0	0
V-9-A	24	2	0	0
V-9-B	4	2	0	0

Table 5.1
Negative Painted Sherds by Context and Subdivision

MOUNDS				
Mound A	1	1	0	0
Mound F	15	278	3	22
O-13-D (Mound I)	26	8	3	1
P-13-C (Mound I)	2	3	0	0
P-15-A (Mound K)	0	22	0	7
P-15-B (Mound K)	0	1	0	0
OTHER CONTEXTS				
T-13-C (terrace edge)	0	0	0	1
no information	0	4	0	1

amount of work the resist painting technique required of the prehistoric potter. Glynn Isaac (1984) used the phrase "feasibility studies" for such replication or experimental projects. Feasibility studies indicate how something could or could not have been done or used but not necessarily how it was done or used. The following research design and results (Hilgeman 1988b) are presented in this spirit.

Comments in *Ceramics for the Archaeologist* (Shepard 1956:207) and correspondence between Glenn Black and Anna Shepard (Black 1952; Shepard 1952) indicate that Shepard studied several negative painted sherds from Angel. Her discussion of the resist painting technique is based in part on her examination of these sherds. The following paragraphs summarize her thoughts on the technique.

Earlier I noted the distinction Shepard made between a negative style and the painting techniques that will yield that appearance. Examination of Angel Negative Painted sherds indicated that it was unlikely that the negative style was achieved by either painting in the background with a dark-colored paint or by painting in the design in a light paint on a dark background. There was no evidence of either a darker-colored paint or a lighter-colored paint. Thus, the negative style is probably produced by a resist painting technique.

Shepard (1956:207) noted that, in the case of the sherds she examined, the black color is a carbon pigment. The gray or black color turns gray and becomes increasingly light when oxidized at low temperatures (500–600°C). These temperatures are probably comparable to or lower than those at which the vessels were fired, indicating that the black carbon pigment is produced by a postfiring technique. A postfiring technique is consistent with the general resist painting technique. A resist is added to the surface of an already fired vessel to block out the areas that will be the designs. The carbon pigment is added to the exposed, background areas, and the resist is then removed.

The black carbon pigment may be produced in a number of ways, and Shepard (1956:207) suggested three that seemed likely. First, some organic substance is painted or washed onto the vessel surface after the resist is applied, and then the vessel is reheated just enough to char the organic paint. Second, soot may be rubbed into the surface of the prepared vessel, and third, the surface of the vessel may be smudged.

Shepard's (1956) comments indicate that a number of possibilities needed to be evaluated. The resist may have been either wax or clay. She noted that if the resist had been wax, then the technique of decorating pottery may have been derived from batik fabric dyeing. She also noted that if the black color was produced by a process involving heat, clay might have been the resist. The black pigment may have been the result of charring an organic paint, rubbing soot into the vessel surface, or smudging the surface (Shepard 1956:207–208).

Because of the number of combinations that needed to be evaluated, I made small round tiles as surrogates for whole plates. The tiles were made from a high-quality, closed-texture clay that is surface mined for, among other things, pottery making near Selvin, Warrick County, Indiana. This is one of the extensive clay deposits in the southwestern Indiana coal sequences. Because the deposit occurs close to the surface, it would have been available to prehistoric potters either at the sources or as secondarily deposited clay in the Ohio River.

The amount and fineness of the shell temper and the polish of the prehistoric sherd surfaces were approximated as closely as possible when making the test tiles. At the leather-hard stage, thirty of the polished tiles were painted with slips made from an orange-red clay dug in Evansville, Indiana, or from ground limonite (from a hematite/limonite concretion) mixed with some of the clay used to make the tiles. The slipped surfaces were then polished again. After drying, the tiles were fired to Cone 020 (about 635°C) in a 100 percent oxidizing atmosphere in an electric kiln to replicate the characteristics of a low-fired piece. The fired tiles provided the assumed starting point of the resist painting process.

Simple designs were painted on the tiles with two resists, clay and pure beeswax. Each of the three methods of producing a black carbon color suggested by Shepard was tried in combination with both resists. The following discussion summarizes the feasibility of each of the carbon painting techniques and both resists. Acceptability was judged, as Shepard suggested, by an appearance that was similar to the prehistoric examples.

Charring

Two substances potentially high in sugar and therefore easy to burn (see Shepard 1956:33–35) and prehistorically available were used as organic paints. One was the juice pressed from unsweetened blackberries; the other was the "milk" pressed from fresh corn *(Zea mays)*. These liquids were brushed onto the tiles, the tiles were allowed to dry thoroughly, and then the tiles were refired under a kitchen range broiler and over a charcoal fire.

The charring of organic paint did not produce satisfactory results. The blackberry juice soaked into and lightly stained the surface of the tiles, but during reheating there was minimal charring of the juice, and the staining faded with increasing heat. The corn milk did not soak into the surface, and when the deposit charred, it scaled. The scales readily peeled off the surface, and the surface was not greatly discolored. These results may be due in part to the non-adsorptive quality of the clays and to the consistency of the paints, especially that of the corn milk paint (Shepard 1956:34).

Sooting

Finely ground charcoal and soot were rubbed on the surfaces of wet, wax-resisted tiles. Neither substance adhered. Soot was then deposited directly onto the surface of a clay-resisted tile. The soot deposit readily washed off with the clay resist in warm water. Therefore, this method also does not seem to be viable.

Smudging

Twelve red-slipped and unslipped clay-resisted tiles were smudged over a charcoal fire in a closed patio grill. The uncovered surfaces and the clay resist were blackened, but the resist was not fired and washed off easily. The red-slipped and unslipped design areas under the resist were not discolored. The appearance of the tiles was very similar to that of the prehistoric sherds. Of the three methods of producing a black color attempted, only smudging produced results similar to the prehistoric examples.

Wax Resist

Melted pure beeswax was brushed onto the tile surfaces as a resist. In a heatless process, wax is an acceptable resist; it is easy to apply and remove. The edges of the resist lines were well sealed to the tile surfaces and did not allow the blackberry juice to seep into the design area. This produced sharp edges between the different color areas. The wax slowly melted off the tiles in hot, but not boiling, water. One drawback was that the melted wax discolored the tile surfaces as it was brushed on, producing an unattractive appearance (*contra* Rice 1987:149).

As Shepard predicted, wax is unsuitable for any process requiring heat. As the wax-resisted tiles were heated under the broiler and over the fire, the wax melted and burned off before any charring or smudging had occurred. After smudging, the surfaces of the wax-resisted tiles were blackened, and only the faint impression of the resist covered areas remained.

Clay Resist

Shepard (1956:208) noted that if the carbon pigment was the result of smudging, clay would make a suitable resist. Furthermore, making pots produces scraps of clay that are easily slaked to an appropriate consistency, similar to that of stiff cake icing. Also, there is no additional "expense" incurred in acquiring a different resist material. Kellar (1967:473) specifically considers a clay resist as a possibility.

The clay resist was easy to apply. When brushed, it was as easily and quickly applied as melted wax; when trailed, application was much faster and only a little less accurate. Ease of application was complemented by ease of removal. During refiring, the clay resist trail did not bond with the surface of the tile, and it was easily brushed off or washed off with water. This ease of removal is important because there is no indication that the design areas of the prehistoric sherds were produced by rubbing or scraping away some substance.

The clay resist, in combination with smudging, produced resist painted results that closely resembled the prehistoric sherds. There was one undesirable aspect of the clay resist, however. The resist trail cracked and occasionally detached from the tile surface as it dried. If the crack was wide enough, a faint black line often crossed the light colored area. If the resist trail was partially detached but not corrected, a faint blurring of the edge of the line work resulted. If detected, the condition was easily corrected with a wet brush.

Results

As noted earlier, replication experiments may indicate how the resist painting technique could or could not have been done but not necessarily how it was done. These experiments evaluated three different methods of producing a black surface color—a charred organic paint, sooting, or smudging—and wax and clay resists. The results indicate that resist painted vessels may be produced by relatively simple and "inexpensive" postfiring smudging technique using a clay resist. The technique is thus a variant of another Southeastern pottery decoration, all-over black filming, which is also probably the result of a smudging or reducing firing (see Steponaitis 1983:25–27). Some speculations concerning the relation between potter and painter are considered later in this chapter.

Design Structure

The analytic concepts defined by Margaret Hardin Friedrich (1970) in her analysis of the San Jose painting style are used herein to organize and describe something of the design structure of the Angel Negative Painted plates. She described the San Jose style as exhibiting "a complex structure including: 1. a hierarchically organized system for subdividing the surface to be painted; and 2. a number of distinct design elements that can be combined into a much greater number of more complex arrangements" (Friedrich 1970:332). This appears to be an apt way of analyzing the designs on Angel Negative Painted plates.

Hardin's approach sees the design structure as a cognitive system, or body of knowledge, through which the painter "decodes" (or encodes) the decorative structure. She defined three analytical concepts: spatial divisions, design elements, and design configurations (Friedrich 1970:335). Spatial divisions are the bounded areas of the vessel's surface that are filled with design configurations. Elements are "the smallest self-contained units." Configurations are "arrangements of design elements that are of sufficient complexity to fill a spatial division" (Friedrich 1970:335).

Sample

This description of the design structure of Angel Negative Painted plates is based on 868 plate sherds, or more than 20 percent of the negative painted plate sherds from the Angel site. This number represents all of the sherds that are unfaded and sufficiently complete so that recognizable portions of design elements and configurations are preserved.

It is difficult, if not impossible, to estimate the minimum number of vessels represented by the sample of sherds. For the purposes of this analysis, I am assuming the 868 sherds represent hundreds of plates. I can be no more accurate for two reasons.

First, the resist painting technique imposes limitations on my ability to decide whether very similar sherds are from one vessel or a number of similar vessels. The clay resist must be thick enough so that the carbon does not penetrate it and begin to deposit on the concealed vessel surface. Therefore, line widths are fairly uniform because the technique imposes limits on how thin lines can be. Moreover, washing off the resist removes individual strokes and overlaps, which are some of the indicators frequently used to identify the work of different artists (Hardin 1977:120–128). Eliminating sherds that are specifically similar to others in color and design details, those aspects that were most helpful in making refits, only reduces the maximum number of vessels by less than a hundred.

Second, design content is circumscribed, and thus many vessels look like each other. Furthermore, it is plausible that a small number of vessels are being produced by one or a few pottery or ritual specialists. A number of vessels might have been produced in a single decorating episode, or over a few episodes, and these may be sufficiently similar to each other so that sherds from them would appear to be from the same vessel.

The Sherd: Spatial Divisions, Design Elements, and Configurations

If the negative painted plate sherd is taken as the unit of analysis, three basic spatial division schemes can be recognized (Hilgeman 1991:8–9). The most common, representing about 54 percent of the sherds in the sample, divides the rim area into a series of bounded triangular areas by means of a zigzag line or a negative band formed by two adjacent zigzag lines (Figure 5.1). The triangular areas are filled with configurations of geometric elements (Figures 5.2, 5.3). Most frequently, these configurations are composed of line segments painted parallel to one of the interior sides of the bounded triangular areas and arranged obliquely to the line segments in the adjacent triangles (Figure 5.1, B and C). Less commonly, these line segments form crosshatches, nested chevrons, and nested diamonds (Figure 5.3, C and D). Unadorned line segments painted concentrically to the rim and well edges are rare, but rows of small brush strokes or small triangles commonly are appended to the horizontal lines (Figure 5.3, A, B, and E). If the bounded triangular area "hangs" from the rim, the triangle or stroke elements tend to point toward the rim. If the area "rises" from the well, they tend to point toward the well. Less frequently, groups of dots may also fill the triangular areas (Figure 5.3, E).

The second most common group of spatial divisions consists of implied panels that are filled with multiple Southeastern Ceremonial Complex motifs or alternating panels and bounded triangular areas. By far the most numerous of the SCC motifs are representations of the cross-in-circle and the suncircle (Figures 5.4–5.7). Three hundred and forty of these motifs were recorded; these represent about 85 percent of the recognizable SCC motifs. The cross-in-circle/suncircle motifs are configurations of either of two central elements, one or two outer rings, and optional triangles or brush strokes. The seven basic variations illustrated in Figure 5.5 represent 93 percent of these motifs. The "swastika" central element occurs about three and one-half times as often as the "cross," and the "single ring-plain" and "double ring-rayed" variants represent 75 percent of the ring-and-ray sets. There is also a group of infrequent, but more elaborate suncircles with unusual variations of the central element, petal-form rays, and interior rings of dots (Figure 5.7).

Infrequent SCC motifs include bilobed arrows, bird heads (pileated or ivory-billed woodpeckers and owls), and a group of motifs that are most similar to

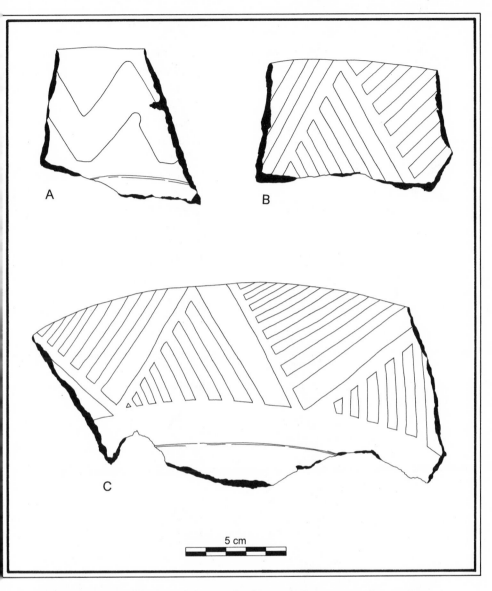

Figure 5.1. Basic line-filled bounded triangular designs. (Hilgeman 1991:Figure 1. Copyright 1990 the Kent State University Press. Used by permission.)

Figure 5.2. Design configurations that fill the bounded triangular areas. *Left column,* "Hanging" triangles; *right column,* "rising" triangles. (Hilgeman 1991:Figure 2. Copyright 1990 the Kent State University Press. Used by permission.)

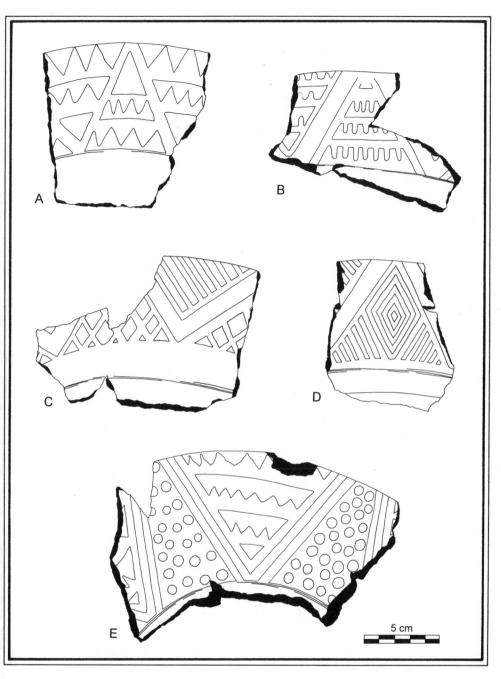

Figure 5.3. Examples of filled bounded triangular areas. (Hilgeman 1991:Figure 3. Copyright 1990 the Kent State University Press. Used by permission.)

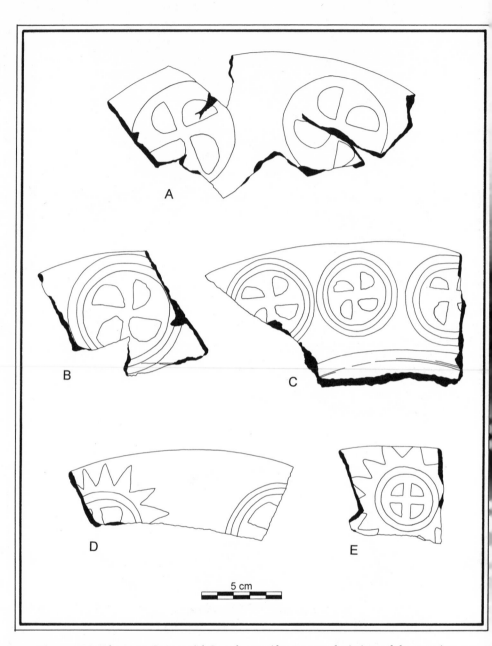

Figure 5.4. Southeastern Ceremonial Complex motifs: common depictions of the cross-in-circle and suncircle. (Hilgeman 1991:Figure 4. Copyright 1990 the Kent State University Press. Used by permission.)

Figure 5.5. Common central elements and ring and ray sets combined to form the usual cross-in-circles and suncircles. *Left column,* "Cross" central element; *right column,* "swastika" central element. *First row,* "Single ring-plain"; *second row,* "single ring-rayed"; *third row,* "double ring-plain"; *fourth row,* "double ring-rayed." (Hilgeman 1991:Figure 5. Copyright 1990 the Kent State University Press. Used by permission.)

Angel Negative Painted Plates 179

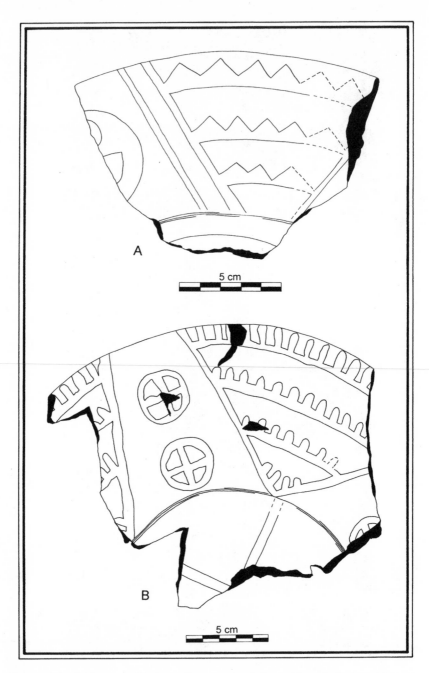

Figure 5.6. Design layouts with alternating cross-in-circles and bounded triangular areas. (Hilgeman 1991:Figure 6. Copyright 1990 the Kent State University Press. Used by permission.)

Figure 5.7. Southeastern Ceremonial Complex motifs: "elaborate" suncircles. (Hilgeman 1991:Figure 7. Copyright 1990 the Kent State University Press. Used by permission.)

Waring's (1968b:88–89, Figure 21) striped or spotted pole (Figure 5.8). Other uninterpretable motifs occur rarely (Figure 5.9, B and C; Figure 5.10, D).

The most infrequently occurring spatial division divides the rim into a series of concentric rings. Triangles and semicircles are attached to the rings, and dots are placed between the rings (Figure 5.10, A to C, E, F). Of course, hybrids of these spatial divisions occur (Figure 5.9, A).

The Plate: Design Composition

In addition to Hardin's three-level design structure, a fourth level of analysis, "design composition" as defined by Shepard (1956:264–266), is included (Hilgeman 1991:9–10). Design composition is the overarching theme that dictates the manner in which the decorative field is divided and filled. It is possible to study design structure from sherds, but design composition requires whole vessels or a suitable substitute. Because there are no whole negative painted plates from Angel, fourteen plates were reconstructed on paper using measurements taken from sherds. The reconstructions assume the following: (1) there are no additional design elements or configurations other than those present on the sherds, and (2) the design compositions are symmetrical, or the elements and configurations repeat around the entire plate rim in the order and in the approximate spacing as that preserved on the sherd.

The reconstructions are shown in Figures 5.11 to 5.24. It is obvious that there are two closely related design compositions. The plate rim decorative field is divided and filled so that the plates are themselves depictions of the cross-in-circle and suncircle motifs.

The idea that the decorated lower Ohio and middle Mississippi Valley plates, both painted and incised, have a common theme is hardly new. Curry (1950:36) noted that if the center of the Angel Negative Painted plate, which is generally undecorated, is seen as the center of the rim motifs, "the idea of a radiating circle for a basic design can be presented." Similarly, John Kelly (1984:10) recognized that when a Wells Incised plate "is viewed as a whole, the various elements combine to represent the rays of the sun." Curry and Kelly described the two design compositions: the plate is itself a suncircle (Figures 5.11–5.17). The plate seen from above presents a circular decorative field, and the triangles "rising" from the well stand in the position of the suncircle rays. The rays encircle the undecorated well, which would hold the material identified with the equal-arm cross. The fractal, or scaled relationship between suncircle motif and plate design composition also holds between the group of more elaborate suncircles, those with petal-form rays and interior rings of dots (Figure 5.7) and the concentric ring designs (Figure 5.10, E). As whole plates these concentric layouts also represent radiating circles (Figure 5.16). One of the previously uninterpretable design configurations (Figure 5.10, D) also represents the rays of an elaborate suncircle (Figure 5.17).

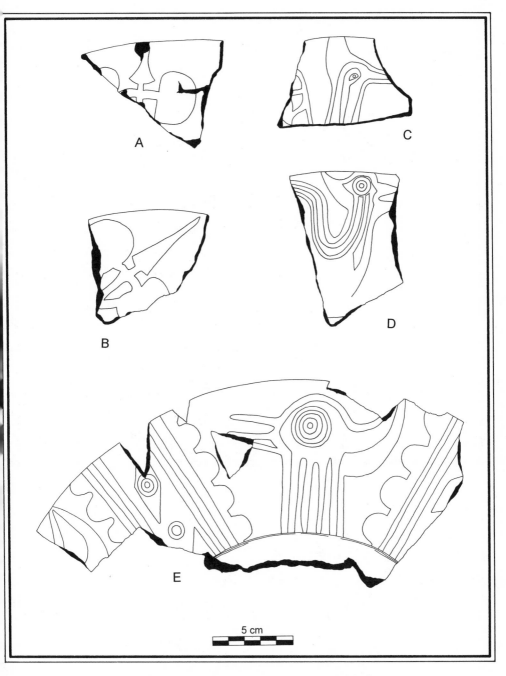

Figure 5.8. Southeastern Ceremonial Complex motifs. *A and B*, bilobed arrows; *C to E*, woodpeckers; and *E*, striped/spotted pole. (Hilgeman 1991:Figure 8. Copyright 1990 the Kent State University Press. Used by permission.)

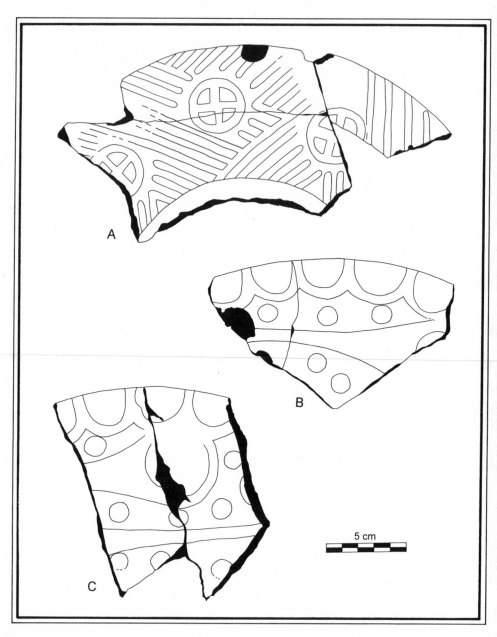

Figure 5.9. *A*, Hybrid design layout; *B and C*, uninterpretable motifs.

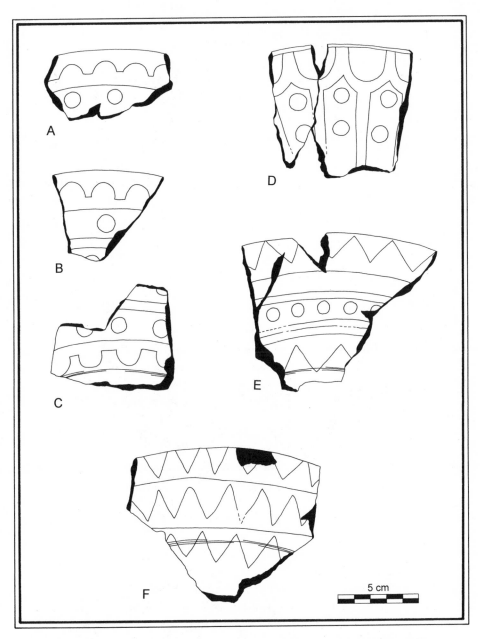

Figure 5.10. *A to C, E, and F,* Concentric circle design layouts; *D,* uninterpretable motifs. (A-C, E, F from Hilgeman 1991:Figure 9. Copyright 1990 the Kent State University Press. Used by permission.)

Figure 5.11. Plate reconstruction: a line-filled, bounded triangular area plate based on a number of similar sherds; see Figure 5.1, B, for an example. (Hilgeman 1991:Figure 10, A. Copyright 1990 the Kent State University Press. Used by permission.)

The second related, or equivalent, design composition is the cruciform layout of those plates with repeated SCC motifs or the alteration of those motifs with bounded triangular areas. Here the plates are representations of the cross-in-circle symbol. Two have alternating cross-in-circles and bounded triangular areas (Figure 5.6), and in both cases the cross-in-circles occupy the bar area on the cruciform layout (Figure 5.18, 5.19). A third is a stylized rendering of the cruciform theme (Figure 5.20). The cruciform layout is repeated in the two plates with alternating bird heads (owls in one case and woodpeckers in the other) and striped and spotted poles; the poles occupy the bar area (Figures 5.21, 5.22). The same eight-part division of decorative space is evident, but not

Figure 5.12. Plate reconstruction: a line-filled, bounded triangular area plate with a negative band separating the triangular areas based on a number of similar sherds; see Figure 5.1, C, for an example. (Hilgeman 1991:Figure 10, B. Copyright 1990 the Kent State University Press. Used by permission.)

demarcated, on two plates with eight cross-in-circles or suncircles around the rim (Figures 5.23, 5.24). These two plates are simplifications of the plate in Figure 5.20.

The artists who created the decorated plates subtly emphasized the relationship between the SCC motifs and the design compositions by the many fractal roles played by the simplest design elements, the small triangles, strokes, and semicircles. These are appended to the horizontal line segments that fill the bounded triangular areas and result in "triangles within triangles", or "rays within rays." The same elements are attached to the outer ring of a cross-in-

Figure 5.13. Plate reconstruction: a line-filled, bounded triangular area plate based on the sherd in Figure 5.3, A (the plate would have been about 32 cm in diameter). (Hilgeman 1991:Figure 11, A. Copyright 1990 the Kent State University Press. Used by permission.)

circle to form a suncircle; they also embellish the striped and spotted pole motifs. Finally, they are attached to the concentric ring spatial divisions to form the outer rings of a suncircle.

Design Structure and Plate Morphology

Plate rim width has an impact on the design layout and content of the Angel Negative Painted standard plates and deep rim plates. The plates with increasingly larger plate rim widths have correspondingly greater rim surface areas. Therefore, there is more rim space available for the artist to develop the design. The impact may be paralleled in the incised types. The morphological transition between standard plate and deep rim plate roughly corresponds to the re-

Figure 5.14. Plate reconstruction: a line-filled, bounded triangular area plate with a negative band separating the triangular areas based on the sherd in Figure 5.3, B (the plate would have been about 32 cm in diameter). (Hilgeman 1991:Figure 11, B. Copyright 1990 the Kent State University Press. Used by permission.)

placement of incising by engraving in the lower Tennessee–Cumberland (R. B. Clay 1991, personal communication). This change in execution may or may not occur in the American Bottom–Illinois Valley sequence—Wells Incised to Crable Deep Rimmed plates—but designs do become more complex (Kelly 1984, 1991; Smith 1951).

The occurrence and frequency of the negative painted design layout and elements and SCC motifs by standard plate and deep rim plate categories defined in Chapter 3 are summarized in Table 5.2. Design layouts on small standard plates are restricted to bounded triangular areas, and the most common fillers are parallel line segments, the element requiring the least amount of space. Suncircles make their first appearance on large standard plates. These are pri-

Figure 5.15. Plate reconstruction: a bounded triangular area plate, with extra lines separating the triangular areas, based on the sherd in Figure 5.3, E (the plate would have been about 30 cm in diameter). (Hilgeman 1991:Figure 12, A. Copyright 1990 the Kent State University Press. Used by permission.)

marily the forms that take up relatively little space, the "single ring-plain" and "double ring-plain" variants. The dominant design layout remains the bounded triangular areas. Elements requiring more space for effective execution than parallel line segments, such as nested diamonds and chevrons or triangles and strokes on horizontal lines, are more important area fillers on large standard plates.

The appearance of small deep rim plates is accompanied by design layouts other than bounded triangular areas; these are the cruciform and concentric circle layouts. Such layouts would be difficult to execute effectively on the narrower-rimmed standard plate. SCC motifs become relatively more common, presumably because the cruciform panels afford the artists more space

Figure 5.16. Plate reconstruction: a concentric circle layout plate based on the sherd in Figure 5.10, E (the plate would have been about 32 cm in diameter). (Hilgeman 1991:Figure 12, B. Copyright 1990 the Kent State University Press. Used by permission.)

than do the bounded triangular areas. The trend away from bounded triangular design layouts to cruciform layouts and more frequent use of SCC motifs continues in the large deep rim plates.

New Fire Ceremony Plates?

The Angel Negative Painted plates have a consistent, recurrent design theme; they are representations of the cross-in-circle and suncircle motifs. Waring (1968a:33) believed that of all the SCC motifs, the cross-in-circle and suncircle "are most easily identified with a conceptual complex on the historic level," which he termed the "fire-sun-deity complex." At the center of the

Figure 5.17. Plate reconstruction: a unique design layout based on the sherd in Figure 5.10, D (the plate would have been about 32 cm in diameter).

Southeastern Indian belief system was a supreme life-giving force, called "Breath Master" by the Creek (Swanton 1928a:207) and "One Who Is Breath" by the Yuchi (Speck 1909:27). This force was identified with the sun, "the great holy fire above us" according to the Chickasaw (Adair 1930:46; Swanton 1928a:208). Its/their earthly representative was fire, particularly the "holy" fire kept in perpetuity by the Natchez and Caddo, made as a part of four major annual feasts by the Cherokee, or kindled anew every year by the Creek and Yuchi during the complex of rites commonly known as the green corn ceremony (Hilgeman 1991:11–13).

The linkage between the fire and the cross motif is illustrated by the following two myths and artifacts and practices that may be related to them (Hilgeman 1991:3). According to a Cherokee story, fire first came to earth when a light-

Figure 5.18. Plate reconstruction: a cruciform plate layout based on the sherd in Figure 5.6, A (the plate would have been about 30 cm in diameter). (Hilgeman 1991:Figure 13, A. Copyright 1990 the Kent State University Press. Used by permission.)

ning bolt struck and ignited a sycamore tree on an island. After a number of animals tried but failed to retrieve the fire, a water spider spun a small bowl on its back, and in the bowl the spider brought back one of the coals (Mooney 1900:239–240). The image of the story is preserved on a number of Late Prehistoric engraved shell gorgets, which depict the spider with the fire—symbolized by an equal arm cross—on its back (Holmes 1883:Plate LXI). A Creek legend (cited in Swanton 1928b:546–548) says that the fire and busk medicines were sent down from "The-One-Above" to ignite four logs. Another version states: "The people from heaven told the [Creek] how to make a fire and that, once a year, the fire was to be extinguished entirely and a new one made, by

Figure 5.19. Plate reconstruction: a cruciform plate layout based on the sherd in Figure 5.6, B (the plate would have been about 28 cm in diameter). (Hilgeman 1991:Figure 13, B. Copyright 1990 the Kent State University Press. Used by permission.)

friction" (Hitchcock 1930:123–124). Thus, a number of Southeastern societies kindle the fire anew every year and use it to light four logs arranged in the form of an equal arm cross.

The most important individual rite that occurred during many of the Southeastern green corn ceremonies was the lighting of a new fire. There are numerous ethnohistoric and ethnographic accounts of new fire rites (Adair 1930:105–117; Ballard 1978; Corkran 1953, 1955; Gilbert 1930:45–58, 1943; Howard 1968; Mooney 1889; Payne 1932; Speck 1909:114–120; Swanton 1911:113–123; Swanton 1928b:546–610; Swanton 1942:227; Waring 1968a; Wetmore 1983; Witthoft 1946, 1949). These accounts span some 200 to 250 years and represent some of the earliest as well as almost present-day descriptions of new fire and green

Figure 5.20. Plate reconstruction: a hybrid line-filled triangle/cruciform plate layout based on the sherd in Figure 5.9, A (the plate would have been about 28 cm in diameter).

corn ceremonies. There are thus some limitations to their applicability to the aboriginal situation. These groups had experienced at least a century, and frequently more than two centuries, of culture change prior to the recording of the observations. In spite of the differences in time and in detail, there are striking similarities over the whole of the Southeast that argue for the probability that many Southeastern groups conducted some variant of the ceremony and that the ceremony may date back to the prehistoric period. The following brief sketch of a green corn ceremony is abstracted from the many Creek examples.

Prior to the beginning of the green corn ceremony, the village and square ground are cleaned and renovated. Frequently, the surface of the square ground is scraped clean, and a fresh layer of earth is spread over it. The hearth in the center of the square ground is either cleaned or rebuilt. If rebuilt, various medi-

Figure 5.21. Plate reconstruction: a cruciform plate layout based on the sherd in Figure 5.8, E (the plate would have been about 32 cm in diameter). (Hilgeman 1991:Figure 14, A. Copyright 1990 the Kent State University Press. Used by permission.)

cines such as tobacco or snake buttonroot are incorporated into it. The walls and supporting posts of the "benches" around the square ground are repainted, and new mats are made for the benches' seats. Household cooking fires are extinguished, and these hearths are also cleaned.

The new fire rite begins at or after daybreak on one of the early days of the four- to eight-day green corn ceremony. An elder or chief (referred to as "fire-priest" in McGillivray's [cited in Swanton 1928b:583] account of the Otciapofa green corn ceremony) kindles a new fire using a fire-drill. This fire is carried to the hearth in the center of the square ground where it is used to ignite four logs that lay aligned to the cardinal directions. The "Breath Master" is thought

Figure 5.22. Plate reconstruction: a cruciform plate layout, on display at Angel Mounds State Memorial, Evansville, Indiana (the plate would have been about 32 cm in diameter). (Hilgeman 1991:Figure 14, B. Copyright 1990 the Kent State University Press. Used by permission.)

to be present in the new fire for a short time. Next, token amounts of the new crops, especially four ears of new maize, and medicines are burned in the new fire. After these sacrifices (and the new fire rite per se) are completed, the "black drink" is brewed and drunk, a portion of the new fire is carried to the edge of the square ground to be used by the women for the rekindling of household cooking fires, and a feast of the new crops is prepared and eaten.

Although pottery vessels are infrequently mentioned, there are a number of contexts in this rite and in the events immediately afterward in which pots are known to have been used or hypothetically could have been used. These generally include food display, preparation, and consumption. Hally (1986) has re-

Figure 5.23. Plate reconstruction: an eight-part (cruciform) design layout based on the sherd in Figure 5.4, D (the plate would have been about 28 cm in diameter). (Hilgeman 1991:Figure 15, A. Copyright 1990 the Kent State University Press. Used by permission.)

viewed the Southeastern ethnohistoric literature concerning the use of pottery vessels for food and "black drink" preparation and consumption. This review will concentrate on contexts that suggest the use of vessels for ritual display.

The use of vessels, particularly plates, for ritual presentation or serving is tenuous but supportable. The plate, because of its open form and interior rim decoration, is more likely to have served for display or consumption than for cooking or storage. Furthermore, the Angel Negative Painted plates are not cooking vessels; the designs would have faded if the plates were heated. Arnold (1985:158–163) makes note of a number of societies that make special pots for ritual eating and drinking activities. It is not uncommon for such vessels to be

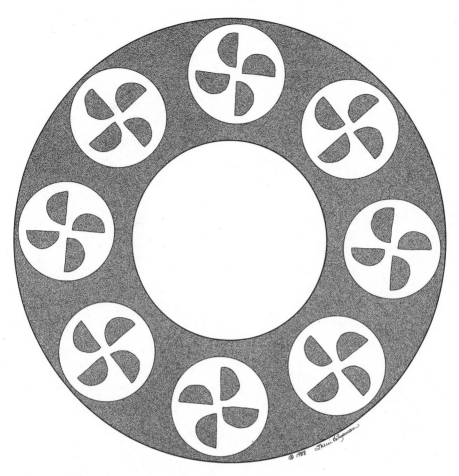

Figure 5.24. Plate reconstruction: an eight-part (cruciform) design layout based on the sherd in Figure 5.4, A (the plate would have been about 28 cm in diameter). (Hilgeman 1991:Figure 15, B. Copyright 1990 the Kent State University Press. Used by permission.)

made specifically for use during that ceremony and to be deliberately broken afterward.

Some evidence in the ethnohistoric literature indicates that pottery vessels were made for use specifically during the Southeastern new fire or green corn ceremony. Payne (1932:176) described the first stomp dance held before the 1835 Tukabatchee green corn ceremony and mentioned that "an order [was] given out for the manufacture of certain articles of pottery to be employed in the ceremonies." Alexander Long, a trader and periodic resident of Overhill Cherokee settlements during 1711–1725 (cited in Corkran 1953:24), stated that the foods to be burnt in the fire were placed in "a new Erten pain pinted all reed."

Table 5.2
Relationship of Plate Layouts, Elements, and Motifs and Plate Form

	PLATE FORM			
	small standard	large standard	small deep rim	large deep rim
LAYOUTS				
bounded triangular areas	35	21	19	7
other triangular layouts	0	2	9	2
cruciform	0	0	11	9
concentric circle	0	2	5	0
indet/other	1	12	10	12
TRIANGULAR AREA FILLERS				
parallel oblique lines	23	10	21	3
horizontal lines	3	0	2	0
cross-hatch lines	1	1	0	0
nested diamonds	0	4	0	0
nested chevrons	7	2	0	1
triangles on horizontal lines	1	3	0	3
strokes on horizontal lines	2	5	0	4
SCC MOTIFS				
suncircles	0	8	29	14
woodpeckers	0	1	1	8
owls	0	0	0	1
striped/spotted poles	0	1	1	6

Speck (1909:27) also identifies a specially made and decorated Yuchi jar that is "used as the receptacle for the sacred concoctions at the annual ceremonies." Similar jars are illustrated in LeMoyne's "Timucua Indians Taking the Black Drink" (in Swanton 1946:Plate 98). Adair (1930:111) noted that the newly kindled spark was carried to the square ground hearth "in an old pottery vessel"; this recapitulates the action and equipment of the mythological water spider. Pottery vessels may also have been used to carry the fire to the edge of the square ground after the first fruits' sacrifice and in turn to individual houses to rekindle household fires. Swanton (1928b:546–610) cited a number of accounts of Creek green corn ceremonies in which foods, particularly the newly harvested crops, and medicines were ceremonially brought into the square ground and displayed. The display of foods in connection with feasting is illustrated by LeMoyne's "Timucua Indians Cooking" (in Swanton 1946:Plate 56) and a photograph of a 1970 Shawnee bread dance (Howard 1981:Plate 38). Finally, a number of the accounts of Creek green corn ceremonies (cited in Swanton 1928b) stated that, during the ritual cleaning of the village prior to the beginning of the green corn ceremony, all old cooking vessels that had contact with the old fire were broken. Presumably because of their contact with the fire during the past year, they had become, like that fire, "a most dangerous pollution" (Howard 1968:23).

The argument that I have been developing concerning the ceremonial role of the Angel Negative Painted plates parallels in many ways Emerson's (1989:62–67) interpretation of the significance of Ramey Incised jars, another special-purpose Mississippian pottery. Ramey Incised is a decorated version of another fineware, Powell Plain, and represents a small proportion of the pottery assemblages from the American Bottom. These facts, taken together, suggested to Emerson that Ramey jars were "meant for special purpose rather than simply being decorations for the elite" (Emerson 1989:63). Ramey jars and sherds have been recovered from both the large centers and the small settlements on the outskirts. If Ramey Incised jars were only prestige goods, we would expect sherds to occur only at the larger sites in the settlement hierarchy, the residences of the elite members of society. As a result, Emerson concluded that Ramey Incised "might be referred to as a 'utilitarian' ritual ware" (Emerson 1989:65) made at specific times of the year and by a limited number of potters. Given the distribution of Ramey Incised in both small sites and centers, Emerson also concluded that at the end of the ceremonies in which they were used, some of the Ramey jars were carried back to the households.

Angel Negative Painted plates are also decorated versions of other more common Bell ware potteries, in this case Old Town Red and Bell Plain. The addition of designs to the Old Town Red and Bell Plain plates indicates that they were something more than simply elite prestige goods or each household's "best china." The content of the designs, the cross-in-circle and suncircle layouts and motifs, strongly suggests that these are ceremonial pieces. The layouts and motifs further link the plates to the Southeastern "fire-sun-deity complex" (Waring 1968a:33) and, by extension, to the new fire and green corn ceremonies or other similar local (harvest) ceremonies. The plate form indicates the role the vessels filled in the ceremony; they are ceremonial display and serving platters. The designs are on the interior, upper surface of the plates. In this position, the messages conveyed by the design and its mode of execution—these plates were made for use during a harvest ceremony like the green corn ceremony at Angel (as opposed to another ceremony at any other town)—could be read by all the participants and observers of the ceremony. Because the designs were limited to the rims, the plates could be used as containers without obscuring the designs or their messages.

The Angel Negative Painted plates had a limited use-life; there is little use-wear on the bases of the plates. The context of disposal, in the midden with other pottery debris, conveys more than the fact that the plates were not burial furniture. Once their finite use-life was over, it was acceptable to break the plates and discard the fragments with other household debris. They were no longer important. Emerson's phrase, utilitarian ritual ware, is an apt characterization of the Angel Negative Painted plates.

That the plates are special-purpose ritual ware is underscored by the stability of the design symbolism through the years. Approximately 250 years (see Chapter 6) are represented by the Angel Negative Painted plate sequence, but the design structure and content are remarkably consistent. True, the width of the plate rim is related to the specific content of the designs: the shift from the narrower-rimmed standard plate to the wider-rimmed deep rim plate is paralleled by the shift from a rayed, suncircle layout to a cruciform, or cross-in-circle layout. These two layouts, however, are equivalent, as demonstrated by the fact that the rays and equal-arm cross are frequently combined into a single motif.

If we accept for now the results of my replication of the resist painting technique and the reconstruction of the plates' ceremonial significance, we can go on to speculate about the relationship between potter and painter and the significance of the negative painting technique. The painter of the designs need not have been the potter of the plates. Because resist painting is a postfiring technique, the painter does not require the skill necessary to form and fire pottery vessels. The plates may have been made and fired by a potter and then passed on to the painter. The painter needed only minimal ceramic skills to smudge vessel surfaces. The painter did require the more critical knowledge of the appropriate design structure so that the finished plate was ceremonially correct. Rather than a full-time or even part-time ceramic specialist, this person would more likely have been some kind of part-time ritual specialist.

The probable timing of decorating and using the plates makes a postfiring technique an attractive decorative option. If the plates were made for a harvest ceremony, it implies that they were at least decorated during the busy late summer harvest, a time when there would be minimal time available to make pottery. If, however, a stockpile of new plates was already available, the task becomes trivial, the time required is greatly reduced, and the responsibility falls to one who already may be involved in aspects of ritual preparation.

In spite of the fact that these plates are ceremonial vessels—as witnessed by their structured and constrained symbolism—they are being disposed of with the household cooking, storage, and eating pots. Their ubiquity at Angel, plus their occurrence at smaller sites, indicates that the primary, or at least final, focus of their use was within the households.

The ethnohistoric material presented earlier indicates that the plates— through their symbolism—were linked to rituals concerned with agriculture, fertility, and basic life forces. The ethnohistoric literature also indicates that, although the rituals may have been "elite sponsored" (Pauketat and Emerson 1991:922), of more importance was that they were integrative festivals in which all members of society participated. The plates may have been decorated by a chiefly sponsored ritual specialist, but it seems likely that they were distributed to clan or household heads for use during the ceremonies. Afterward, many were carried back to individual households.

The Angel Negative Painted plates might have been broken as a part of the ritual cleaning of the village at the end of the old ceremonial year, rather than at the end of the ceremony for which they were made. If this were the case, it suggests that the plates acquired a ritual energy—through contact with the new fire and first fruits—not unlike that endowing the new fire during the rite. Throughout the ceremonial year both the fire and the plates were used in various rites until by the end of the year both had lost their power or were considered polluted. Both were ritually destroyed and then discarded. New fire and new plates began the ritual cycle anew.

6 Chronology of the Angel Site and Phase

This chapter presents a pottery chronology for the Angel site and phase. As I noted at the beginning of Chapter 1, there have been many studies of the Angel society, and they have provided a great deal of information. They lacked a time scale with which to examine issues related to the growth and decline of Angel, however. Researchers were forced to treat the four centuries assigned to the site and phase as a single chronological unit, with no developmental trajectory.

Schurr's (1989a, 1989b) relative fluorine chronology of the Angel human burials was a breakthrough in the Angel chronological impasse. By ordering a sample of the burials from the eastern village on the basis of their mean fluorine content and then establishing their relative chronological relationship with other structural features in this part of the site, Schurr demonstrated that the burials in the eastern village represent a continuous episode of mortuary activity that occurred relatively late in the occupation of the site. Nevertheless, he was unable to determine the absolute dating of the episode of mortuary activity.

The major goal of this research has been to provide a chronological framework for the prehistoric Angel society to facilitate future studies of these people. Such a framework is in place for Kincaid, the other large Mississippian town in the lower Ohio Valley, and for the Wickliffe site, a smaller town located at the confluence of the Ohio and Mississippi Rivers (Figure 6.1). The Angel, Kincaid, and Wickliffe pottery assemblages exhibit many stylistic similarities. Thus, the three-phase sequence for the A.D. 1000/1100 to 1450 time period in the Kincaid and lower Tennessee–Cumberland region and the three-phase sequence for the A.D. 1100 to 1350 time period for the Wickliffe site and their diagnostic pottery assemblages form an essential background for the Angel phase chronology developed in this chapter.

Kincaid and Environs

Kincaid was excavated from 1934 to 1944 by a group from the University of Chicago (Cole et al. 1951). These excavations explored portions of four mounds in the western mound group (Mx4, Mx7, Mx8, and Mx9), one mound in the eastern mound group (Pp2), portions of the western plaza (Mx1D), vil-

Figure 6.1. Mississippian sites in the lower Ohio Valley region.

lage areas in the extreme western part of the site (Mx1A, Mx1A-41, Mx1B, and Mx1C), and segments of the stockade north and south of the western mound group (Mx36 and Mx31).

An important part of *Kincaid: A Prehistoric Illinois Metropolis* (Cole et al. 1951) was Kenneth Orr's appendix, "Change at Kincaid: A Study of Cultural Dynamics" (Orr 1951). Orr's study documented changes in pottery styles that occurred during the Middle Mississippian "Kincaid" component. Orr used samples from the upper and lower levels of four "domiciliary" mounds, Mx4, Mx1A-35, Mx1A-41, and Mx1B. The samples were assembled into a combined sample; the upper levels constituted a "Late" period sample and the lower levels an "Early" period sample. These assignments were later adjusted as the relative chronological position of each context was assessed.

Many of the chronological trends Orr discerned (Table 6.1) have already been noted in the appropriate discussions in Chapters 3, 4, and 5. Between the Early and Late Periods he interposed a Middle Period, which he described as "one of transition in which the traits show form and frequency characteristics intermediate between the Early and Late periods" (Orr 1951:356).

Orr's work provides a fairly detailed statement on changes in paste, vessel forms, secondary attributes, and decoration. Robert Riordan (1975:145–167) reevaluated Orr's trends using the published counts and percentages and noted that it was difficult to reconstruct numbers, but the trends were generally supported. More recently, Brian Butler (1991:265) echoed this sentiment, albeit with reservations: "Thus, while Orr's study successfully identifies the general style trends in the Mississippian ceramic sequence, the details are fuzzy and there is little information on specific contexts. Orr ultimately divided the occupational sequence into three segments—Early, Middle, and Late—but these units must be viewed with considerable caution. The early and middle units, in particular, suffer badly from chronologically mixed lots of material" (Butler 1991:265).

Jon Muller (1978, 1986) suggested that the Mississippian occupation at Kincaid dates primarily to the A.D. 1200 to 1300 time period (Figure 6.2; Appendix C) because the majority of the extant radiocarbon dates from Kincaid and other Black Bottom Mississippian sites fall into this century.

R. Berle Clay (1963, 1976, 1979) synthesized the University of Kentucky's work on Mississippian sites in the lower Tennessee and Cumberland Valleys south of Kincaid and defined two local phases. The earlier of these, the Jonathan Creek phase, is defined on the basis of assemblages from the Jonathan Creek site (15Ml4), the lower midden at Tinsley Hill (15Ly18), and Dedmon (15Ml68). The later of the two phases, the Tinsley Hill phase, is defined on the basis of assemblages from Goheen (15Ml14), Roach (15Tr10), Birmingham (15Ml8), Rodgers (15Tr17), a portion of Jonathan Creek, and the upper midden at Tinsley Hill.

Clay (1979) recognized that there is a stylistic and temporal gap between the Jonathan Creek and Tinsley Hill phases that is filled by the Angelly phase, as defined by Riordan (1975). The pottery characteristics and absolute dating of the Angelly phase are based on assemblages from the Angelly hamlet (11Mx66) and a number of excavated farmsteads (BBMx213, BBMx164, and BBPp105) in the Black Bottom around Kincaid. More recently, analysis of material recovered during the Kentucky Heritage Council's salvage of the Chambers site (15Ml109) (Pollack and Railey 1987), located on the East Fork Clarks River, a tributary of the Tennessee River, indicates it is also a late Angelly phase village.

The Jonathan Creek phase is dated to the period A.D. 1000/1100 to 1200 on the basis of two radiocarbon dates from the Dedmon site and one date from the lower midden at Tinsley Hill (Figure 6.3). (This is a slightly different span

Table 6.1
Pottery Characteristics of Orr's Early and Late Periods[1]

	EARLY PERIOD	LATE PERIOD
ware	plates, bottles, and bowls tend to be made of a finer (Bell) paste	plates, bottles, and bowls tend to be made of a coarser (Mississippi) paste
vessel forms	bowls relatively more common	pans supplanting bowls in popularity
pans	heavier, thicker, fabric-impressed exteriors	thinner with a beveled lip, plain surfaces more common
jars	shorter, flared rims, more handles, fewer lugs, thinner lugs, loop and intermediate loop-strap handle forms, nodes, jars rarely decorated, decoration includes lobed bodies with incised arcs (Matthews Incised, *variety Matthews*)	longer rims, more lugs, fewer handles, thinner lugs, wide strap handles, incising rare, lobed jars with double row of punctations (Matthews Incised, *variety Manly*)
bottles	black-on-red negative painting more common, elaborate owl heads on hooded bottles, effigy modeling more detailed/elaborate	black-on-buff negative painting more common, human and animal heads on hooded bottles, modeling simplified
plates	more curved rim, more horizontal, short rim, punctations or incised designs, black-on-red negative painting more common	straighter, steeper, longer rims, black-on-buff negative painting more common
bowls	fish, human hand, and bird effigies cruder	frog and "snout" bowls occur, modeling of features more refined/conventionalized, fewer birds, more humans and animals

[1] Table compiled from Orr 1951.

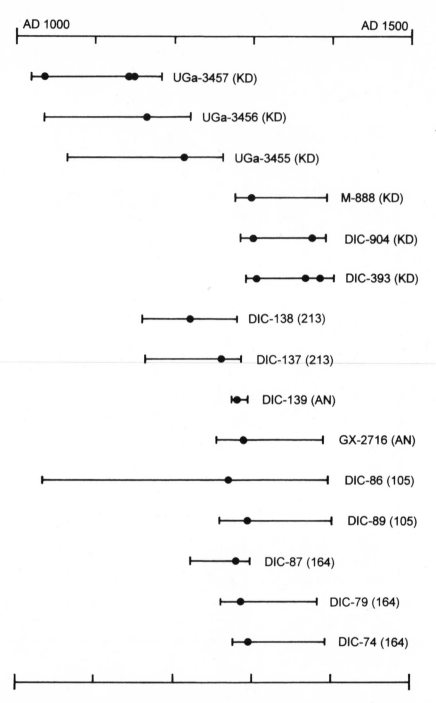

Figure 6.2. Kincaid and Black Bottom sites radiocarbon dates. Letters or numbers in parentheses following lab number identify the site: *(KD)*, Kincaid; *(AN)*, Angelly (11Mx66); *(105)*, BBPp105; *(164)*, BBMx164; *(213)*, BBMx213.

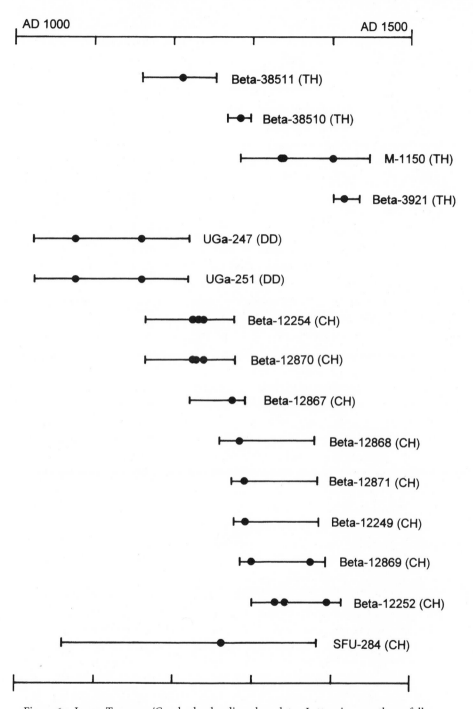

Figure 6.3. Lower Tennessee/Cumberland radiocarbon dates. Letters in parentheses following lab number identify the site: *(TH)*, Tinsley Hill; *(DD)*, Dedmon; *(CH)*, Chambers.

of time from that cited by Muller [1986:185] and Butler [1991:226]. The difference lies with the different radiocarbon calibration curves used [Klein et al. 1982; Stuiver and Reimer 1993; Stuiver et al. 1998] and the recently acquired radiocarbon date from Tinsley Hill.) Clay (1979) stresses the simplicity of the Jonathan Creek assemblage. Old Town Red (1.6 percent of the assemblage) and McKee Island Cord Marked are the important decorated types. Most of the lower Ohio Valley and Tennessee-Cumberland decorative modes—incising, engraving, punctating, and negative and direct painting—are missing (see also Wolforth 1987:Table 3). The most important temporal marker of this phase is the loop handle on jars.

Muller (1986:184) and Butler (1991:266) questioned Clay's depiction of the Jonathan Creek phase pottery assemblage as simple because Clay's samples from the Jonathan Creek and Tinsley Hill sites were small. Wolforth's (1987) reanalysis of a larger sample of pottery from twelve house basins from Jonathan Creek, however, corroborates Clay's earlier description of the phase assemblage. Work on contemporary early Mississippian assemblages in the Mississippi River counties of western Kentucky—the late half of the James Bayou phase (A.D. 900 to 1100) and the early half of the Dorena phase (A.D. 1100 to 1300) (Lewis 1991:281–290; Lewis and Mackin 1984)—demonstrates that these assemblages are as undecorated as the Jonathan Creek phase assemblages to the east.

The Angelly phase dates to the A.D. 1200 to 1300 period and is relatively well dated when compared with the preceding and succeeding phases. Radiocarbon dates from the small Black Bottom sites are similar to those from Chambers (Figures 6.2 and 6.3). The Black Bottom Angelly phase decorated pottery assemblages include sherds of the types Matthews Incised, O'Byam Incised, *variety O'Byam*, Old Town Red, and Angel Negative Painted. Plates are the standard plate form. Three loop and three intermediate handles occur (Riordan 1975:Appendix 1). The Chambers assemblage includes O'Byam Incised, *variety O'Byam* standard plate sherds and pieces of Mound Place Incised, Matthews Incised, Beckwith Incised, Barton Incised, Old Town Red, Angel Negative Painted, and Kincaid Negative Painted. Handles are the narrow and wide intermediate forms (Pollack and Railey 1987:74–88).

Finally, the Tinsley Hill phase is dated to the A.D. 1300 to 1450 period. There are two accepted radiocarbon dates from the Tinsley Hill site, with calibrated intercepts of A.D. 1334, 1336, and 1400 (M-1150) from the cemetery and A.D. 1416 (Beta-3921) from a house support post in the village (Figure 6.3). Clay (1984:106) considers the very late, post–A.D. 1500 dates from Tinsley Hill, Roach, and Goheen erroneous because they are far more recent than radiocarbon assays run in the last few years on samples with equivalent pottery associations.

The Tinsley Hill phase decorated pottery assemblage includes McKee Island Cord Marked, Old Town Red, Matthews Incised, Beckwith Incised, O'Byam

Incised, *variety Stewart* deep rim plates, Angel Negative Painted, and Kincaid Negative Painted. Jars have wide strap handles (Clay 1979). As Butler notes, "There are substantial amounts of later ceramic material (Tinsley Hill phase) at Kincaid" (1991:271).

Rather than rework Orr's tripartite Kincaid phase chronology, the Kincaid area researchers (Butler 1991:266–267; Muller 1986:183–185; Riordan 1975:168–180) have chosen to adopt the combined lower Tennessee–Cumberland and Black Bottom phase chronology. Although Butler cautions against equating Early Kincaid with Jonathan Creek, Middle Kincaid with Angelly, and Late Kincaid with Tinsley Hill, the handle forms illustrated as being Early, Middle, and Late Kincaid (Cole et al. 1951:Plate XXII) appear to be the same forms that distinguish the Jonathan Creek, Angelly, and Tinsley Hill phases. Thus, it does seem likely that the two sequences are roughly equivalent.

Wickliffe Phase Chronology

A second relevant phase chronology with distinctive pottery markers has been defined by Kit Wesler (1991a, 1991b, 1991c) for the Wickliffe site (15Ba4), located just south of the confluence of the Ohio with the Mississippi River. The pottery characteristics of the three Wickliffe phases are similar to the characteristics of the Jonathan Creek and Angelly assemblages. It thus demonstrates that many of the stylistic trends and pottery markers just discussed are useful beyond the immediate Kincaid and lower Tennessee–Cumberland area.

The Early Wickliffe phase (A.D. 1100 to 1200) assemblage is characterized by a relatively high frequency of red-slipped pottery, Old Town Red (2.5 to 3.5 percent) to incised pottery (0.5 to 1.0 percent) and loop handles on jars. The Middle Wickliffe (A.D. 1200 to 1250) assemblage is marked by the appearance of O'Byam Incised, *variety Adams* decorations on short rim plates and intermediate handles. Red-slipped and incised sherds are represented in roughly equal proportions (1.5 to 3.0 percent) in the assemblage. During the Late Wickliffe phase (A.D. 1250 to 1350), the standard plate and O'Byam Incised, *variety O'Byam* replaces the short rim plate and *variety Adams*. The jar handle shape remains the intermediate form, but the proportion of incised sherds exceeds that of red-slipped sherds. The increasing rarity of red-slipped pottery is illustrative of a widely noted regional pattern whereby red slipping gradually drops out of the later Mississippian decorative repertoire in the confluence region (Lewis 1990a). Also, given that Late Wickliffe ends at about A.D. 1350, it is not surprising that strap handles, deep rim plates, O'Byam Incised, *variety Stewart*, and other post–A.D.1300/1350 pottery styles present in Tinsley Hill phase assemblages are absent or occur as singular pieces at Wickliffe.

Regional Pottery Stylistic Trends

One of the purposes of the formal classification of the Angel pottery assemblage was to identify any morphological or stylistic pottery attributes that might have chronological significance and to determine which of these occur frequently enough to be useful in constructing a pottery chronology for Angel. This research was not carried out in an intellectual vacuum, however. The majority of the morphologies and decorations that occur in sufficient frequency in the excavated contexts so as to be useful in a seriation are known to have temporal significance. The most important of these are the handle and plate morphologies, two jar decorations, and two bowl decorations.

Handles

Previous studies in the Ohio Valley and adjacent regions have indicated that the morphologies of handles have temporal significance (Butler 1991; Clay 1963, 1976, 1979; Orr 1951:331; Phillips, Ford, and Griffin 1951:152; Pollack and Railey 1987; Riordan 1975; Smith 1969; Wesler 1988, 1991a, 1991b, 1991c; Williams 1954:114). Loop handles are diagnostic of the early Kincaid "phase," the Jonathan Creek phase in the lower Tennessee–Cumberland Valleys (A.D. 1000/1100 to 1200), and Early Wickliffe phase (A.D. 1100 to 1200). Intermediate handles are diagnostic of the middle Kincaid "phase," the Angelly phase (A.D. 1200 to 1300), and the Middle Wickliffe and Late Wickliffe phases (A.D. 1200 to 1250 and A.D. 1250 to 1350, respectively). Strap handles are diagnostic of the late Kincaid "phase" and the Tinsley Hill phase (A.D. 1300 to 1450).

The morphologies of the Angel handles were defined metrically using a ratio of middle thickness to middle width (see Chapter 4; Figure 4.3). The range of this ratio is from 0.1 to greater than 1.2 (a thin strap handle to a thick loop handle). For the purposes of this study, strap handles are those with ratios of 0.10 to 0.38, wide intermediate handles are those with ratios of 0.39 to 0.56, narrow intermediate handles are those with ratios of 0.57 to 0.74, and loop handles are those with ratios of 0.75 to greater than 1.0.

Plates

As is the case with handles, the morphologies of plates have temporal significance. In the Ohio Valley and contiguous regions, plates are generally assigned to one of five types—Bell Plain, Old Town Red, Angel Negative Painted, O'Byam Incised, or Wells Incised—depending on the absence or presence and kind of decoration (Clay 1963, 1976; Griffin 1949:56, Plate III; Kelly 1984, 1991; Lewis and Mackin 1984:193; Phillips 1970:144; Vogel 1975:104–106; Williams 1954:220–223). The validity of Orr's chronological pattern—earlier plates tend to have shorter rims and later plates have wider rims—has been demonstrated for the lower Ohio Valley (O'Byam Incised plates) and for the American

Bottom–Illinois Valley (Wells Incised plates) (Clay 1976; Conrad 1991; Kelly 1984, 1991; Lewis 1990a, 1990b, 1991; Lewis and Mackin 1984:194; Vogel 1975:104; Wesler 1991a).

Short rim plates with O'Byam Incised, *variety Adams* decorations are diagnostic of the Dorena phase (A.D. 1100 to 1300) and the Middle Wickliffe phase (A.D. 1200 to 1250) of the Ohio-Mississippi confluence area. Short rim plates with Wells Incised, *variety Broad Trailed* designs, which are similar to O'Byam Incised, *variety Adams* decorations, are diagnostic of the earlier part of the Morehead phase (A.D. 1200 to 1275) in the American Bottom and the Orendorf phase (A.D. 1200 to 1275) in the middle Illinois Valley. (Calendrical dating of the American Bottom phases follows the chronology suggested by Hall [1991:Figure 1.3]. Calendrical dating of the middle Illinois Valley phases are rough corrections of the phase chronology outlined by Conrad [1991].)

Standard plates with O'Byam Incised, *variety O'Byam* decorations are diagnostic of the Medley phase (A.D. 1300 to 1500) and the Late Wickliffe phase (A.D. 1250 to 1350). Standard plates in the Kincaid and lower Tennessee–Cumberland area, with either O'Byam Incised, *variety O'Byam* or Angel Negative Painted designs, date to the Angelly phase (A.D. 1200 to 1300). Standard plates with Wells Incised, *variety Broad Trailed* and *variety Fine Incised* occur during the later Morehead and Sand Prairie phases (A.D. 1200 to 1275 and A.D. 1275 to 1350, respectively) in the American Bottom and during the Orendorf and Larson phases (A.D. 1200 to 1275 and A.D. 1275 to 1325, respectively) in the middle Illinois Valley.

Deep rim plates with O'Byam Incised, *variety Stewart* motifs are diagnostic of the Tinsley Hill phase (A.D. 1300 to 1450) of the Kincaid and lower Tennessee–Cumberland area. The same plate form with Crable Incised designs is diagnostic of the Crabtree and Crable phases (A.D. 1300 to 1350 and A.D. 1350 to 1425, respectively) of the middle Illinois Valley.

The morphologies of the plates from Angel are also defined metrically (see Chapter 3; Figure 3.3). Short rim plates have plate rim widths that are less than 28 millimeters, standard plates have plate rim widths that are between 28 and 65 millimeters, and deep rim plates have plate rim widths that are between 66 millimeters and 122 millimeters. The short rim plates are further divided into two groups. One consists of those with "triangular theme" rim decorations; these include Angel Negative Painted, O'Byam Incised, *variety Adams,* or scalloped lip decorations. The second group consists of those with the Vanderburgh Stamped decorations.

Jar Decorations

Two jar decorations, Ramey Incised, *variety Green River* and Parkin Punctated, *variety Parkin* are relatively common in the Angel assemblage. Ramey Incised, *variety Green River,* a new variety designation for the material occurring at Angel, is similar to American Bottom Morehead phase (A.D. 1200 to 1275) Ramey Incised (J. Kelly, G. Holley, and G. Milner 1988, personal communication). Ramey Incised is absent from later American Bottom Sand Prairie phase (A.D. 1275 to 1350) assemblages (Milner et al. 1984:173–181). Parkin Punctated, in contrast, occurs no earlier than A.D. 1350 or 1400 (Morse and Morse 1983:278) in the central Mississippi Valley.

Bowl Decorations

Two secondary modifications of bowls have chronological significance. These are the beaded rim and notched applique strip. Smith (1992:123) notes that bowls with notched applique strips are diagnostic of the Thruston phase (A.D. 1250 to 1450) of the middle Cumberland Valley. Polhemus (1990:41) indicates that bowls with notched applique strips and beaded rims are characteristic of the Middle Dallas phase (A.D. 1450 to 1525) in eastern Tennessee.

Seriation And Chronology

The succession of handle and plate morphologies and jar and bowl decorations (Figure 6.4) is well dated elsewhere in the Midsouth. It would be easy at this point to create a pottery chronology—and to define a chronological series of phases—by cross-dating these elements of the Angel assemblage to better-dated assemblages in the Midsouth. However, if I were content with creating a chronology in this way, there would always be questions, in my mind at least, concerning the validity and applicability of such a chronology. For example, Kreisa (1993) has noted that there is geographical and temporal variation in the incorporation of key pottery types into Mississippian assemblages in western Kentucky. Therefore, the temporal significance of any pottery marker must be evaluated anew as it is encountered in a new geographical area. It is important to establish the chronological markers and trends independently for Angel. This was done by selecting a number of archaeological contexts and seriating them and then evaluating the seriation results by means of other available chronological information.

Context and Attribute Selection

Angel does not present a textbook case for the application of seriation to create a pottery chronology, and in this respect it probably represents the usual situation, not an exception. A pottery chronology based on the seriation of grave lots, such as that created by Steponaitis (1983) for Moundville, was simply not an option. Pottery is not commonly associated with Angel burials (Schurr 1989a:133–134). Only 24 (or 6.5 percent) of the burials have clearly associated pottery vessels, and many of these vessels do not have temporally diagnostic attributes.

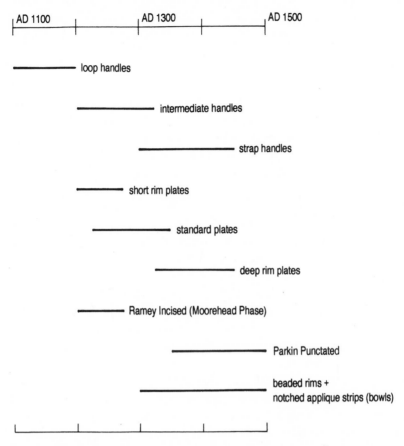

Figure 6.4. Estimated duration of diagnostic pottery types and attributes during the A.D. 1100 to 1500 time period.

Pottery was a common fill item in the thousands of excavation block levels and features. Such contexts are often considered less desirable for seriation because their deposition occurred over an extended period of time. Nevertheless, they are perfectly acceptable (Marquardt 1978) and yield useful results, as exemplified by the Summerville phase chronology that was created by using a combination of feature and excavation level contexts (Peebles and Mann 1983), provided some care is exercised in their selection.

There are potentially thousands of possible contexts at Angel that could be selected for seriation. The majority of these are in the eastern village. Deposits in this part of the site were up to 2.8 feet in depth (Black 1967:Figures 85, 118), and in places up to seven arbitrary 0.4-foot levels were excavated. Thus, some stratigraphic relationships were preserved. Inspection of the plan maps (Black 1967:Figures 78, 89, 130, 176, 270, and 310) suggests that the occupational and depositional history of the eastern village and the majority of the midden were badly disturbed by aboriginal earthmoving activities. Some selection criteria are necessary to identify any relatively undisturbed contexts that remain.

Parkin Punctated and Ramey Incised are useful as context selection criteria for at least two reasons. First, there should be a chronological gap between the occurrence of the two on the order of seventy-five to one hundred years. If sherds of both Ramey and Parkin occur in the same feature or level, then the span of time represented by the feature or level contents is likely to be greater than the desired phase duration of 100 to 150 years. Second, they are more useful than plate and handle forms because they are unambiguous. A sherd is Ramey Incised or not, or it is Parkin Punctated or not. Of all of the different kinds of items in the Angel pottery assemblage, they most closely approximate horizon markers (Willey and Phillips 1958:32–33). In contrast, the characterizations of plate and handle forms are based on somewhat arbitrary lines drawn on a continuum, no matter how well informed the lines are from study of this and other assemblages. Also, in any normally distributed population of handles (or plates) produced over a short period of time, there will be some that are atypical. Put another way, if the "style" of handle at some point in time is the intermediate form, I would expect a few loops and few straps also to have been produced.

The occurrences of handle and plate forms and Ramey Incised and Parkin Punctated were tabulated by feature, burial, and excavation block level. All archaeological contexts having one or none of these morphologies or decorations were eliminated from further consideration. This is because seriation programs eliminate contexts with only one attribute, or attributes that occur once, and because seriation programs order the attributes and contexts based on the *combination* of attributes within individual contexts. Then, all contexts having both Ramey Incised and Parkin Punctated or, in the case of the excavation blocks, having a sherd of Ramey Incised in the same level as or in a level stratigraphically above a Parkin Punctated sherd were eliminated as being either of too great a duration or too badly mixed.

After these sequential eliminations, twelve features remained. Two areas in the eastern village midden were also identified as being minimally disturbed. These areas were in the southwestern part of X-11-C (Black 1967:Figure 89) and the south central part of W-11-A (Black 1967:Figure 176). Inspection of the floor plans of these two areas showed that features were less dense in these areas, and the strata were probably less mixed due to aboriginal earthmoving. Levels from these areas could be selected and seriated with a degree of confidence.

Within these general guidelines, levels were selected and in some cases combined to represent as wide a range as possible of co-occurring pottery types and attributes. The goal was to eliminate mixed contexts but not to predetermine the results of the seriation on the basis of which contexts were selected and which were not.

Seriation Procedure

Initially I performed a seriation of thirty-three features and levels, four handle forms, three plate forms, Ramey Incised, Parkin Punctated, and two groups of short rim plate decorations using the Bonn Seriation program, Version 4.1 (Scollar and Herzog 1991) for presence-absence data (cemetery module) in stable iteration mode. The presence-absence procedure is more appropriate than the abundance procedure because single occurrences and very low frequencies of the proposed diagnostic morphologies and attributes are the norm in the Angel contexts. Marquardt (1978) provides an extensive review of the theory and practice of seriation as a chronological tool, and the Bonn program manual (Scollar and Herzog 1991; see also Ihm and van Groenewoud 1984; Read 1989; Scollar, Weidner, and Herzog 1985) discusses the particular seriation algorithms, which are based on correspondence analysis, used by the programs.

The results of the preliminary seriation runs were successful. The criteria for success were that the repeated runs of the program using different random number starting points produced results in which the stratigraphic relationships of levels were preserved and the succession of pottery types and attributes was reasonable.

I then selected an additional twenty-three levels and combinations of levels using the same criteria as before in an attempt to increase the number of pottery types and attributes considered and to sample other parts of the village midden. The pottery assemblage from each feature and level was tabulated, and fifty-six contexts, including twelve features and forty-four levels and level combinations, and twenty-two pottery types, morphologies, or attributes (Tables 6.2 and 6.3) were seriated. A total of five seriation runs were completed. The orders of archaeological contexts and pottery characteristics were similar in all five cases. Figure 6.5 reproduces the results of one run.

Acceptability of Results

A seriation program produces a best-fit order of artifacts and archaeological contexts based on the available data. Therefore, it is a statistical construct, and its validity as a chronological order needs to be evaluated on the basis of all relevant independent chronological information. In the case of these results, the validity of the seriation order as a chronological order is corroborated by the applicable stratigraphy, absolute radiocarbon dates, and relative fluorine assays.

STRATIGRAPHY

Inspection of the relative placement of the stratigraphic levels (Figure 6.5) reveals that the basal levels of the midden (1.6–2.0, 2.0–2.4, 2.4–2.8 feet below surface) are generally at the bottom (i.e., the earlier) end of the seriation order

Table 6.2
Pottery Types, Morphologies, and Attributes Utilized in the Seriation

VESSEL MORPHOLOGIES

short rim plate -- triangular theme decorations
 (this plate with Angel Negative Painted,
 O'Byam Incised, *variety Adams*, or scalloped
 lip decorations
short rim plate -- Vanderburgh Stamped
 decorations
standard plate
deep rim plate
colander

CLOSED HANDLE MORPHOLOGIES

loop handle
narrow intermediate handle
wide intermediate handle
strap handle

CLOSED HANDLE SECONDARY MODIFICATIONS

single groove	finely notched single
single horn	scallop
double horn	notched single scallop
single scallop	small scallops/horns
double scallop	

**BOWL DECORATIONS
& SECONDARY MODIFICATIONS**

Mound Place Incised
beaded rim
notched applique strip

JAR DECORATIONS

Ramey Incised
Parkin Punctated

and that the upper levels (0.4–0.8, 0.8–1.2 feet below surface) are generally at the upper, more recent end of the order. More specifically, never does a lower stratigraphic level, such as W11A/2R4/1.6-2.0, occur higher in the seriation order than does a higher stratigraphic level, such as W11A/2R4/0.8-1.2, in the same or an adjacent block. Thus, the physical stratigraphic placement of the excavation block levels is preserved in the seriated order.

Table 6.3
Features and Excavation Block Levels Used in the Seriation

FEATURES

F9/O-13-D	F23/O-13-D	F4/S-11-D	F5/S-11-D
F6/S-11-D	F13/X-11-B	F26/X-11-C	F46/X-11-C
F88/X-11-C	F1/X-11-D	F1/V-09-A	F10/W-10-D

LEVELS

X-11-C/4-R-5&X-11-D/4-L-5/0.8-1.2[1]	X-11-C/5-R-5&X-11-D/5-L-5/1.2-2.0
X-11-B/0-L-4&0-L-5/1.2-2.0	X-11-B/1-R-1/0.4-0.8
X-11-B/3-L-3&3-L-4&3-L-5/0.8-1.6	X-11-B/3-R-2/0.4-0.8
X-11-B/5-L-1&5-R-1/0.4-0.8	X-11-B/0-L-4&0-L-5&W-11-A/0-R-5/2.4-2.8
W-11-A/3-L-1&3-R-1/1.6-2.0	W-11-A/7-L-3&7-L-4/0.4-1.6
W-11-A/1-R-3&1-R-4/2.0-2.4	W-11-A/1-L-1/0.4-1.2
W-11-A/1-R-2/0.4-1.2	W-11-A/2-R-4/1.6-2.0
W-11-A/7-R-1/1.6-2.0	W-11-A/2-L-2/0.8-1.6
W-11-A/2-R-3/2.0-2.4	W-11-A/2-R-1&2-R-2/1.6-2.0
W-11-A/2-R-4/0.8-1.2	W-11-A/5-L-1/1.6-2.0
X-11-C/9-L-5/1.6-2.0	X-11-C/7-L-4/1.6-2.0
X-11-C/5-L-5/0.8-1.6	X-11-C/4-L-3/1.6-2.4
X-11-C/1-L-2&2-L-2/1.2-1.6	X-11-C/4-R-4/1.2-1.6
X-11-C/9-L-5/0.4-1.2	X-11-C/5-L-4/2.0-2.4
X-11-C/1-I-2/0.4	X-11-C/1-L-5/1.2-2.0
X-11-C/0-L-3/0.4-1.2	X-11-C/5-R-2/1.2-1.6
X-11-C/4-R-3/0.4-1.2	W-10-D/0-L-5/2.0
W-10-D/1-L-4/2.0	W-10-D/1-L-4/1.2-1.6
W-10-D/2-L-3/1.2-1.6	W-10-D/3-L-3/0.4-1.2
W-10-D/4-L-3/0.4-1.2	W-10-D/5-L-5&5-L-4/0.8-1.2
W-10-D/0-L-5&0-L-4/0.8-1.6	W-10-D/0-R-2/0.4-0.8
W-10-D/0-R-2/1.6-2.0	W-10-D/2-L-3&3-L-3/1.6-2.0

---

[1] Read: subdivision X-11-C, block 4-R-5 and subdivision X-11-D, block 4-L-5, level 0.8 to 1.2 ft below surface.

```
          ----------+----------------------------------------------------
F    W10D/4L3/0.4-1.2          |                           |      |    | ||
     X11C/1L2/0.4              |                           |      |    | |
e    F88/X11C             (f1) |                           |      |    | |
     W11A/1L1/0.4-1.2          |              |      | | | |      |    | ||
a    W10D/0L5&0L4/0.8-1.6      |                 | |  | | |      |    | ||
     W10D/1L3/1.2-1.6          |                |      | |      |    | ||
t    W11A/7L3&7L4/0.4-1.6      |               |   | | | |    | | | | ||
     X11C/1L5/1.2-2.0          |             |      | |      | |      ||
u    X11C/0L3/0.4-1.2          |                   |      | | |      |
     W10D/5L5&5L4/0.8-1.2      |                |      | | |      |
r    X11B/5L1&5R1/0.4-0.8      |                      | | |      |
     X11C/4R3/0.4-1.2          |              | |    | | |      ||
e.   X11B/3L5&3L4&3L3/0.8-1.6  |              | |  | | |    | |  |
     F4/S11D                   |                   |      |      |
s    W11A/2L2/0.8-1.6          |                    |      |      |
     F6/S11D              (c14)|           | | |  | | |    | | |  | ||
/    X11C/5L5/0.8-1.6          |             | |  | |      | |      |
     W11A/1R2/0.4-1.2          |             | | | |  | | |      |
L    W11A/2R4/0.8-1.2          |               |    | |      |
     F10/W10D                  |                 |      |      |
e    F5/S11D              (c14)|          |   |      | |    |      |
     W10D/3L3/0.4-1.2          |             | |  | | | |      |
v    F26/X11C                  |             |      | | |      |
     X11C/5L4/2.0-2.4          |               |  | |      |
e    X11C/4L3/1.6-2.4          |           | | |  | |    | |  |
     X11B/3R2/0.4-0.8          |             |      |      |
l    W10D/2L3/1.2-1.6          |        |    | |      |  | .    |
     W10D/0R2/0.4-0.8          |       |      | |      |      |
s    - - - - - - - - - - - - - - - - - - - - - - - - - - - - - -
     F13/X11B              (f1)|         | | |  | |    |
     X11C/1L2&2L2/1.2-1.6      |       |      | |  |      |
     F1/V9A                    |         | | |  |
     X11B/1R1/0.4-0.8          |      |    |      |    |      |
     X11C/9L5/0.4-1.2          |       |    | |  |
     F9/O13D             (f1,c14)|       | | |  |
     X11C/5R5&X11D/5L5/1.2-2.0 |      |    | | |  |
     X11B/0L5&0L4/1.2-2.0      |       |    | |  |
     F1/X11D                   |         |    |      |
     F23/O13D              (f1)|    |    | |  |
     W10D/1L4/2.0              |    |    | |  |
     W10D/0R2/1.6-2.0          |    |      |      |
     X11C/4R5&X11D/4L5/0.8-1.2 | |    |    | |    |
     W11A/3L1&3R1/1.6-2.0      | |    |      |      |
     X11B/0L4&0L5&W11A/0R5/2.4-2.8 | |    | |  |
     W11A/1R3&1R4/2.0-2.4      | |    |  | |
     W11A/2R1&2R2/1.6-2.0      | |  | |  |      |
     X11C/4R4/1.2-1.6          | |    |      |
     W11A/2R4/1.6-2.0          | |    |
     W10D/2L3&3L3/1.6-2.0      | |  |      |
     X11C/5R2/1.2-1.6          |  | | |  |
     W11A/5L1/1.6-2.0          | |  |    |
     W11A/2R3/2.0-2.4          | |  |
     X11C/7L4/1.6-2.0          | |    |
     W10D/0L5/2.0              | |  |
     F46/X11C                  | | | |
     W11A/7R1/1.6-2.0          | | |
     X11C/9L5/1.6-2.0          | | |
          --------------------------------------------------------------|
```
Figure 6.5. Angel seriation order. Dashed line divides it into Angel 2 and Angel 3 phases.

Three of the features that were seriated have associated radiocarbon dates. F9/O-13-D has one acceptable date with a corrected intercept of A.D. 1278 (Beta-39234). F5/S-11-D has two dates with corrected intercepts of A.D. 1299 and 1375 (Beta-44768) and A.D. 1302, 1369, and 1382 (Beta-44769). F6/S-11-D also has two dates with corrected intercepts of A.D. 1334, 1336, and 1400 (Beta-44771) and A.D. 1412 (Beta-44770). The chronological ordering of these three features—from earlier to later, F9/O-13-D, F5/S-11-D, and F6/S-11-D—based on radiocarbon dates is preserved in the seriation order.

FLUORINE ASSAYS

Four features in the seriated order are also ordered on the basis of mean fluorine content (in parts per million [ppm]) of deer metapodials from those features (Schurr and Hilgeman 1991). The order of three, F23/O-13-D (0.400544 ppm), F9/O-13-D (0.187078 ppm), and F13/X-11-B (0.078598 ppm), is the same as that produced by the seriation. However, F88/X-11-C (0.188600 ppm) is placed prior to F9/O-13-D on the basis of fluorine content and after F13/X-11-B in the seriated order. This discrepancy is not a serious problem because F88/X-11-C has relatively few chronologically important markers and may be misplaced in the seriation order.

The Angel Pottery Chronology in Regional Perspective

The seriated order is divided into two segments in Figure 6.5, which represent two chronological phases; these will be discussed as the Angel 2 and Angel 3 phases in the next section. I chose the place indicated by the horizontal line to divide the seriation order into two segments; this area seemed to minimize the within-group differences and maximize the between-group differences. Put another way, at this point in the seriation order the important pottery characteristics of the earlier Angel 2 phase—short rim plate with triangular theme decorations, Ramey Incised, loop handles, standard plates and narrow intermediate handles—are occurring less frequently and at the same time the important characteristics of the later Angel 3 phase—deep rim plates, strap handles, short rim plates with Vanderburgh Stamped decorations, beaded bowl rims and colanders—are occurring more frequently. The radiocarbon dates and cross-dating of the diagnostics suggest that the seriated order represents the A.D. 1200 to 1450 time period.

The pottery types, morphologies, and attributes contribute to varying degrees to the seriated order. The plate and handle morphologies and jar decorations form the backbone of the order, as expected. The handle top and body secondary modifications contributed little additional information to the succession of handle morphologies. This was unexpected but is due to the fact that most of the secondary modifications occur on specific handle shapes. Mound Place Incised also was relatively unimportant. The colander, a minor bowl form, and the bowl secondary modifications, beaded rim and notched applique strip, are valuable late markers.

In the conclusion of Chapter 3, I noted that two important regional patterns serve to distinguish the Angel pottery assemblage from contemporaneous Mississippian assemblages elsewhere in the Ohio Valley. First, the Angel assemblage is plain; less than 0.8 percent of the sherds that have been recovered are decorated (see Table 3.5). The Angel assemblage is similar to the lower Tennessee–Cumberland assemblages with respect to the proportion of decorated sherds. The Angel assemblage exhibits a smaller proportion of decorated sherds than do the Ohio-Mississippi confluence area assemblages.

When the total pottery assemblages from the seriated contexts are tabulated it is evident that the Angel assemblage gets plainer through time. To examine this trend, I divided the seriated order into quarters to approximate earlier and later halves of the two chronological phases, Angel 2 and Angel 3. For each quarter, I tabulated the major decorated types and converted the counts into percentages (Table 6.4). During the earlier half of the Angel 2 phase, decorated sherds make up a little less than 3 percent of the total sherds, but by the later half of the Angel 3 phase decorated sherds make up only about 0.6 percent of the total sherds.

The second pattern I noted in Chapter 3 was that painting—as opposed to other decorative techniques such as incising, engraving, or punctating—was the important decorative mode. The dominance of painted decoration distinguishes the Angel assemblage from assemblages recovered from sites to the southwest of Angel. Red slipping (Old Town Red, *variety Knight*) and negative painting (Angel Negative Painted, Kincaid Negative Painted, Nashville Negative Painted, and Sikeston Negative Painted) together represent about 0.75 percent of the Angel pottery assemblage. In contrast, all other decorative modes—including all incised, trailed, and engraved sherds, as well as Parkin Punctated and Pouncey Pinched sherds—represent only about 0.03 percent of the assemblage.

The valleywide trend is one of decreasing frequency of painted pottery through time. In the western Kentucky and the lower Tennessee–Cumberland assemblages, Old Town Red is the dominant decorated type prior to about A.D. 1200; after A.D. 1200, incising replaces red-slipping as the dominant decorative mode (see Clay 1963:Tables 4, 7, 12, 15, 18, 21, and 28; Pollack and Railey 1987:Tables 25 and 26; Riordan 1975:Appendix 1; Wesler 1991a, 1991b, 1991c).

The Angel assemblage does follow the trend of decreasing importance of painting through time (Table 6.4). During the earlier half of the Angel 2 phase,

Table 6.4
**Summary Counts and Percentages
for Some Decorated Pottery Types in the Seriated Contexts**

	Total Sherds	Old Town Red, *variety Knight*	Black-on-red negative painted[1]	Black-on-buff negative painted[2]	Incised[3]	Parkin Punctated
Later Angel 3[4]	14,302	57 (0.40)[5]	18 (0.13)	6 (0.04)	0	12 (0.08)
Earlier Angel 3[6]	9578	75 (0.78)	44 (0.46)	17 (0.18)	1 (<0.01)	15 (0.16)
Later Angel 2[7]	8746	82 (0.94)	40 (0.46)	13 (0.15)	11 (0.13)	0
Earlier Angel 2[8]	4515	45 (1.00)	34 (0.75)	22 (0.48)	17 (0.38)	0

---

[1] Includes Angel Negative Painted, *variety Angel* and Kincaid Negative Painted, *variety Kincaid.*

[2] Includes Angel Negative Painted, *variety Nurrenbern* and Kincaid Negative Painted, *variety Massac.*

[3] Includes O'Byam Incised, Ramey Incised, Mound Place Incised, Oliver decorated, and miscellaneous incised.

[4] Contexts included are: X-11-B/3-L-3 & 3-L-4 & 3-L-5/0.8-1.6, X-11-C/4-R-3/0.4-1.2, X-11-B/5-L-1 & 5-R-1/0.8-1.2, X-11-C/0-L-3/0.4-1/2, X-11-C/1-L-5/1.2-2.0, W-11-A/7-L-3 & 7-L-4/0.4-1.6, W-11-A/1-L-1/0.4-1.2.

[5] Count (percentage of total sherds)

[6] Contexts included are: X-11-B/3-R-2/0.4-0.8, X-11-C/4-L-3/1.6-2.4, X-11-C/5-L-4/2.0-2.4, W-11-A/2-R-4/0.8-1.2, W-11-A/1-R-2/0.4-1.2.. X-11-C/5-L-5/0.8-1.6, W-11-A/2-L-2/0.8-1.6.

[7] Contexts included are: W-11-A/1-R-3 & 1-R-4/2.0-2.4, X-11-B/0-L-4 & 0-L-5 & W-11-A/0-R-5/2.4-2.8, W-11-A/3-L-1 & 3-R-1/1.6-2.0, X-11-B/0-L-5 & 0-L-4/1.2-2.0, X-11-C/9-L-5/0.4-1.2, X-11-C/1-L-2 &2-L-2/1.2-1.6.

[8] Contexts included are: X-11-C/9-L-5/1.6-2.0, W-11-A/7-R-1/1.6-2.0, X-11-C/7-L-4/1.6-2.0, W-11-A/2-R-3/2.0-2.4, W-11-A/5-L-1/1.6-2.0, X-11-C/5-R-2/1.2-1.6, W-11-A/2-R-4/1.6-2.0, W-11-A/2-R-1 & 2-R-2/1.6-2.0.

red-slipped sherds make up about 1 percent and negative painted sherds make up about 1.2 percent of the total sherds. By the later half of the Angel 3 phase, however, red-slipped sherds make up only about 0.4 percent and negative painting make up only about 0.2 percent of the total sherds. Incising, never an important decorative technique at Angel, virtually drops out by the earlier Angel 3 years and is replaced by punctating (Parkin Punctated).

The Angel Phase Chronology

The seriated contexts and sherds encompass two cultural-historical phases; these are designated the Angel 2 and the Angel 3 phases. The pottery characteristics and absolute dating of these phases, plus a sketch of an earlier phase, are described in the following sections.

Stephan-Steinkamp Phase (Angel 1?), Earlier Than A.D. 1100 to 1200

The proposed Stephan-Steinkamp phase is not represented in the seriated order and is poorly represented, if at all, within the excavated contexts at Angel. It is included in this phase chronology and discussion primarily as a place holder. It is known from work at the Stephan-Steinkamp site (12Po33) and seems to be the period of the earliest Middle Mississippian occupations in the Angel vicinity.

Analysis of the surface collections from Stephan-Steinkamp (Schurr 1989c) suggests that the site is the result of two overlapping "Angel phase" (*sensu* Honerkamp 1975) components. Excavations in the area of overlap (Hilgeman 1989; Hilgeman and Schurr 1987) produced evidence of two chronologically distinct components, the earlier (Stephan-Steinkamp phase) of which is similar in pottery characteristics and absolute dating to the Jonathan Creek and Early Wickliffe phases to the southwest. At Stephan-Steinkamp, cord-marked (McKee Island Cord Marked) body sherds represent approximately 5 percent by weight of the total excavated body sherd collection, and Old Town Red sherds represent a little less than 2 percent by weight of the total excavated sherds. Two loop handles are also associated with deposits from this component.

Two plain-surfaced, shell-tempered body sherds from a basin-shaped pit (Feature 2) have thermoluminescence dates of A.D. 1010±160 and A.D. 1090±230 (Figure 6.6; Appendix B). The dating of the Stephan-Steinkamp phase, from before A.D. 1100 to 1200 is therefore very preliminary. (The more reasonable of the two Ellerbusch site [12W56] [Green 1977] radiocarbon dates, with a corrected intercept of A.D. 1160, also dates to this time period, but examination of pottery from the site suggests the date is too early [see also Green and Munson 1978:306].)

If a recognizable pre–A.D. 1200 assemblage, which is similar to the Stephan-Steinkamp assemblage, is identified at Angel in the future, the phase name

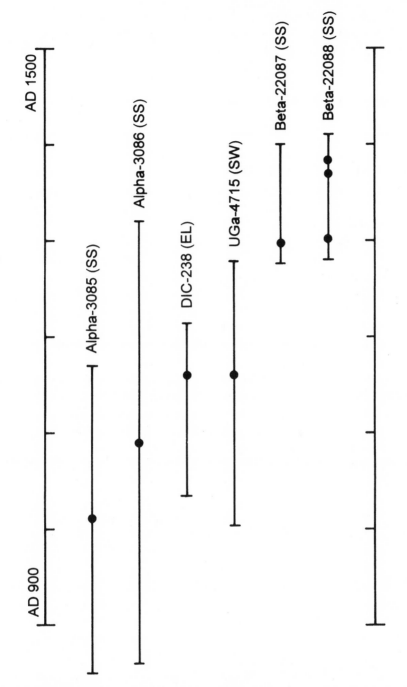

Figure 6.6. Angel phase radiocarbon and thermoluminescence dates. Letters in paren theses following lab number identify the site: *(EL)*, Ellerbusch; *(SS)*, Stephan-Steinkamp; *(SW)*, Southwind.

should be changed to Angel 1. (At present I am reluctant to name the phase "Angel 1" in the absence of deposits clearly dating to this time period at Angel.) In any case, more work is required at Angel, Stephan-Steinkamp, and similar sites to define more precisely the diagnostic pottery (Figure 6.7), absolute dating, and settlement characteristics of the Middle Mississippian presence in the Angel vicinity during this time period.

Angel 2 Phase, A.D. 1200 to 1325

The diagnostic characteristics of the Angel 2 phase assemblage include Ramey Incised, *variety Green River,* incised (O'Byam Incised, *variety Adams*), negative painted (Angel Negative Painted), and scalloped triangular designs on short rim plates and standard plates, and loop and narrow and wide intermediate handles (Figure 6.7).

The seriation diagram and cross-dating of the diagnostics suggest that it may be possible to recognize earlier and later halves of the phase. These subphases parallel the distinction between the Middle and Late Wickliffe phases. The earlier subphase of Angel 2 is distinguished by Ramey Incised jars, O'Byam Incised and scalloped lip short rim plates, and loop and intermediate handles. The sporadic presence of loop handles in the Angel 2 phase levels appears to be a real phenomenon; however, their presence may result from incorporation of relatively sparse earlier (Stephan-Steinkamp/Angel 1) materials into later deposits. The later half of the phase is recognizable by the presence of Old Town Red, Angel Negative Painted, and the rare O'Byam Incised, *variety O'Byam* standard plates and narrow and wide intermediate handles.

Only one of the Angel 2 features has an associated radiocarbon date. This feature is F9/O-13-D; the date has a corrected intercept of A.D. 1278 (Beta-39234; Figure 6.8). (A second date for this feature [Beta-39235] from an extremely small sample [<0.5 g after pretreatment] appears to be about 100 years too early.) One of the early Michigan dates, A.D. 1276 (M-7), is approximately contemporary with the F9/O-13-D date. It is from an unspecified house wall trench in the eastern village (block 9-L-4 in subdivision W-11-A). There is a considerable amount of Angel 2 pottery in the basal levels of adjacent blocks; thus the date is tentatively accepted as dating Angel 2 deposits.

The pottery assemblage from Southwind (12Po265) (Munson 1994) appears to date to the late Angel 2 period. It includes two loop handles, one narrow intermediate handle, four wide intermediate handles, two strap handles, sixteen standard plates, and two deep rim plates. In terms of plate and handle forms, the Southwind assemblage resembles the late Angelly phase Chambers site (15Ml109) (Pollack and Railey 1987). Four of the radiocarbon dates from Southwind have been shown to be coal contaminated (UGa-4645, -4646, -4647, -4716). The corrected intercept of the fifth date, A.D. 1161 (UGa-4715) (Munson

1994; Tankersley et al. 1987:Table 1), appears to be too early for this plate and handle assemblage, but the one sigma maximum range extends into the late A.D. 1200s.

Given the similarities in plate and handle forms of this phase to the Angelly and Middle and Late Wickliffe phases and the similar radiocarbon dates, the Angel 2 phase is assigned to the A.D. 1200 to 1325 time period. (A number of people have questioned the wisdom of using the seemingly precise date of A.D. 1325, rather than 1300 or 1350, as the cut point between the Angel 2 and Angel 3 phases. I chose it because it is the midpoint of the A.D. 1200 to 1450 time period and results in two phases of equal duration.)

Angel 3 Phase, A.D. 1325 to 1450

The diagnostic characteristics of the Angel 3 phase assemblage include wide intermediate and strap handles on jars, Old Town Red and Angel Negative Painted deep rim plates, Vanderburgh Stamped short rim plates, Parkin Punctated jars, notched applique strips and beaded rims on bowls, and colanders (Figure 6.7).

In comparison to Angel 2, the Angel 3 phase is well dated (Figure 6.8). Two features in the seriation order, F5/S-11-D and F6/S-11-D, each have two radiocarbon dates from the floors or fill of these house basins. The calibrated intercepts range from A.D. 1299 to 1412 (Beta-44768, -44769, -44770, and -44771). A square pit (F12/Mound F) on the "primary mound surface" (second-to-last building stage) of Mound F contains an Angel Negative Painted deep rim plate. Charcoal from a burned cover of the pit has two radiocarbon dates with calibrated intercepts of A.D. 1329, 1343, and 1395 (Beta-39233) and A.D. 1412 (M-4). (A third radiocarbon date from this feature, A.D. 1216 (Beta-39232), is from another small sample [<0.5 g after pretreatment] and is considered erroneous.)

Other areas of the site have similarly late associated radiocarbon dates. Another of the early Michigan dates, of A.D. 1332, 1340, and 1398 (M-5), from an unspecified wall trench in the eastern village (block 0-R-1 in subdivision W-10-D), is overlain by Angel 3 materials. Finally, there are two dates with corrected intercepts of A.D. 1421 (DIC-1024) and A.D. 1491, 1603, and 1609 (DIC-1023), from a habitation area located north of Mound A between the inner and outer stockade lines (in subdivision Q-08-C). The latter date seems too recent, but the one sigma minimum range extends back into the mid-A.D. 1400s. The A.D. 1421 date is consistent with the Old Town Red, *variety Knight* deep rim plate from this area as well as the other Angel 3 dates.

One Angel satellite dates to the Angel 3 phase time period. This is the eastern portion of Stephan-Steinkamp (12P033). One of the excavated house basins, Feature 9, has two associated radiocarbon dates. One, A.D. 1297 (Beta-22087), is from a wall timber or rafter lying horizontally approximately 0.2 feet

Figure 6.7. Hypothetical Stephan-Steinkamp (Angel 1), Angel 2, and Angel 3 pottery assemblages.

Angel 3 assemblage: strap handles (A, C, E, H, I, M, O); Parkin Punctated (C); deep rim plate (B & G); Old Town Red (G & N); Angel Negative Painted (B); Kincaid Negative Painted (F); notched short rim plate (D); beaded rim on bowl (D); notched applique strip on bowl (K); colander (L)

Angel 2 assemblage: intermediate handles (A, C, D, E, G, I, J, L, N); Ramey Incised (B); O'Byam Incised, *variety Adams* (F); short rim plate (F); Kincaid Negative Painted (H); Old Town Red (K & O); Angel Negative Painted (M); standard plates (M & O)

Stephan-Steinkamp assemblage: loop handles (A, B, D, E, G); McKee Island Cord-marked (C & G); Old Town Red (F)

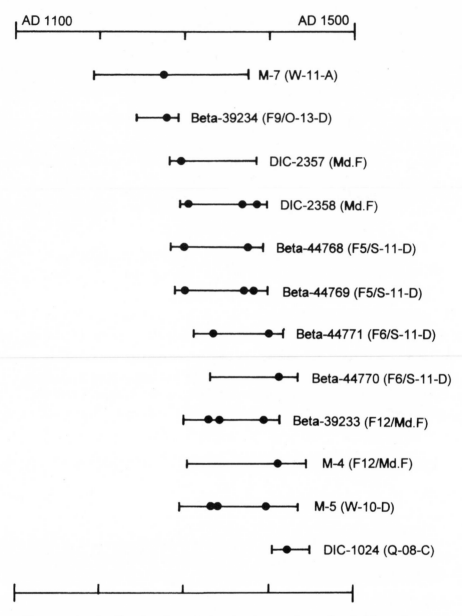

Figure 6.8. Angel radiocarbon dates. Designations in parentheses after the lab number identify the excavation area within the site.

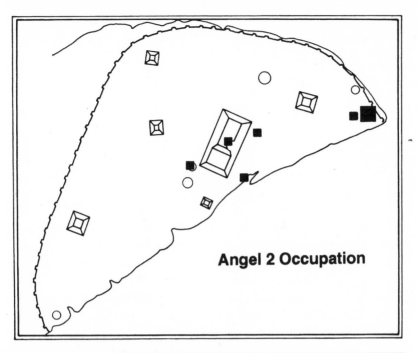

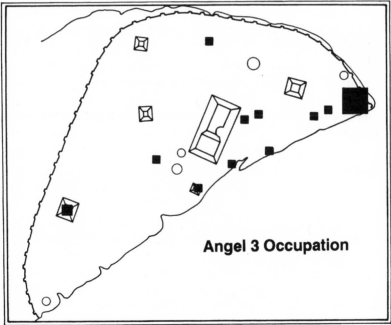

Figure 6.9. *Top,* Excavated areas *(black squares)* with Angel 2 phase materials; *bottom,* excavated areas with Angel 3 phase materials.

above the basin floor. The second, A.D. 1302, 1369, and 1382 (Beta-22088), was from a vertically set post. Four strap handles and an undecorated deep rim plate are associated with this structure.

All of the available radiocarbon dates, plus the dating of the stylistically similar Tinsley Hill phase, suggest a 100- to 150-year duration for this phase, or A.D. 1325 to 1450.

The Occupation of Angel in a Temporal Perspective

The earliest definite Middle Mississippian occupation at Angel occurs during the Angel 2 phase (Figure 6.9, top). The stratigraphic levels from the village area assigned to this phase generally represent the basal levels of the midden deposit. Thus, a number of the house remains and features in this area were probably constructed and used during this period.

The temporal placement of the Mound I features sheds some light on the establishment of the Angel ceremonial precinct. Mound I is a small conical mound at the southwest corner of Mound A (in subdivisions O-13-D and P-13-C). Given the relative sizes, and presumed relative importance, of the two mounds, it seems likely that Mound A was established first and that Mound I was constructed as a part of the Mound A precinct. Therefore, the early stages of Mound A should predate the late A.D. 1200s date for F9/O-13-D. Mound A and, by extension, the plaza and perhaps Mound F were probably established during the early A.D. 1200s.

The pottery assemblage from the small test on the top of Mound A includes a Ramey Incised sherd, two symmetrically scalloped short rim plate sherds and loop, narrow intermediate, and wide intermediate handles. This assemblage dates to the Angel 2 time period. These deposits represent either the final use of the summit or the characteristics of the fill used to cap the mound after the final usage. In either case, the absence of diagnostic Angel 3 pottery materials suggests that Mound A was no longer in active use after the late Angel 2 period. (Interestingly, Butler [1991:270] suggests that the use of Mx10, Kincaid's largest platform mound that is structurally similar to Mound A, also ceased at about A.D. 1300. A radiocarbon date with corrected intercepts of A.D. 1299 and 1375 (DIC-904) is associated with the charred remains of a structure on the uppermost level of Mx10.)

Very little else may be said concerning the probable appearance or size of Angel during the Angel 2 period except to suggest that, given the deposits in the village area and in Mound I, at least one-half of the ultimate site area was probably in use during this phase.

On the basis of all the available evidence, it appears that the most extensive or intensive habitation and use of the Angel site area occurred during the Angel 3 period (Figure 6.9, bottom). In the village, where midden depths average

2.0 feet, the upper 1.2–1.6 feet of deposits are generally Angel 3 deposits; in places the deposits appear to be Angel 3 from ground surface to subsoil.

The chronological placement of the majority of the village midden confirms Schurr's (1989a, 1989b) assessment of the chronological placement of the burials from the eastern village. The individuals interred in the eastern village appear to postdate house wall trenches and all three stockades. Fluorine dating suggests that the forty-four burials that have been assayed represent a single continuous episode of mortuary activity that occurred relatively late in the occupation of the site. In terms of the emerging fluorine chronology for the site (Schurr and Hilgeman 1991), the human burials from the eastern village have less fluorine than any deer bone that has been measured. Therefore, the human burials are later than any of the features that have been ordered on the fluorine content of the deer bone.

The palisade trench contains material characteristic of both Angel 2 and Angel 3 phases, the secondary trench contains diagnostic pottery suggesting an Angel 3 placement, and the heavy trench contains no diagnostic materials. The lack of diagnostic material in the heavy trench may imply that this stockade was built very early (early Angel 2 phase) in the site's history, or at least early in the history of this part of the site, before there was a large quantity of habitation debris present to be mixed in during backfilling of the trench.

Minimally, the palisade and secondary walls must have been taken down during the Angel 3 phase to account for the Angel 3 pottery inclusions. The palisade might have been built during the Angel 2 years, but the trench might just have been dug through some older midden. The secondary wall may be a slightly later construction, possibly to protect and extend the use-life of an increasingly dilapidated palisade structure.

The destruction of the palisade and secondary wall during the Angel 3 time period may mark the end of use of this area for housing. Certainly neither the palisade nor the secondary walls were standing when the area was used as a cemetery. It is not known whether the town was enclosed by a stockade at this very late stage in Angel's life or whether the cemetery was located outside an interior, as yet unknown, stockade.

Most of the other excavated areas of the site were occupied or in use during the final phase of the site's life. The occupations in four areas (subdivisions U-11-D/U-12-A/V-12-B, T-13-C, N-13-D, and P-15-A) scattered throughout the site interior dated to the Angel 3 phase, and that of three other areas (subdivisions R-14-B, R-12-A/R-11-D, and V-11-A) possibly began during the later part of the Angel 2 phase and continued into the Angel 3 phase.

In sum, deposits dating to the Angel 3 phase occur in the northern, eastern, and western portions of the site as well as throughout the interior. This indicates that the maximal site area was in use until late in Angel's history.

7 Angel in Regional Perspective

The research reported in this volume provides a systematic descriptive and chronological analysis of the pottery assemblage from Angel. In this final chapter, I want to address three interrelated issues: the possibility of ancestor-descendant relationships between the Angel phase and the preceding Yankeetown phase and between the Angel phase and the succeeding Caborn-Welborn phase, and the likelihood that the contemporary Angel and Kincaid societies are related polities.

Yankeetown and Angel

The Emergent Mississippian Yankeetown phase circa A.D. 750 to 1000 is marked by "a distinctive ceramic assemblage consisting of grog-tempered . . . vessels decorated with complex incised, stamped, or filleted decorative motifs. Vessel forms most commonly take the form of either smooth or cordmarked globular jars with straight to flared rim profiles, simple rounded bowls, or shallow pans. Some jars and bowls exhibit exterior rim folds and notched lips" (Redmond 1990:7–8).

Kellar (1983:51–52) notes that the Yankeetown pottery assemblage is a unique complex with Woodland and Mississippian elements and that the balance of the artifact assemblage contains a number of Mississippian forms. The most common chipped stone tool is the triangular projectile point that may herald the introduction of the bow and arrow into the lower Ohio Valley. Chipped stone hoes and charred maize remains indicate that Yankeetown populations were in part dependent on horticulture.

Redmond (1990:252–253) has suggested that Yankeetown people engaged in an annual round that was a compromise between a sedentary and shifting lifestyle. From the late spring through the late fall, they lived in settlements of varying sizes on natural elevations in the Ohio and Wabash River floodplains. They grew corn and other crops, gathered wild plants, and hunted animals. From the late fall through the early spring, the Yankeetown people occupied base camps located on terrace edges and upland bluffs. These sites were above the peak seasonal floods and appear to be situated to take advantage of the nut and animal resources available in these zones during this time of the year.

Unfortunately, it has not been possible to generate much new information on the Emergent Mississippian Yankeetown to Middle Mississippian Angel transition. There are no intact deposits from the excavations at Angel that date to the critical period of A.D. 1000 to 1200. This was the period when, more narrowly, shell-tempered pottery replaced grog-tempered pottery and predominantly plain-surfaced pottery replaced the attractively and distinctively incised Yankeetown motifs. In a wider sense, there was a shift from a simpler sociopolitical organization to the simple chiefdom of Angel (see Schurr 1989a).

Redmond argues that the similar settlement-subsistence pattern shared by the Yankeetown and Angel phases, indeed the fact that many Angel phase sites have Yankeetown components, provides "the most convincing evidence of cultural continuity between the Yankeetown and Angel phases" (Redmond 1990:275). He then concedes that comparable data in the form of transitional pottery styles linking Yankeetown and Angel are lacking.

I do not agree with Redmond's suggestion that the co-occurrence of Yankeetown and Angel components is evidence of cultural continuity between the two peoples. Many of these locations also have earlier Archaic or Woodland components and later Euroamerican components. They are, simply, attractive places to settle for a shorter or longer period of time. What is needed in addition to the site distribution data is evidence of continuity in some form of material culture, and in the case of pottery-making peoples, the most obvious place to look for continuity is in the pottery assemblages.

The most recognizable and common decorated Yankeetown pottery is the fineline Yankeetown Incised (Blasingham 1953:32–48; Redmond 1990:50–158). There is nothing like it in the Angel shell-tempered assemblage. In fact, little incised pottery occurs during the Angel 2 phase assemblage, the earliest recognizable Mississippian occupation of the site. Incised pottery that does date to the Angel 2 time period is, for all practical purposes, limited to broadline, curvilinear Ramey Incised, *variety Green River*—possibly an import—and fineline O'Byam Incised, *variety Adams*. Although these are the most common incised pottery types in the Angel assemblage, with totals of 90 and 35, respectively, from the perspective of the assemblage, they are extremely rare. Therefore, if Yankeetown is the cultural ancestor of Angel, then the idea of incising, so important in the Yankeetown decorative repertoire, was lost almost completely in the transition.

A site south of Angel in western Kentucky gives us an idea of what to expect in the way of transitional pottery styles. The Andalex site (15Hk22) is located on a minor tributary of the Green River (Niquette et al. 1991). Here, in addition to grog-tempered Yankeetown Incised, Fillet, and Pseudo-fillet sherds, there are a number of sherds called by the investigators Pond River Incised, *variety Hopkins*, which occur in mound contexts dating to the late A.D. 1200s. These sherds are Yankeetown-like pseudo-fillet designs on shell-tempered paste. Pond River Incised, *variety Hopkins*, is therefore a transitional pottery style. In contrast, in the Ohio Valley around Angel, I know of no examples of Yankeetown decorations on shell-tempered paste (see also Redmond 1990). For example, in the Angel and Stephan-Steinkamp assemblages, Yankeetown decorations occur only on grog-tempered sherds.

The larger question becomes: does the occurrence of Yankeetown decorations on shell-tempered vessels at a distance from Angel and absence of the same in the Ohio Valley around Angel say something about the mode of "Middle Mississippian-ization" of the greater Angel neighborhood? I think so. It suggests that in the immediate vicinity of the large town, the earlier Yankeetown grog-tempered pottery tradition was replaced in a rather abrupt fashion by the Mississippian shell-tempered pottery tradition. Does this indicate, as Clay (1984) suggests, some amount of population displacement or replacement? That is certainly a possibility, but it is not a certainty.

In the Green River hinterlands, away from Angel's immediate presence, the transition between Emergent Mississippian Yankeetown and Middle Mississippian Angel was more gradual. The gradual nature is marked, in pottery terms, by the ready transferability of the older grog-tempered designs onto newer shell-tempered pots and the maintenance of those designs in the potters' decorative repertoire for a period of time. There is no reason to posit any population displacement or replacement. The existing populations were gradually "Middle Mississippian-ized" as a result of contacts with Angel people to the north.

In summary, there are no transitional pottery styles linking the Yankeetown and "Angel phase" (*sensu* Honerkamp 1975; Power 1976) pottery assemblages, similar to Pond River Incised, *variety Hopkins,* in the Ohio Valley around Angel. There is only the weak circumstantial evidence of the co-occurrence of Yankeetown and Angel components in some of the same places along the Ohio River. These components may be separated in time by as much as three or four centuries, a block of time equivalent to that separating the end of the Mississippian occupation and the beginning of the occupation of Mathias Angel's farmstead (Ball, Senkel, and French 1990). Thus, I believe it is premature to posit a cultural ancestor-descendant relationship between Yankeetown and Angel.

Angel and Caborn-Welborn

The Caborn-Welborn phase dates to the A.D. 1400 to 1700 period and includes the block of time following the demise the Angel polity up to the arrival of Euroamericans in the lower Ohio Valley. In a linear area of less than 50 river miles centered on the mouth of the Wabash River, there are more than eighty known Caborn-Welborn phase sites ranging from settlements as small as 0.6 acres in size to a village larger than 35 acres (Green and Munson 1978;

Pollack 1998; Pollack and Munson 1998). There was no single large town comparable to Angel (Green and Munson 1978).

The Caborn-Welborn artifact assemblage is marked by distinctive decorated pottery and chipped stone tools. The decorated pottery assemblage is characterized by the dominant type Caborn-Welborn Decorated, consisting of broadline incised, trailed, and punctated triangular designs on the upper shoulders of standard Mississippian jars (Munson 1984; Pollack and Munson 1998). The chipped stone assemblage includes two new, equally distinctive forms: snub-nose endscrapers and leaf-shaped Nodena points.

The scenario proposed by Pollack and Munson (1998) has some or all of the Angel population moving downstream to the mouth of the Wabash area following the demise of the Angel chiefdom (Pollack 1998; Pollack and Munson 1998). In support of this hypothesis they cite four continuities that link the earlier Angel and later Caborn-Welborn societies: (1) continuation of a settlement hierarchy; (2) similar settlement and subsistence patterns; and (3) similar pottery vessel forms, appendages, and minor decorated types (Pollack 1998:9; Pollack and Munson 1998:179, 189, 192).

For the reasons outlined in the discussion above concerning Yankeetown, I think it is a mistake to use similar settlement locations along the Ohio River as evidence for cultural continuity. These locations offered the same advantages to anyone, Yankeetown, Angel, Caborn-Welborn, or early Euroamerican farmers (such as Mathias Angel), looking for a good place to settle, including an elevation on which to build a dwelling, easily cultivated and relatively fertile soils, and a concentration of wild plant and animal resources. As is the case with Angel and Yankeetown sites, many Caborn-Welborn sites have earlier Archaic and Woodland as well as later Euroamerican components, underscoring the continuing attractiveness of these locations. Determining the degree to which Caborn-Welborn retains part of the Angel settlement hierarchy will require more extensive excavation of Caborn-Welborn sites.

The issue raised by Pollack and Munson that can be address here is the proposed evidence of continuity in the pottery assemblages. Specifically, these include: (1) vessel forms (the utilitarian jars, bowls, pans and bottles); (2) appendage forms (strap handles and bifurcated lugs) (Pollack 1998: 52–53); (3) increase in the number of bowls with beaded rims and notched applique strips and an increase in the number of outflaring bowls, some with scalloped lips (Pollack 1998:53; Pollack and Munson 1998:189); (4) the line-filled triangular motifs shared by Angel Negative Painted and Caborn-Welborn Decorated (Pollack 1998:147; Pollack and Munson 1998:179); and (5) the continued production of a number of minor decorated types, including Old Town Red, Angel Negative Painted, O'Byam Incised, Mound Place Incised, Matthews Incised, *variety Matthews* and *variety Manly*, and Beckwith Incised (Pollack 1998:142; Pollack and Munson 1998:192).

Many of the items cited by Pollack and Munson do not specifically link Angel to Caborn-Welborn. The form of the jars, bowls, pans, and bottles, strap handles and bifurcated lugs are typical of Mississippian assemblages of the lower Ohio Valley to the Ohio-Mississippi confluence area. Bowls with beaded rims and notched applique strips also occur in a larger area than the lower Ohio Valley. It is not possible to evaluate the suggested increase in the number of outflaring bowls, some with scalloped lips, because I did not attempt to reconstruct relative number of vessel forms.

The idea that the line-filled triangular motifs shared by Angel Negative Painted and Caborn-Welborn Decorated demonstrates continuity deserves serious attention. Pollack and Munson (Pollack 1998:147; Pollack and Munson 1998:179) correctly point out the similarities. Although I agree that the motifs on the two types are similar, I want to point out that the designs on Angel Negative Painted plates and on Caborn-Welborn Decorated jars are not unique to Angel Negative Painted, or even Angel. The line-filled triangle motif is in fact widespread. In the lower Ohio Valley and the middle and lower Mississippi Valley, they also occur as Barton Incised and O'Byam Incised. In the north-central Mississippi Valley they occur as Wells Incised and Crable Deep Rim Plates. Pollack and Munson are correct in saying that Angel Negative Painted is an antecedent style in that Angel Negative Painted is one of a number of midsouthern Mississippian pottery decorations that predate Caborn-Welborn Decorated that are based on line-filled triangles. However, it is the combination of the plate and negative painting that makes Angel Negative Painted unique, and Caborn-Welborn Decorated jars shares neither of those characteristics with Angel Negative Painted.

There is another aspect that distinguishes Angel Negative Painted from Caborn-Welborn Decorated, and that is the contexts in which each occur in their respective sites. I know from my own experience surveying and excavating Caborn-Welborn sites in Point Township, Posey County, Indiana, that very often all or most of the Caborn-Welborn Decorated sherds are recovered from those parts of the sites with pieces of human bone. Away from these cemetery areas, the occurrence of Caborn-Welborn Decorated is rare. As I pointed out in Chapter 5, Angel Negative Painted plates are not burial furniture. In fact, as Schurr (1989a:133–134) notes, pottery is not commonly associated with Angel burials; less than 7 percent of the burials have clearly associated pottery vessels. Therefore, not only is there little to uniquely link Angel Negative Painted and Caborn-Welborn Decorated pottery, the uses to which each is put are different.

The final aspect that Pollack and Munson use to demonstrate continuity between Angel and Caborn-Welborn is the continued production of a number of minor decorated types, including Old Town Red, Angel Negative Painted, O'Byam Incised, Mound Place Incised, Matthews Incised, *variety Matthews* and *variety Manly,* and Beckwith Incised (Pollack 1998:142; Pollack and Munson 1998:192). To put this statement into context, it must be noted the inclusion of these pottery types in Caborn-Welborn pottery assemblages is the result of an assumption that "the attributes characteristic of sites containing the distinctive Caborn-Welborn material culture are characteristic of this later Mississippian phase, and are not the results of Angel phase peoples" (Green and Munson 1978:308; see also Pollack 1998:21–23). In other words, if a surface collection contained Caborn-Welborn incised and punctated sherds, the site was considered to be a single-component Caborn-Welborn phase site, and "rare pieces of red-filmed and negative painted ware" (Green and Munson 1978:301) in surface collections with Caborn-Welborn Decorated sherds were considered minor elements of the Caborn-Welborn assemblage rather than indicative of an earlier, Angel-contemporary occupation.

In addition to incorporating these minor pottery types into the Caborn-Welborn pottery assemblage, this assumption has a major consequence. It effectively depopulates the mouth of the Wabash area for the A.D.1100/1200 to 1400 time period. This assumption makes it impossible to identify sites occupied during this period because all of the potential pottery diagnostics, such as Old Town Red, Angel Negative Painted, O'Byam Incised, Mound Place Incised, Matthews Incised, *variety Matthews* and *variety Manly*, and Beckwith Incised, are assumed to be minor types of the Caborn-Welborn assemblage. As a result, Green and Munson's map (1978:Figure 11.3) of Angel and Caborn-Welborn phase sites shows a gap in the distribution of Angel phase sites along the Ohio River in the Posey County area and the absence of any multicomponent, Angel and Caborn-Welborn sites. Pollack (1998:438) describes the mouth of the Wabash as an area not "as intensively or extensively utilized during the earlier Angel chiefdom."

Although it is possible that the mouth of the Wabash area is not occupied during the A.D. 1100/1200 to 1400 time period, it seems unlikely that this is the case. If it were unoccupied, it would represent the only such stretch of the Ohio River from above the mouth of the Green River and the Angel site to the Ohio-Mississippi confluence to be unoccupied (Clay 1999, personal communication). For that reason, I am unwilling to make such an assumption.

The Hovey Lake site (12Po10) is identified as being an early Caborn-Welborn site based on radiocarbon dates and a pottery assemblage showing continuity with the Angel pottery assemblage (Pollack and Munson 1998:166–167, 189). The Hovey Lake site consists of an eight-acre village and cemetery surrounding a central plaza located adjacent to Hovey Lake, a large oxbow lake. Three radiocarbon dates from the site have corrected intercepts of A.D. 1405, 1410, and 1657. Pollack and Munson (1998:167, Table 1) believe that the early A.D. 1400s dates may be more reliable than the mid-A.D. 1600s date.

I have already discussed in the preceding paragraphs the characteristics of an early Caborn-Welborn pottery assemblage that lead Pollack and Munson to conclude that the Hovey Lake assemblage, an example of such an early (A.D. 1400 to 1450; Pollack 1998:18, 168–170) Caborn-Welborn assemblage, shows continuity with the Angel assemblage.

In addition to plain, fabric- and net-impressed, and cord-marked sherds, the Hovey Lake pottery assemblage includes eighty-two incised sherds (seventy-one Caborn-Welborn Decorated sherds, three Matthews Incised, *variety Manly* sherds, three O'Byam Incised sherds, one Beckwith Incised sherd, two Oneota-like sherds, and two Kent Incised-like sherds), eleven Old Town Red sherds, and one Parkin Punctated sherd (Pollack and Munson 1998:Table 2). The incised sherds make up 7.9 percent of the analyzed sherds (decorated + rims greater than 4 cm^2) and 1.1 percent of the estimated sherd totals.

In the next section I will argue that I am not in favor of assuming that the Angel polity extended as far west as the mouth of the Wabash area, and for the reasons discussed here earlier I am equally unwilling to assume that the mouth of the Wabash area was unoccupied during the A.D.1100/1200 to 1400 time period. I am also unwilling to extend the Angel phases to the mouth of the Wabash area not because I want to equate "polity" with "phase," but because I expect, based on the regional trends discussed in Chapters 3 and 6, that pottery assemblages recovered from the mouth of the Wabash area during this time period will be recognizably different. They will contain the same painted (Old Town Red, Angel Negative Painted and Kincaid Negative Painted), incised (O'Byam Incised, Mound Place Incised, Matthews Incised, and Beckwith Incised), and punctated (Parkin Punctated) types that occur in assemblages upstream and downstream from the mouth of the Wabash, but these types will occur in different relative proportions, something intermediate between the relative proportions of the contemporary lower Tennessee-Cumberland assemblages and the relative proportions of the two newly defined Angel phases (see discussions in Chapters 3 and 6, and Table 6.4).

For example, removing the Caborn-Welborn elements from the list of decorated pottery types recovered at Hovey Lake leaves eleven Old Town Red sherds, three Matthews Incised, *variety Manly* sherds, three O'Byam Incised sherds, one Beckwith Incised sherd, and one Parkin Punctated sherd. This assemblage is midway, in both a geographical sense and a stylistic sense, between the Tinsley Hill assemblages of the lower Tennessee–Cumberland, in which incising replaced painting, and the Angel 3 assemblage, in which incising—never an important decorative mode—has vanished and painting (red slipping and negative painting) continue to be the preferred decorative mode (Table 6.4). Furthermore, there is nothing in the absolute dating to disprove that the Hovey Lake site is a multicomponent Mississippian site, with an earlier component that is contemporary with Tinsley Hill phase sites and the Angel 3 phase occupation of Angel, and a later Caborn-Welborn component.

Taking a step back, this discussion indicates that, as is the case with the

Yankeetown-to-Angel transition, it is premature to speak of a cultural ancestor-descendant relationship linking Angel and Caborn-Welborn. No specific pottery styles link the two assemblages, no Caborn-Welborn Decorated sherds were recovered at Angel, and the two phases occupy different geographic areas. It will first be necessary to conduct research to determine whether there is a Middle Mississippian occupation at the mouth of the Wabash during the A.D. 1100/1200 to 1400 time period and, minimally, the characteristics of its pottery assemblage. It is within that local tradition, when identified, within its settlement hierarchy, subsistence patterns, and pottery vessel forms, appendages, and decorated types, within a pottery-making tradition that retains the idea of incising, that the connections to later Caborn-Welborn should be sought. Once that is accomplished, it will then be appropriate to consider the extent to which Caborn-Welborn is an in situ development or the result of the movement of Oneota-related peoples or some lower Mississippi Valley peoples, or both, into the mouth of the Wabash area to join or replace peoples previously there (Hall 1991:18–19; Lewis 1996:147–148; Muller 1986:257–258).

Angel and Kincaid

With a greater knowledge of the absolute dating of the Angel site and the patterns of occupation within the stockade, it is possible to evaluate some ideas concerning the sociopolitical relationship between Angel and Kincaid. In his examination of Mississippian in the Ohio Valley, Jon Muller suggested that Angel and Kincaid might have been the two major settlements in a single polity. As part of the supporting evidence for this idea, he suggests that the occupations of the two sites are roughly contemporaneous.

As I noted in Chapter 6, Muller (1978:275; 1990, personal communication) concluded that the majority of the Mississippian occupations, at Kincaid and at the smaller sites, date to the Angelly phase or about A.D. 1200 to 1300. He went on to say: "The dates from the Angel vicinity seem to run a little later than those from Kincaid, but it is by no means certain that Mississippian settlement there persisted longer than was the case at [Kincaid]" (Muller 1986:180–181).

Although all of the small Mississippian sites that have been excavated in the Black Bottom do date to the Angelly phase (Riordan 1975), I am not at all convinced that the majority of Kincaid's Mississippian occupation dates to that time period. Both Butler (1991) and Clay (1979) noted the presence and apparent quantity of post-A.D. 1300 Tinsley Hill phase pottery in the Kincaid volume illustrations. Orr (1951:357) also observed: "Remains of the Late period are found in the uppermost layers of most of the Kincaid features, indicating the most extensive occupation of the site." Unfortunately, it is difficult to estimate the relative proportions of Angelly and Tinsley Hill phase sherds in the Kincaid assemblage based on pictures. Kincaid must have had a sizeable Tinsley Hill phase (A.D. 1300 to 1450) occupation, but it is not possible to say whether it was larger or smaller than, or roughly the same size as, the Angelly phase (A.D. 1200 to 1300) occupation.

In contrast to Muller's ideas concerning the chronology of the Angel site, the research reported herein indicates that the most extensive or intensive use of the Angel site postdated A.D. 1300. The presence of Parkin Punctated at Angel and its apparent absence at Kincaid does suggest that Angel might have remained an active town after the decline and abandonment of Kincaid. Thus, although both Angel and Kincaid have post–A.D. 1300 components, it may be that Kincaid reached its zenith about a century prior to the zenith at Angel and that Kincaid was the first to decline. If that is the case, then the plausibility of Muller's idea, that Angel and Kincaid are the two settlements in a single polity, is lessened.

Geography also calls into question Muller's idea. Angel is 150 river miles upstream of Kincaid. Hally (1987) and Blitz (1993) suggest that the maximum radius of a Mississippian chiefdom was one day's travel out from the center, "the practical limit to which effective administrative control could be extended" (Hally 1987:5). Hally also noted that middle-range societies worldwide have a similarly scaled spatial pattern.

By foot, one day's travel is approximately 12 miles (20 kilometers), the specific scenario Hally and Blitz consider. This would place the western boundary of the Angel polity in the vicinity of the present-day Vanderburgh–Posey County, Indiana, line. However, considering that many Mississippian towns, including Angel and Kincaid, are located close to or on major rivers, one day's travel by water may be a more appropriate distance. Lafferty (1977:Appendix II) suggested that 60 miles is a little more than one day's travel by water downstream. One day's travel upstream is less. This latter measure places the maximal downstream boundary of the Angel polity between the Southwind site at Mount Vernon, Indiana (50 river miles downstream) and the Ohio-Wabash confluence (70 river miles downstream). Given that on this issue it is probably better to be conservative, the boundary should be assumed to be no further west than Southwind, if as far. Using the generous estimates of the Kincaid polity's eastern boundary being 30 river miles upstream of Kincaid and the Angel polity's western boundary being 50 river miles downstream of Angel, there is a minimum gap between the two boundaries on the order of 60 to 70 river miles.

The gap between the boundaries of the Angel and Kincaid polities was undoubtedly considerably larger because the distance over which each was able to exert political control was probably considerably less than the 80 river miles—50 downstream and 30 upstream—allotted to each polity. Cahokia, the largest Mississippian chiefdom, is not thought to have been able to extend its political control beyond a 50-mile (25-mile radius) stretch of the central Mississippi Valley (Blitz 1993:182; Milner 1990:7–8). Furthermore, Lubbub Creek, which is 33 miles by foot from Moundville, produced no evidence of direct Moundville political control (Blitz 1993:182). Therefore, it is extremely unreasonable to expect that Kincaid was able to exert any political control over Angel, or vice versa, because the distance involved is simply too great.

This interpretation of the Angel chiefdom as having a limited sphere of political control is corroborated by looking at the influence of Angel from the perspective of a small mound center located outside of the Angel polity. Andalex (15Hk22) (Niquette et al. 1991; Clay 1991) is located about 40 miles south of Angel. Prior to the early A.D. 1200s, the site was a village. Then, in the mid- to late-A.D.1200s, the inhabitants built a substructure mound over some earlier domestic structures. The building on top of the mound was burned down in the late-A.D. 1200s, and the mound was abandoned for a period of perhaps a century. Then the mound was leveled off, and another structure was built on top of it.

Clay (1991) interprets the "on-again, off-again" importance of the mound and its surmounting structure as reflecting the imperfect and sporadic incorporation of the small Andalex community into the sphere of the Angel polity. The small mound was first constructed during the A.D. 1200s. This is coeval with the establishment of the major features of the ceremonial precinct at Angel. Clay believes that the construction of the Andalex mound indicates the alliance of one particular Andalex kin group with a highly ranked kin group elsewhere, at Angel.

> It is probable, therefore, that the changes in Andalex are related to the emergence of Angel as the regional seat of chiefly power. Likewise the temporary nature of this first excursion in mound building at Andalex is also, no doubt, a measure of the nature of the linkage with the larger center. This would suggest that, if Andalex represents a start at the emergence of a typical site hierarchy in the Angel region with single mound sites, it was an emergence which was both halting and incomplete, halting because it resulted in only one mound stage at Andalex, and incomplete in that it did not result in the widespread occurrence of single mound centers in the Angel system (Clay 1991:11).

Today, Clay, favoring a more "decoupled" view of Mississippian polities (Clay 1997), would not place Andalex in the Angel system, which seems reasonable given the distances involved. It is too far away for the leaders of Angel to exert any direct political control on Andalex. Yet, I concur with Clay's assessment that Andalex was responding to sociopolitical events in the region, most likely the establishment of Angel.

Finis

A three-phase pottery chronology for the Middle Mississippian occupation at Angel was created as a result of this research. The initial phase, the Stephan-Steinkamp phase (A.D. 1100 to 1200) is represented poorly, if at all, within the excavated contexts at Angel. On the basis of the available information, the initial late prehistoric occupation of the Angel site began during the Angel 2 phase (A.D. 1200 to 1325). During this period, the layout of the ceremonial precinct in the center of the town was established, and at least one-half of the one-hundred-acre site area was occupied. The use of the largest mound, Mound A, as a substructure mound apparently ceased by about the end of the phase. The most extensive occupation of the site occurred during the Angel 3 phase (A.D. 1325 to 1450). Deposits dating to the Angel 3 phase occur at the northern, eastern, and western margins of the site as well as throughout the interior. This indicates that the maximum site area was in use until late in Angel's history. Near the end of the phase, and the termination of the town's occupation, Angel may have no longer been surrounded by a stockade. It appears that the town was abandoned by its prehistoric inhabitants at about A.D. 1450.

This research is a first step. In the future it should be possible to refine this chronology further as the data become available and the refinements become necessary to meet the needs of new research. We should be able to add to our knowledge of the timing of the events in the occupation of Angel, correlate those events with similar events in the occupation of Kincaid, and set both towns into a new perspective in the Mississippian world.

Appendix A

Appendix A
SUMMARY OF THE EXCAVATIONS AT ANGEL: 1939-1989

WPA EXCAVATIONS

Subdivision	Year(s)	Area (sq ft)	Purpose // Findings
			Third Terrace
X-07-D	1939	2400	examined the natural soil profiles in the area in the walls of an old cellar // prehistoric and historic artifacts and three historic firepits
X-08-A	1939	1800	examined strata in the bank from terrace to slough // two pottery filled aboriginal pits
Y-08-B	1939	2600	continuation of excavation of X-08-A // more aboriginal pits
X-07-C	1939	400	continued observation of soil profiles composing the terrace north and east of the slough // no aboriginal material encountered
Y-07-C	1939	500	eastward continuation of X-07-D excavations // two fragmentary burials, one with three pottery vessels
			Eastern Village
X-11-D	1939-40	5460	Thomas (1894) and Purdue (1897) maps indicated the stockade terminated in X-11-D; much occupation debris in division X-11 // the southeastern termini of two stockade trenches, dwellings, and associated facilities
X-11-C	1939	9300	continuation of excavations in X-11-D // continuation of stockade trenches; numerous postholes, house wall trenches, pits, puddled clay hearths, burials, etc
X-11-A	1940	250	// stockade bastion and continuation of secondary trench
X-11-B	1940-41	8300	continuation of excavation in this area of the site, with special interest in bastion spacing

Subdivision	Year(s)	Area (sq ft)	Purpose // Findings
X-10-C	1940	1650	continuation of stockade course
W-11-A	1940-41	10,000	desire to find a house with hypothesized semi-subterranean floor intact // evidence of intense use of this area
W-10-D	1941-47	9600	expose more of the stockade tenches and more of a group of wall trenches // discovery of bastion on the heavy trench (the earlier stockade), part of a circular structure
W-11-B	1941-??	10,000?	slightly lower elevation than to east – might reflect less debris and building-filling-building than to east // felt depth of debris was diminishing toward the west (subdivision never completed to subsoil)
Stockades			
U-08-B	1939-40	7000	examined stockade line in an area where the course was marked by an embankment and little habitation debris // palisade and secondary trenches, little habitation debris
U-08-A	1940	2300	// continuation of stockade to southeast; little debris
U-08-D	1940	1900	// continuation of stockade to southeast; little debris
V-08-C	1940	4200	// continuation of stockade to southeast; increasing amount of debris to southeast
V-09-B	1940	380	// continuation of stockade to southeast; increasing amount of debris to southeast
V-08-D	1940	400	// continuation of stockade to southeast; increasing amount of debris to southeast
V-09-A	1940	2320	// continuation of stockade to southeast; debris and humus becoming common, post molds plainly visible in stockade trench
J-14-B	1943	200	excavation in Ziener's (Black 1967) Transect I to check correlation between vegetation and stockade line indication seen on surface // stockade trench located
Mound			
Mound F	1940-41	44,000	seeking in Mound F strata evidence of flood seen in Kincaid excavations (Black 1967); comparison of western part of site with eastern // excavated in "primary mound" (second-to-last building episode

FIELDSCHOOL EXCAVATIONS: 1946-1961

Village-Habitation Areas

Subdivision	Year(s)	Area (sq ft)	Purpose // Findings
W-10-C	1948	1100	excavate remainder of circular structure located in W-10-D // circular structure most recent structure; bastion of still-earlier stockade; portion of intact semi-subterranean house pit
S-11-D	1949, 51	3660	habitation less intensely used than eastern village, therefore dwellings with less rebuilding // remains of three "intact" semi-subterranean house pits
R-14-B	1957	400	examine unusual vegetation patterns // wall trenches and postholes; shallow deposits and few artifacts
O-08-D	1957	600	test of linear concentration of daub fragments and unusual vegetation patterns // three superimposed structures ; very shallow deposits and few artifacts [area possibly cleared for plaza east of Mound E]
U-11-D,U-12-A, V-12-B	1959	1310	examine projected habitation area between S-11-D and eastern village // shallower deposits than in eastern village; area may have been borrowed or scraped clean
V-11-A	1961	800	examine habitation area between U-11-D/U-12-A/V-12-B and eastern village // shallower deposits than in eastern village

Stockades

Subdivision	Year(s)	Area (sq ft)	Purpose // Findings
Q-09-A, Q-09-D	1946	1620	test a vegetation pattern which suggested the course of interior stockade and spacing of bastions (this stockade seen by Stinson (1883), Purdue (1897), and Thomas (1894)) // stockade, bastion, and paralleling secondary trench located; no evidence of houses on ridge extending from this area to Mound B
U-09-A, V-09-B	1958	1200	test an elevation which might be part of the inner stockade // found intersecting stockade and bastion, clay borrow pit

Subdivision	Year(s)	Area (sq ft)	Purpose // Findings
M-12-B	1959	700	test Purdue's (1897) suggestion that inner stockade extended southwest of Mound C // area badly disturbed by crayfish burrowings, no cultural deposits and few artifacts found
H-20-A, H-20-B	1960	600	test to locate stockade in western corner of site // H-20-B badly disturbed historically; stockade trench located in H-20-A
T-13-C	1960	1200	test for stockade along river edge of site // irregular pits and several historic features
P-09-D	1961	1110	initial use of proton magnetometer to locate stockade line // backhoe excavation uncovered stockade line and bastion
Mounds			
O-13-D, P-13-C	1952, 1954?	1600	determine whether Mound I is natural or man-made // mound built over semi-subterranean pit and other wall trenches; mound possibly surmounted by circular structure
Mound A	1955	300	test relationship of conical offset to rest of Mound A // double row of postholes, fill of Mound A relatively sterile (unlike Mound F)
P-15-A	1955	300	test whether Mound K is natural or man made // mound at least in part man-made, built over two structures which were in turn built over a filled-in "ditch" excavation
R-12-A, R-11-D	1957	400	examine a ramp on eastern side of Mound A // ramp an artificial construction, corner of a structure within which there was an unusual, partially cremated burial (charnel structure with elite individual?)
Plaza			
N-11-A,N-11-D, N-12-A,N-12-D, N-13-A,N-13-D	1950	6000	investigation of the plaza // "clean" plaza, portion of inner stockade northeast of Mound C, wall trenches south of the plaza in N-13-D
MAGNETOMETER INVESTIGATIONS OF STOCKADES: 1962-1964			
K-11-B, K-11-A	1962	400	// two stockade trenches located

Subdivision	Year(s)	Area (sq ft)	Purpose // Findings
K-11-D	1962	50	// burned area, associated with stockade?
K-10-A, L-10-B	1962	800	// two stockade trenches located
N-07-B, N-07-C, N-08-B	1962	800	// one (outer) stockade trench located, unable to see inner trench
O-07-A, O-07-D	1962	400	// one (outer) stockade trench located, unable to see inner trench
O-10-A	1962	250	// stockade trench located
R-07-C	1962	300	// stockade trench not located
O-07-B, O-07-C	1963	270	// outer stockade bastion located, no sign of inner stockade trench
R-07-D	1963	240	// stockade trench not located
S-07-C, S-08-B	1963	470	// located the junction of the interior and more recent eastern stockade
R-07-C, R-07-D	1963	130	// stockade trench not located
U-08-C	1963	150	// no features located
U-08-D	1963	440	// features located, stockade trench not located
P-07-A	1964	190?	// stockade trench located
Q-07-C, Q-07-B	1964	160	// stockade trench located
R-07-C?	1964	30	// stockade trench located
R-07-D	1964	190?	// stockade trench not located
S-07-C	1964	350	// stockade trench located

MOUND F EXCAVATION: 1964-1965

Subdivision	Year(s)	Area (sq ft)	Purpose // Findings
Mound F	1964-65	8480	examine construction sequence below the primary mound // documented one and possibly two mound stages earlier than the primary mound, as well as wall trench structures on the original ground surface
FIELDSCHOOL EXCAVATIONS: 1976, 1977, 1989			
R-09-B	1976	800	(with Q-08-C) looking for different house wall orientations on either side of the interior stockade // badly disturbed stone box graves
Q-08-C	1976-77	1250	// house wall trenches of both orientations
N-16-D	1989	300	looking for a possible southern terminus of the interior stockade // site of Mathias Angel's cabin
INTERIOR STOCKADE EXCAVATIONS: 1983			
M-11-D, M-12-A, M-12-D	1983	1740	Trenches 1 and 2, test vegetation line west of Mound C // stockade trench not located, structure in M-12-D
M-13-A, N-13-B	1983	510	Trench 3, in plaza // stockade trench located
M-13-D, N-13-C	1983	500	Trench 4, southern edge of plaza where line turns southeast // stockade trench located
N-14-A, N-14-B	1983	280	Trench 5, intercept line after it turns southeast // stockade trench and habitation area
M-13-A, N-13-B, M-13-D, N-13-C	1983	710	Trench 6, between Trenches 3 and 4 // stockade trench and bastion located

Appendix B

Appendix B
RADIOCARBON AND THERMOLUMINESCENCE DATES FOR THE ANGEL SITE AND PHASE

Sample No.	C14 Years	Calendrical Years AD min range (cal ages) max range[1]	Comments
		ANGEL (12Vg1)	
M-2	1340+/-120		charcoal, secondary mound mantle, 4 ft below surface, Block 13R4, Mound F, sample collected in 1941 and submitted in 1949, not acceptable
M-4	530+/-100	1304 (**1412**) 1445	charcoal, F12/Mound F, primary mound surface, collected in 1941 and submitted in 1949, acceptable
M-5	580+/-100	1296 (**1332 1340 1398**) 1435	charcoal, house wall trench, Block 0R1, W-10-D, collected in 1941 and submitted in early 1950s, acceptable
M-7	760+/-100	1192 (**1276**) 1376	charcoal, house wall trench, Block 9L3, W-11-A, collected in 1941 and submitted in early 1950s, acceptable
M-9	1980+/-130		mussel shell, primary mound surface, Block 8R5, Mound F, collected in 1941 and submitted in 1949, not acceptable
M-10	1850+/-120		mussel shell, 0.4-0.8 ft level, Block 9R5, W-11-A, collected in 1941 and submitted in early 1950s, not acceptable
DIC-1023	360+/-50	1452 (**1491 1603 1609**) 1635	wood charcoal, F5/Q-08-C, 0.8 ft below surface, Block 1R2, collected and submitted in 1977, somewhat late
DIC-1024	510+50/-40	1404 (**1421**) 1438	wood charcoal (FS#Q-08-C/883), F24B-1/Q-08-C, 2.4 ft below surface, Block 1R1, collected in 1976 and submitted in 1977, acceptable
DIC-2357	680+/-50	1282 (**1296**) 1385	wood charcoal, on R3.5 line between Blocks 7R4 and 8R4, exposed in profile at elevation 378.47 ft, Mound F, collected in 1964 and submitted in 1981, acceptable

Sample No.	C14 Years	Calendrical Years AD min range (cal ages) max range[1]	Comments
DIC-2358	630+/-45	1296 (1304 1367 1385) 1397	wood charcoal, elevation 380.26 ft, Mound F, collected in 1965 and submitted in 1981, acceptable
DIC-2359	90+/-110		wood charcoal, corner post of house on second building stage, Block 13R1, Mound F, collected in 1965 and submitted in 1981, not acceptable
Beta-39232	840+/-80 (adj)	1060 (1216) 1277	wood charcoal (FS# Md.F/4499), F12/Mound F, primary mound surface, collected in 1941 and submitted 9-5-90, <0.5 g after pretreatment, date not acceptable (C-13 adjusted C-14 age)
Beta-39233	590+/-60	1300 (1329 1343 1395) 1413	wood charcoal (FS# Md.F/4499), F12/Mound F, primary mound surface, collected in 1941 and submitted 9-5-90, date acceptable and corroborates M-4
Beta-39234	750+/-50	1245 (1278) 1291	wood charcoal (FS# O-13-D/395), F9/O-13-D, collected in 1952 and submitted 9-5-90, acceptable
Beta-39235	950+/-80 (adj)	1003 (1037 1143 1148) 1205	wood charcoal (FS# O-13-D/547), F9/O-13-D, collected in 1952 and submitted 9-5-90, , <0.5 g after pretreatment, date not acceptable (C-13 adjusted C-14 age)
Beta-44768	660+/-60	1284 (1299 1375 1375) 1393	wood charcoal (FS# S-11-D/783), from the floor of Black's house pit #2 (F5/S-11-D), at or below 1.6 ft BS, collected in 1949 and submitted 5-6-91, somewhat early but acceptable
Beta-44769	640+/-60	1289 (1302 1369 1382) 1398	wood charcoal (FS# S-11-D/819), from the fill of Black's house pit #2 (F5/S-11-D), in the 1.2 to 1.6 ft level BS, collected in August 1949 and submitted 5-6-91, acceptable
Beta-44770	530+/-50	1331 (1412) 1435	wood charcoal (FS# S-11-D/2760A), from the floor of Black's house pit #3 (F6/S-11-D), at or below 1.6 ft BS, collected in October 1951 and submitted 5-6-91, acceptable

Sample No.	C14 Years	Calendrical Years AD min range (cal ages) max range[1]	Comments
Beta-44771	570+/-50	1312 (1334 1336 1400) 1417	wood charcoal (FS# S-11-D/2760B), from the floor of Black's house pit #3 (F6/S-11-D), at or below 1.6 ft BS, collected in October 1951 and submitted 5-6-91, acceptable
ELLERBUSCH (12 W 56)			
DIC-237	1690+/-60		wood charcoal, Feature 11, N1050/E495, 1.1-1.45 ft BS, collected in 1973 and submitted in 1974, not acceptable
DIC-238	900+50/-60	1035 (1160) 1215	wood charcoal, Posthole 78, N970/E520, 1.0-1.7 ft BS, collected in 1973 and submitted in 1974, appears too early (Green and Munson 1978:306)
SOUTHWIND (12 Po 265)			
UGa 4645	1085+/-85	887 (980) 1022	wood charcoal, charred wood post in RS 28b, J-1, Sec. 32, Level 4, collected in 1981 and submitted in 1982, too early (coal contaminated)
UGa-4646	955+/-115	984 (1036 1144 1146) 1216	wood charcoal, on floor RS 52, Feature N-1, Sec. 25, Level 3, collected and submitted in 1982, too early (coal contaminated)
UGa-4647	1005+/-65	984 (1021) 1152	wood charcoal, charred wood in hearth of RS 58c, Feature 16 in BB-4, Level 3, collected in 1981 and submitted in 1982, too early (coal contaminated)
UGa-4715	890+/-135	1005 (1161) 1278	carbonized maize and charcoal, Feature PH-WB-21, small smudge pit, collected in 1982 and submitted in 1983, adjusted for isotopic fractionation, somewhat early
UGa-4716	995+/-125	899 (1022) 1188	carbonized maize, PH-EB-105, small smudge pit, collected in 1981 and submitted in 1982, adjusted for isotopic fractionation, not acceptable (coal contaminated)

Sample No.	C14 Years	Calendrical Years AD min range (cal ages) max range[1]	Comments
		STEPHAN-STEINKAMP (12 Po 33)	
Beta-17509	1230+/-60	690 (**778**) 888	wood charcoal from a hardwood log, Feature 2 (a bathtub-shaped pit), collected and submitted in 1986, too early
Alpha-3085	940+/-160	1010	shell-tempered sherd from a globular jar, Feature 2, collected and submitted in 1986, acceptable (although the large standard deviation bothers me)
Alpha-3086	860+/-230	1090	shell-tempered sherd from a globular jar, Feature 2, collected and submitted in 1986, acceptable (although the large standard deviation bothers me)
Beta-22087	670+/-90	1276 (**1297**) 1398	wood charcoal from a log lying horizontally approximately 0.2 ft above the house basin floor, Feature 8, collected and submitted in 1987, acceptable
Beta-22088	640+/-100	1280 (**1302 1369 1382**) 1409	wood charcoal from what appeared to be a vertically-set wall support post in Feature 8, collected and submitted in 1987, acceptable and corroborates Beta-22087

List compiled from data on file at the Glenn A. Black Laboratory of Archaeology, Indiana University, Bloomington, Black (1967), Green (1977), Hilgeman (1989), Hilgeman and Schurr (1987), Munson (1994:Table 15.3), Munson (1999, personal communication), and Tankersley et al. (1987).

1. All radiocarbon determinations are corrected using CALIB (version 4.1.2; Stuiver and Reimer 1993) using the INTCAL98.14C dataset (Stuiver et al. 1998). No laboratory error multipliers are used. The calibrated age(s) are given in parentheses and are bracketed by the one sigma minimum and maximum range.

Appendix C

Appendix C
RADIOCARBON DATES FROM THE KINCAID - LOWER TENNESSEE-CUMBERLAND REGION

Sample No.	C14 Years	Calendrical Years AD min range (**cal ages**) max range[1]
		WESTERN KENTUCKY
		Tinsley Hill (15 Ly 18)
I-478	300+/-80	1480 (**1637**) 1662
M-1150	570+/-150	1284 (**1334 1336 1400**) 1448
Beta-3921	520+/-40	1402 (**1416**) 1435
Beta-38511	850+/-50	1160 (**1212**) 1256
Beta-38510	720+/-50	1268 (**1284**) 1298
		Roach (15 Tr 10)
I-479	410+/-85	1427 (**1452**)1629
		Goheen (15 Ml 18)
I-477	350+/-85	1443 (**1516 1599 1616**) 1647
		Dedmon (15 Ml 68)
UGa-247	905+/-85	1023 (**1074 1076 1159**) 1221
UGa-251	905+/-75	1024 (**1074 1076 1159**) 1219
UGa-249	690+/-90	1263 (**1293**) 1393
		Chambers (15 Ml 109)
B-12251	1040+/-60	904 (**1000**) 1025
B-12867	760+/-60	1221 (**1276**) 1291
B-12252	590+/-60	1300 (**1329 1343 1395**) 1413
B-12869	660+/-60	1284 (**1299 1375 1375**) 1393
B-12249	690+/-60	1278 (**1293**) 1385
B-12250	490+/-60	1405 (**1430**) 1445
B-12871	700+/-60	1276 (**1290**) 1382
B-12868	720+/-70	1259 (**1284**) 1379

Sample No.	C14 Years	Calendrical Years AD min range (**cal ages**) max range[1]
B-12253	380+/-60	1442 (**1481**) 1631
B-12254	810+/-60	1165 (**1224 1231 1239**) 1279
B-12870	810+/-60	1165 (**1224 1231 1239**) 1279
SFU-283	1100+/-200	689 (**904 910 976**) 1160
SFU-284	780+/-140	1060 (**1263**) 1382
15 McN 24		
UGa-3574	490+/-85(?)	1333 (**1430**) 1455
UGa-3575	550+/-69(?)	1315 (**1406**) 1434
15 McN 38		
UGa-3573	235+/-70	1533 (**1657**) 1946
BLACK BOTTOM, SOUTHERN ILLINOIS		
Kincaid		
M-888	675+/-75	1278 (**1297**) 1393
DIC-393	630+/-65	1291 (**1304 1367 1385**) 1402
DIC-904	660+/-55	1285 (**1299 1375 1375**) 1392
DIC-903	1110+/-65	886 (**902 917 962**) 999
UGa-3455	850+/-65	1066 (**1212**) 1262
UGa-3456	890+/-65	1035 (**1161**) 1220
UGa-3457	950+/-70	1018 (**1037 1143 1148**) 1183
Angelly (11 Mx 66)		
GX-2714	940+/-40	1024 (**1040 1100 1116 1141 1151**) 1160
DIC-136	1100+90/-95	783 (**904 910 976**) 1021
GX-2716	705+/-95	1255 (**1288**) 1390
GX-2715	3205+/-145	
DIC-139	730+35/-45	1276 (**1282**) 1294
BB Pp 105		
DIC-86	770+180/-190	1036 (**1271**) 1397
DIC-89	680+/-110	1259 (**1296**) 1401

Sample No.	C14 Years	Calendrical Years AD min range (**cal ages**) max range[1]
BB Mx 164		
DIC-74	680+70/-75	1277 (**1296**) 1392
DIC-75	1250+105/-100	
DIC-79	710+75/-70	1261 (**1287**) 1383
DIC-87	740+70/-75	1222 (**1280**) 1298
BB Mx 213		
DIC-138	820+75/-80	1160 (**1221**) 1281
DIC-137	790 +/-80	1165 (**1259**) 1287
Table compiled from Clay (1979; personal communication), Butler (1991), Butler, Penny, and Robison (1981), Muller (1986) and Pollack and Railey (1987).		

1. All radiocarbon determinations are corrected using CALIB (version 4.1.2; Stuiver and Reimer 1993) using the INTCAL98.14C dataset (Stuiver et al. 1998). No laboratory error multipliers are used. The calibrated age(s) are given in parentheses and are bracketed by the one sigma minimum and maximum range.

Appendix D

Appendix D

CATALOG AND SHERD NUMBERS OF THE ILLUSTRATED SPECIMENS

Figure 3.5 A, W-10-D/13900 (11724) + W-11-B/5671 (796); C, W-11-A/9154 (795) + W-11-A/9606 (794); D. W-11-A/9201 (606); E. X-11-B/3543 (19796)

Figure 3.6 X-11-B/3481 (437) + W-11-A/2597 (436) + W-11-A/11405 (435)

Figure 3.7 X-11-B/3499 (624) + X-11-C/1886 (625) + X-11-C/1392 (626) + X-11-C/1242 (616)

Figure 3.8 A, X-11-B/2678 (612); B, X-11-B/3365 (19883); C, X-11-B/510 (394); D, X-11-B/1155 (392); E, Md.F/3307 (393)

Figure 3.9 A, X-11-C/613 (524); B, W-10-D/4015 (461)

Figure 3.10 A, W-10-D/1973 (560); B, X-11-C/1266 (562); C, X-11-C/1814 (565); D, X-11-C/421 (602)+X-11-D/365 (603); E, X-11-C/1959 (605); F, X-11-C/696 (604)

Figure 3.11 A, X-11-C/1755 (591); B, W-11-B/3195 (588); C, X-11-B/7399 (533); D, W-11-A/5562 (553); E, X-11-C/438 (444); F, W-11-A/4855 (445); G, W-11-A/5760 (548)

Figure 3.12 A, X-11-B/5046 (600) + X-11-C/1104 (598); B, X-11-B/5707 (19761); C, X-11-C/1596 (448); D, X-11-C/1174 (447)

Figure 3.13 A, X-11-B/1460 (340); B, W-11-B/8624 (337)

Figure 3.14 A, X-11-D/195 (346); B, W-11-B/8145 (20299); C, X-11-C/534 (348); D, X-11-B/7404 (20869); E, X-11-C/422 (20866)

Figure 3.15 X-11-C/941 (22443)+X-11-C/996 (22444)+X-11-C/1037 (22445)+X-11-C/1121 (22446) + X-11-C/1787 (22447)

Figure 3.19 X-11-C/1512 (22410)

Figure 3.20 X-11-C/1472 (22538)

Figure 3.21 Y-07-C/14 (22497)

Figure 3.22 X-11-C/37 (22439)

Figure 3.23 W-11-B/799 (22399)

Figure 3.24 A, Md.F/3008 (14178); B, W-11-A/5233 (17439); C, X-11-B/3611 (19902); D,

Md.F/5494 (17379); E, X-10-C/81 (17420); F, X-10-C/99 (17418); G, X-10-C/642 (17416);

H, X-10-C/373 (19907)

Figure 3.25 A, W-11-A/11272 (17598); B, W-11-A/9237 (17599) + W-11-A/11272 (17600)

Figure 3.26 A, W-10-D/2046 (20724); B, X-11-C/1240 (20728); C, W-10-D/2170 (20756); D,

Md.F/2599 (21387); E, X-11-B/2798 (21379); F, W-11-A/7362 (21378); G, W-11-A/10693

(21376); H, W-10-D/18074 (21377); I, X-11-B/18 (21386); J, W-11-A/6140 (21380)

Figure 3.29 A, W-11-A/1908 (350); B, W-11-A/520 (368)

Figure 3.30 A, X-11-D/171 (17748); B, X-11-B/4810 (17490); C, W-11-A/12289 (17464); D, X--

11-D/184(20984)

Figure 3.31 X-11-C/1163 (8794)

Figure 3.32 A, Md.F/2160 (194); B, Md.F/2824 (193); C, Md.F/2824 (198); D, X-11-B/7390

(204); E, Md.F/3759 (205); F, X-11-B/1457 (199); G, X-11-D/173 (197)

Figure 3.33 A, S-11-D/1775 (20462); B, Y-08-B/9 (20464); C, Y-08-B/9 (20463)

Figure 3.34 A, X-11-C/1525 (410); B, X-11-C/1520 (409); C, W-10-D/16918 (423)

Figure 3.35 A, X-11-B/3393 (19732); B, V-11-A/1027 (21131); C, W-11-B/3031(21128)

Figure 3.36 A, X-10-C/141 (20733); B, R-12-A/130 (20754); C, W-10-D/623 (20753); D, W-11-A/11687 (20747); E, W-11-B/7639 (20738)

Figure 3.37 A, Md.F/2889 (20751); B, W-10-C/894 (20742); C, W-11-B/7016 (20750); D, W-11-B/6660 (20737); E, W-11-A/2473 (20745); F, S-11-D/2422 (20734)

Figure 3.38 A, W-10-D/8140(20708); B, X-11-C/718 (20591); C, S-11-D/2465 (20503); D, W-10-D/1526 (20719); E, W-10-D/14892 (20710); F, W-11-A/1766 (20613); G, W-10-D/15219 (20700)

Figure 3.39 A, W-11-B/1338 (20649); B, X-11-D/216 (20539); C, W-11-A/8421 (22434); D, W-10-C/3001 (20522); E, X-11-C/1026 (20605); F, W-10-C/421 (20531); G, W-10-D/13784 (20712); H, X-11-C/12 (20604); I, X-11-D/102 (20546); J, X-11-B/398 (20568); K, W-11-B/7493 (20673); L, R-12-A/19 (20529)

Figure 3.40 A, W-11-A/3686 (20616); B, X-11-C/848 (20598); C, X-11-B/478 (20577); D, W-11-B/644 (22437); E, R-14-B/67 (20509); F, W-11-A/3625 (20635); G, W-10-D/3024 (20703); H, V-11-A/446 (20513)

Figure 3.41 A, X-11-C/1816 (20590); B, W-10-D/14475 (20690) C, W-11-B/8155 (20650); D, W-11-A/2481 (20646); E, W-11-A/14153 (20641); F, W-11-A/2612 (20620); G, O-13-D/526 (20516);

Figure 3.42 A, X-11-B/1397 (20576); B, X-08-A/13(20515); C, W-11-A/10906 (20642); D, X-11--C/1236 (20599); E, W-10-D/16878 (20677); F, X-10-C/130 (20547); G, X-11-B/505 (20588);

H, W-11-A/1003 (20634); I, W-11-B/581 (20659); J, W-10-D/14901 (20721)

Figure 3.43 A, X-11-C/1439 (22432); B, Md.F/4178 (20535); C, W-11-A/2670 (20621); D, X-11-C/458 (20594); E, X-11-B/1186 (205790); F, X-11-B/900 (20573); G, W-10-D/4990 (20693)

Figure 3.44 A, X-11-C/1587 (22436); B, W-10-D/6785 (20718); C, V-08-C/240 (20536); D, W-10-D/3159 (20910); E, W-11-B/9857 (20912)

Figure 3.45 A, W-11-B/8040 (22532); B, W-10-D/6337 (22463)

Figure 3.46 A, W-10-D/8439 (20797); B, S-11-D/523 (20824); C, W-10-D/313 (20799); D, W-10-D/4976 (20798); E, W-10-D/1472 (20819); F, X-11-B/1917 (20803); G, W-11-B/7155 (21161); H, W-11-B/1621 (20836)

Figure 3.47 X-11-B/1476 (20790)

Figure 3.48 W-11-B/263 (20760)

Figure 3.49 A, W-11-A/1020 (20791); B, W-11-A/13770 (20792); C, V-11-A/179 (20780); D, W-11-B/610 (20768)

Figure 3.56 A, X-11-C/875 (208); B, X-11-B/4763 (258); C, X-10-C/1286 (206); D, W-10-D/16749 (21300)

Figure 3.57 A, S-11-D/2413 (14893); B, W-11-A/6221 (164); C, X-11-C/1610 (177); D, X-11-B/3734 (171); E, Md.F/2512 (188); F, Md.F/5184 (184); G, Md.F/2112 (187)

Figure 3.58 A, X-11-C/493 (153); B, W-10-D/767 (15741); C, X-11-B/4592 (161); D, W-10-D/692 (21209); E, W-11-B/8776 (21207); F, X-11-D/734 (156)

Figure 3.59 A, X-11-B/753 (295); B, W-10-D/13287 (21267); C, W-11-A/7719 (294); D,

Md.F/216 (282); E, X-11-D/253 (329)+X-11-D/255 (330)

Figure 3.60 X-11-C/1514 (22403)

Figure 3.61 A, W-10-D/1086 (136); B, X-11-B/6479 (140); C, W-11-A/3601 (138); D, W-10-D/2109 (144)

Figure 3.62 A, W-11-A/14208 (391+20388); B, W-11-A/13245 (386); C, X-11-C/1336 (390); D, X-11-B/1540 (21176); E, W-11-A/6827 (21175); F, V-08-C/16 (21177)

Figure 3.63 A, X-11-C/481 (769); B, W-11-A/7347 (22331) + X-11-B/5967 (22332); C, W-11-A/11893 (22321) + W-11-A/12120 (22360)

Figure 3.64 A, X-11-C/1363 (22378); B, X-11-B/4024 (22384); C, X-11-C/1077 (22377); D, Md.F/834 (22373); E, Md. F/532 (22372); F, X-11-B/4139 (22380); G, W-11-A/4858 (22366); H, X-11-C/472 (20863); I, W-11-A/2248 (1389)

Figure 3.65 X-11-C/1893 (22493)

Figure 4.4 A, W-11-B/657 (15984); B, W-10-D/13706 (15720); C, X-11-C/650 (1413)

Figure 4.5 A, X-10-C/401 (19916); B, X-11-C/1778 (1429); C, X-11-D/196 (1368)

Figure 4.6 A, W-11-A/5575 (1447); B, X-11-B/5936 (14971); C, W-10-D/13597 (15775)

Figure 4.7 A, X-11-B/1574 (1390); B, Md.F/221 (14964); C, W-10-C/500 (16053)

Figure 4.8 A, W-10-D/2916 (16350); B, V-09-B/477 (17615); C, W-11-A/9613 (14809); D, V-08-D/8 (17643); E, W-10-D/13281 (15778)

Figure 4.9 A, W-10-D/462 (1458); B, X-11-C/426 (1557); C, X-11-C/715 (1522); D, X-11-C/597 (1468)

Figure 4.10 A, W-10-D/12776 (15761); B, W-11-A/3295 (1485); C, X-11-B/189 (1538)

Figure 4.11 A, W-11-A/11170 (1484); B, W-10-D/3187 (1443); C, W-11-A/3670 (1501)

Figure 4.12 A, W-10-D/16124 (1572); B, W-11-B/510 (1472); C, X-11-C/264 (1502)

Figure 4.16 B, X-11-C/1781 (21065)

Figure 4.19 A, X-11-B/2715 (1399); B, W-11-A/7356 (1400); C, W-11-A/2774 (1402)

Figure 4.20 A, X-11-B/3706 (1623); B, W-10-D/1172 (15762); C, X-11-C/708 (1628) + X-11-

   C/680 (15021); D, W-10-D/1041 (21430); E, X-11-D/229 (1575); F, W-10-D/1295 (1573)

Figure 4.21 W-11-A/12468

Figure 4.22 A, (270); B, W-10-D/3807 (281); C, W-10-D/5665 (15290)

Figure 4.23 A, W-10-C/923 (744); B, X-11-C/437 (742); C, X-11-C/70 (771)

Figure 4.26 A, X-11-C/464 (666); B, W-11-A/2559 (11939)

Figure 4.27 A, X-11-B/3933 (627); B, W-11-B/456 (636); C, W-11-A/6814 (727); D, W-11-

   A/4993 (673); E, W-10-D/1560 (642)

Figure 4.28 A, X-11-C/1300 (659); B, X-11-C/1707 (653); C, W-11-A/13136 (12220)

Figure 5.1 A, X-11-B/2832 (834); B, X-11-B/323 (992); C, X-11-B/3527 (1024)

Figure 5.3 A, W-11-A/10817 (1040); B, X-11-C/1960 (1045) + X-11-C/572 (1044); C, X-11-

   B/2723 (1051); D, W-10-D/8217 (1035) + W-10-D/723 (1036); E, X-11-B/1658 (1041)+X-11-

   B/1671 (1042)+ X-11-B/1668 (1043)

Figure 5.4 A, X-11-B/1504 (1329) + X-11-B/1624 (1330) + X-11-B/1569 (1331); B, X-11-B/933

   (911); C, X-11-B/2303 (909); D, X-11-B/1512 (926); E, X-11-B/3892 (912)

Figure 5.6 A, X-11-C/720 (1334); B, X-11-C/1622 (22441) + X-11-C/676 (22442)

Figure 5.7 A, X-11-C/1387 (958) + X-11-C/1305 (959); B, X-11-B/1504 (956) + X-11-B/1569 (957); C, X-11-C/1686 (955)

Figure 5.8 A, X-11-D/232 (1347); B, W-11-A/13511 (1343); C, X-11-D/242 (22430); D, X-11-D/257 (1342); E, W-11-B/522 (1337) + W-11-B/559 (1338) + W-10-D/606 (1339) + W-11-B/960 (1340)

Figure 5.9 A, X-11-B/5352 (1111)+X-11-B/3485 (1112)+ X-10-C/953 (112); B, W-10-D/609 (1288); C, W-11-A/2929 (1309)

Figure 5.10 A, X-11-C/639 (1209) + X-11-C/674 (1210); B, W-11-A/2165 (1216) + W-11-A/1651 (1217); C, W-11-A/1651 (1212); D, W-10-D/5418 (1225)+W-10-D/3999 (9902); E, X-10-C/139 (1204) + X-10-C/568 (1205); F, W-10-D/6885 (1218) + W-11-B/8404 (1219)

References Cited

Adair, James
    1930   *The History of the American Indians.* New edition by Samuel Cole Williams. Wautauga Press, Johnson City, Tennessee.

Adams, William R.
    1949   *Archaeological Notes on Posey County, Indiana.* Indiana Historical Bureau, Indianapolis.

Arnold, Dean
    1985   *Ceramic Theory and Cultural Process.* Cambridge University Press, New York.

Ball, Stephen J., Dianne Senkel, and Shawn French
    1990   Historical Archaeology at the Angel Site: Mathias Angel's Farmstead. In *Current Research in Indiana Archaeology and Prehistory: 1989,* edited by C. S. Peebles, p. 1. Research Reports No. 11. Glenn A. Black Laboratory of Archaeology, Indiana University, Bloomington.

Ballard, W. L.
    1978   *The Yuchi Green Corn Ceremonial: Form and Meaning.* American Indian Studies Center, University of California, Los Angeles.

Bareis, Charles J., and James W. Porter
    1965   Megascopic and Petrographic Analysis of a Foreign Pottery Vessel from the Cahokia Site. *American Antiquity* 31(1):95–101.

Black, Glenn A.
    1952   Letter to A. O. Shepard, dated July 5, 1952. Correspondence on file, Glenn A. Black Laboratory of Archaeology, Indiana University, Bloomington.
    1967   *Angel Site: An Archaeological, Historical, and Ethnological Study.* 2 vols. Indiana Historical Society, Indianapolis.

Black, Glenn A., and Richard B. Johnston
    1962   A Test of Magnetometry as an Aid to Archaeology. *American Antiquity* 28:199–205.

Blasingham, Emily J.
    1953   Temporal and Spatial Distribution of the Yankeetown Cultural Manifestation. Unpublished Master's thesis, Department of Anthropology, Indiana University, Bloomington.

Blitz, John H.
    1993   Big Pots for Big Shots: Feasting and Storage in a Mississippian Community. *American Antiquity* 58(1):80–96.

Brain, Jeffrey P.
    1988   *Tunica Archaeology.* Papers of the Peabody Museum of Archaeology and Ethnology Vol. 78. Harvard University, Cambridge, Massachusetts.

Bronitsky, Gordon, and Robert Hamer
1986 Experiments in Ceramic Technology: The Effects of Various Tempering Materials on Impact and Thermal-Shock Resistance. *American Antiquity* 51(1):89–101.

Burt, Allen, Gregory Cook, William Meadows, and Seth Shteir
1989 The Fickas Farm Project: Mississippian Farmsteads in the Vicinity of the Angel Site, Vanderburgh County, Indiana. In *Current Research in Indiana Archaeology and Prehistory: 1987 and 1988,* edited by C. S. Peebles, pp. 5–7. Research Reports No. 10. Glenn A. Black Laboratory of Archaeology, Indiana University, Bloomington.

Butler, Brian M.
1991 Kincaid Revisited: The Mississippian Sequence in the Lower Ohio Valley. In *Cahokia and the Hinterlands: Middle Mississippian Cultures of the Midwest,* edited by T. E. Emerson and R. B. Lewis, pp. 264–273. University of Illinois Press, Urbana.

Butler, Brian M., Jo-Anne M. Penny, and Cathy A. Robison
1981 *Archaeology Survey and Evaluation for the Shawnee 200 M.W. A.F.B.C. Plant, McCracken County, Kentucky.* Research Paper No. 21. Center for Archaeological Investigations, Southern Illinois University, Carbondale.

Childress, Mitchell R.
1992 Mortuary Vessels and Comparative Ceramic Analyses: An Example from the Chucalissa Site. *Southeastern Archaeology* 11:31–50.

Clay, R. Berle
1963 Ceramic Complexes of the Tennessee-Cumberland Region in Western Kentucky. Unpublished Master's thesis, Department of Anthropology, University of Kentucky, Lexington.
1976 A Mississippian Cultural Sequence from the Lower Tennessee–Cumberland and Its Significance. Manuscript on file, Office of State Archaeology, University of Kentucky, Lexington.
1979 A Mississippian Ceramic Sequence from Western Kentucky. *Tennessee Anthropologist* 4(2):111–128.
1984 Morris Plain: and Other West Kentucky Ceramic Smoking Guns. *Tennessee Anthropologist* 9(2):104–113.
1991 Political Evolution of a Hinterland Mississippian Site. Paper presented at the Midwestern Archaeological Conference, LaCrosse, Wisconsin.
1997 The Mississippian Succession on the Lower Ohio. *Southeastern Archaeology* 16(1):16–32.

Cole, Fay–Cooper, Robert Bell, John Bennett, Joseph Caldwell, Norman Emerson, Richard MacNeish, Kenneth Orr, and Roger Willis
1951 *Kincaid: A Prehistoric Illinois Metropolis.* University of Chicago Press, Chicago.

Conrad, Lawrence A.
1991 The Middle Mississippian Cultures of the Central Illinois River Valley. In *Cahokia and the Hinterlands: Middle Mississippian Cultures of the Midwest,* edited by T. E. Emerson and R. B. Lewis, pp. 119–156. University of Illinois Press, Urbana.

Cordell, Ann S.
1993 Chronological Variability in Ceramic Paste: A Comparison of Deptford and Savan-

nah Period Pottery in the St. Marys Region of Northeast Florida and Southeast Georgia. *Southeastern Archaeology* 12:33–58.

Corkran, David H.
1953   The Sacred Fire of the Cherokees. *Southern Indian Studies* 5:21–26.
1955   Cherokee Sun and Fire Observances. *Southern Indian Studies* 7:33–38.

Curry, Hilda J.
1950   *Negative Painted Pottery of the Angel Mounds Site and Its Distribution in the New World.* Memoir 5. Indiana University Publications in Anthropology and Linguistics, Baltimore.
1954   *Archaeological Notes on Warrick County, Indiana.* Indiana Historical Bureau, Indianapolis.

Deam, Charles
1953   *Trees of Indiana.* 3rd ed. Division of Forestry, Indiana Department of Conservation, Indianapolis.

Dickens, Roy S., Jr.
1976   *Cherokee Prehistory.* University of Tennessee Press, Knoxville.

Dorwin, John T.
1965   "F" Mound—1965. Manuscript on file, Glenn A. Black Laboratory of Archaeology, Indiana University, Bloomington.
1971   *The Bowen Site: An Archaeological Study of Culture Process in the Late Prehistory of Central Indiana.* Prehistory Research Series Vol. 4, No. 4. Indiana Historical Society, Indianapolis.

Dragoo, Don W.
1955   *An Archaeological Survey of Gibson County, Indiana.* Indiana Historical Bureau, Indianapolis.

Dunnell, Robert C.
1986   Five Decades of American Archaeology. In *American Archaeology Past and Future,* edited by D. Meltzer, D. Fowler, and J. Sabloff, pp. 123–149. Smithsonian Institution Press, Washington, D.C.

Emerson, Thomas E.
1989   Water, Serpents, and the Underworld: An Exploration into Cahokian Symbolism. In *The Southeastern Ceremonial Complex: Artifacts and Analysis,* edited by P. Galloway, pp. 45–92. University of Nebraska Press, Lincoln.

Emerson, Thomas E., and R. Barry Lewis
1991   Preface. In *Cahokia and the Hinterlands: Middle Mississippian Cultures of the Midwest,* edited by T. E. Emerson and R. B. Lewis, pp. vii–xi. University of Illinois Press, Urbana.

Fischbeck, Helmut J., J. Daniel Rogers, Stuart R. Ryan, and Fern E. Swenson
1990   Sourcing Ceramics in the Spiro Region: A Preliminary Study Using Proton-induced X-ray Emission (PIXE) Analysis. *Midcontinental Journal of Archaeology* 14(1):3–17.

Ford, James A., and Gordon Willey

1941 An Interpretation of the Prehistory of the Eastern United States. *American Anthropologist* 43:325–363.

Friedrich, Margaret Hardin

1970 Design Structure and Social Interaction: Archaeological Implications of an Ethnographic Analysis. *American Antiquity* 35:332–343.

GBL

n.d. Site survey files. Forms on file, Glenn A. Black Laboratory of Archaeology, Indiana University, Bloomington.

Gibson, Jon L.

1993 Ceramics. In *The Development of Southeastern Archaeology,* edited by J. K. Johnson, pp. 18–35. University of Alabama Press, Tuscaloosa.

Gifford, J. C.

1960 The Type-Variety Method of Ceramic Classification as an Indicator of Cultural Phenomena. *American Antiquity* 25:341–347.

Gilbert, William H., Jr.

1930 New Fire Ceremonialism in America. Unpublished Master's thesis, Department of Anthropology, University of Chicago, Chicago.

1943 *The Eastern Cherokees.* Anthropological Papers No. 23, Bulletin 133. Bureau of American Ethnology, Smithsonian Institution, Washington, D.C.

Green, Thomas J.

1972a An Archaeological Survey of the Wabash River Valley in Posey and Gibson Counties, Indiana. Manuscript on file, Glenn A. Black Laboratory of Archaeology, Indiana University, Bloomington.

1972b The Vegetation of Southwestern Indiana in 1800: An Archaeological Perspective. Manuscript on file, Glenn A. Black Laboratory of Archaeology, Indiana University, Bloomington.

1977 Economic Relationships Underlying Mississippian Settlement Patterns in Southwestern Indiana. Unpublished Ph.D. dissertation, Department of Anthropology, Indiana University, Bloomington.

Green, Thomas J., and Cheryl A. Munson

1978 Mississippian Settlement Patterns in Southwestern Indiana. In *Mississippian Settlement Patterns,* edited by B. D. Smith, pp. 293–330. Academic Press, New York.

Griffin, James B.

1949 The Cahokia Ceramic Complexes. In *Proceedings of the Fifth Plains Conference for Archaeology,* edited by J. L. Champe, pp. 44–58. Notebook 1. Laboratory of Anthropology, University of Nebraska, Lincoln.

1966 *The Fort Ancient Aspect.* Reprinted. Originally published 1943. Anthropological Papers No. 28. Museum of Anthropology, University of Michigan, Ann Arbor.

Griffith, Roberta Jean

1981 *Ramey Incised Pottery.* Circular No. 5. Illinois Archaeological Survey, Urbana.

Hall, Robert L.

1991 Cahokia Identity and Interaction Models of Cahokia Mississippian. In *Cahokia and the Hinterlands: Middle Mississippian Cultures of the Midwest,* edited by T. E. Emerson and R. B. Lewis, pp. 3–34. University of Illinois Press, Urbana.

Hally, David J.

1983a The Interpretive Potential of Pottery from Domestic Contexts. *Midcontinental Journal of Archaeology* 8(2):163–196.

1983b Use Alteration of Pottery Vessel Surfaces: An Important Source of Evidence for the Identification of Vessel Function. *North American Archaeologist* 4(1):3–26.

1984 Vessel Assemblages and Food Habits: A Comparison of Two Aboriginal Southeastern Vessel Assemblages. *Southeastern Archaeology* 3(1):46–64.

1986 The Identification of Vessel Function: A Case Study from Northwest Georgia. *American Antiquity* 51(2):267–295.

1987 Platform Mounds and the Nature of Mississippian Chiefdoms. Paper presented at the Southeastern Archaeological Conference, Charleston, S.C.

Hanson, Lee H., Jr.

1960 The Analysis, Distribution, and Seriation of Pottery from the Green River Drainage as a Basis for an Archaeological Sequence of the Area. Manuscript on file, Office of State Archaeology, University of Kentucky, Lexington.

1970 *The Jewell Site, Bn21, Barren County, Kentucky.* Miscellaneous Paper No. 8, Tennessee Archaeological Society, Knoxville.

Hardin, Margaret Ann

1977 Individual Style in San Jose Pottery Painting: The Role of Deliberate Choice. In *The Individual in Prehistory: Studies of Variability in Style in Prehistoric Technologies,* edited by J. N. Hill and J. Gunn, pp. 109–136. Academic Press, New York.

1981 The Identification of Individual Style of Moundville Engraved Vessels: A Preliminary Note. *Southeastern Archaeological Conference Bulletin* 24:108–110.

1984 Models of Decoration. In *The Many Dimensions of Pottery: Ceramics in Archaeology and Anthropology,* edited by S. E. van der Leeuw and A. C. Pritchard, pp. 79–127. Universiteit van Amsterdam, Amsterdam.

Heimlich, Marion Dunlevy

1952 *Guntersville Basin Pottery.* Museum Paper No. 32. Geological Survey of Alabama, Tuscaloosa.

Helman, Vernon R.

1950 The Cultural Affiliations and Relationships of the Oliver Farm Site, Marion County, Indiana. Unpublished Master's thesis, Department of Anthropology, Indiana University, Bloomington.

Henn, Robert

1971 A Preliminary Report on the Leonard Site. *Proceedings of the Indiana Academy of Science* 80:67–73.

Hilgeman, Sherri L.

1985 Lower Ohio Valley Negative Painted Ceramics. *Midcontinental Journal of Archaeology* 10:195–213.

1988a Artificial Cranial Deformation at the Angel Site, Vanderburgh County, Indiana. *Proceedings of the Indiana Academy of Science* 98:83–91.

1988b Replicating Lower Ohio Negative Painted Ceramics. Paper presented at the annual meeting of the Society for American Archaeology, Phoenix.

1989   A Mississippian House Basin at the Stephan-Steinkamp Site (12P033). In *Current Research in Indiana Archaeology and Prehistory: 1987 & 1988*, edited by C. S. Peebles, pp. 42–43. Research Reports No. 10. Glenn A. Black Laboratory of Archaeology, Indiana University, Bloomington.

1991   Angel Negative Painted Design Structure. *Midcontinental Journal of Archaeology* 16:3–33.

Hilgeman, Sherri L., and Mark R. Schurr

1987   The 1986 IU/GBL Excavations at the Stephan-Steinkamp Site (12P033). *Proceedings of the Indiana Academy of Science* 95:83–90.

Hitchcock, Ethan Allen

1930   *A Traveler in Indian Territory.* Edited by Grant Foreman. Torch Press, Cedar Rapids, Iowa.

Hoffman, Michael A.

1966   *An Archaeological Survey of the Newburgh and Uniontown Lock and Dam Areas.* National Park Service, Southeast Regional Office, Richmond, Virginia.

Holley, George R.

1989   *The Archaeology of the Cahokia Mounds ICT-II: Ceramics.* Cultural Resources Study No. 11. Illinois Historic Preservation Agency, Springfield.

Holmes, W. H.

1883   Art in Shell of the Ancient Americas. *Second Annual Report of the Bureau of American Ethnology,* pp. 179–305. Smithsonian Institution, Washington, D.C.

Honerkamp, Marjorie

1975   The Angel Phase: An Analysis of a Middle Mississippian Occupation in Southwestern Indiana. Unpublished Ph.D. dissertation, Department of Anthropology, Indiana University, Bloomington.

Howard, J. H.

1968   *The Southeastern Ceremonial Complex.* Memoir 6. Missouri Archaeological Society, Columbia.

1981   *Shawnee! The Ceremonialism of a Native American Tribe and Its Cultural Background.* Ohio University Press, Athens.

Ihm, P., and H. van Groenewoud

1984   Correspondence Analysis and Gaussian Ordination. In *Lectures in Computational Statistics,* edited by J. M. Chambers, J. Gordesch, A. Klas, L. Lebart, and P. P. Sint, pp.5–60. Physica-Verlag, Wurzburg.

Isaac, Glynn L.

1984   The Archaeology of Human Origins: Studies of the Lower Pleistocene in East Africa, 1971–1981. *Advances in World Archaeology* 3:1–87.

Johnston, R. B.

1957   The Physical Relationship of Certain Middle Mississippian and Southeastern Groups. Unpublished Master's thesis, Department of Anthropology, Indiana University, Bloomington.

1964a   *Proton Magnetometry and Its Application to Archaeology: An Evaluation At Angel Site.* Prehistory Research Series Vol. 4, No. 2. Indiana Historical Society, Indianapolis.

1964b Summary Remarks Concerning the 1964 Excavation in Mound F. Manuscript on file, Glenn A. Black Laboratory of Archaeology, Indiana University, Bloomington.

Joukowski, Martha
1980 *A Complete Manual of Field Archaeology: Tools and Techniques of Field Work for Archaeologists.* Prentice Hall, New York.

Kellar, James H.
1956 *An Archaeological Survey of Spencer County, Indiana.* Indiana Historical Bureau, Indianapolis.
1958 *An Archaeological Survey of Perry County, Indiana.* Indiana Historical Bureau, Indianapolis.
1967 Material Culture. In *Angel Site: An Archaeological, Historical, and Ethnological Study,* edited by Glenn A. Black, pp. 431–487. Indiana Historical Society, Indianapolis.
1983 *An Introduction to the Prehistory of Indiana.* Indiana Historical Society, Indianapolis.

Kelly, John
1984 Wells Incised Or O'Byam Incised, *variety Wells,* and Its Context in the American Bottom. Paper presented at the 1984 Paducah Ceramic Conference, May 30, Paducah, Kentucky.
1991 Wells Incised Plates: Symbolic Antecedents and Spatial Affinities. Paper presented at the 36th Annual Midwestern Archaeological Conference, LaCrosse, Wisconsin.

Klein, Jeffrey, J. C. Lerman, P. E. Damon, and E. K. Ralph
1982 Calibration of Radiocarbon Dates. *Radiocarbon* 24(2):103–150.

Kreisa, Paul P.
1991 Ceramic Analysis. In *Excavations at the Andalex Village (15Hk22), Hopkins County, Kentucky,* edited by C. M. Niquette, pp. 72–112. Contract Publication Series 91–03. Cultural Resource Analysts, Lexington, Kentucky.
1993 Ceramics, Radiocarbon Dates, and Mississippian Chronology Building in Western Kentucky. Paper presented at the annual meeting of the Society for American Archaeology, St. Louis, Missouri.

Lafferty, Robert
1977 The Evolution of Mississippian Settlement Patterns and Exploitative Technology in the Black Bottom of Southern Illinois. Unpublished Ph.D. dissertation, Department of Anthropology, Southern Illinois University at Carbondale.

Lewis, R. Barry
1982 *Excavations at Two Mississippian Hamlets in the Cairo Lowland of Southeast Missouri.* Special Publication No. 2. Illinois Archaeological Survey, Urbana.
1990a The Late Prehistory of the Ohio-Mississippi Rivers Confluence Region, Kentucky and Missouri. In *Towns and Temples along the Mississippi River,* edited by David Dye and Cheryl Cox, pp. 38–58. University of Alabama Press, Tuscaloosa.
1990b Mississippi Period. In *The Archaeology of Kentucky: Past Accomplishments and Future Directions,* vol.2, edited by D. Pollack, pp. 375–466. State Historic Preservation Comprehensive Plan Report No. 1. Kentucky Heritage Council, Frankfort.
1991 The Early Mississippi Period in the Confluence Region and Its Northern Relationships. In *Cahokia and the Hinterlands: Middle Mississippian Cultures of the Midwest,* edited by T. E. Emerson and R. B. Lewis, pp. 274–294. University of Illinois Press, Urbana.

1996   Mississippian Farmers. In *Kentucky Archaeology,* edited by R. B. Lewis, pp. 127–159. The University Press of Kentucky, Lexington.

Lewis, R. Barry (editor)
1986   *Mississippian Towns of the Western Kentucky Border: The Adams, Wickliffe, and Sassafras Ridge Sites.* Kentucky Heritage Council, Frankfort.

Lewis, R. Barry, and Lynne M. Mackin
1984   The Adams Site Ceramic Assemblage in Regional Perspective. In *Late Prehistoric Research in Kentucky,* edited by D. Pollack, C. Hockensmith, and T. Sanders, pp. 187–204. Kentucky Heritage Council, Frankfort.

Lewis, Thomas M. N., and Madeline Kneberg
1946   *Hiwassee Island: An Archaeological Account of Four Tennessee Indian People.* University of Tennessee Press, Knoxville.

Lilly, Eli
1937   *Prehistoric Antiquities of Indiana.* Indiana Historical Bureau, Indianapolis.

Maher, Thomas O.
1989   The Middle Woodland Ceramic Assemblage. In *The Holding Site: A Hopewell Community in the American Bottom,* edited by Andrew C. Fortier, Thomas O. Maher, Joyce A. Williams, Michael C. Meinkoth, Kathryn E. Parker, and Lucretia S. Kelly, pp. 125–318. FAI-270 Site Reports Vol. 19. University of Illinois Press, Urbana.

Mann, Cyril B.
1983   Classification of the Ceramics from the Lubbub Creek Archaeological Locality. In *Prehistoric Agricultural Communities in West Central Alabama,* vol. 2, edited by C. S. Peebles, pp. 2–63. Interagency Archaeological Services, Atlanta, and the U.S. Army Corps of Engineers, Mobile District.

Marquardt, William H.
1978   Advances in Archaeological Seriation. In *Advances in Archaeological Method and Theory,* edited by M. B. Schiffer, pp. 257–314. Academic Press, New York.

McCullough, Robert G.
1991   A Reanalysis of Ceramics from the Bowen Site: Implications for Defining the Oliver Phase of Central Indiana. Unpublished Master's thesis, Department of Anthropology, Ball State University, Muncie.

Million, Michael G.
1975a   Ceramic Technology of the Nodena Phase Peoples (ca. A.D. 1400–1700). *Southeastern Archaeological Conference Bulletin* 18:201–208.
1975b   Research Design for the Aboriginal Ceramic Industries of the Cache River Basin. In *The Cache River Archaeological Project,* edited by M. B. Schiffer and J. H. House, pp. 217–222. Research Series 8. Arkansas Archeological Survey, Fayetteville, Arkansas.
1976   Preliminary Report on Zebree Site Ceramics. In *A Preliminary Report of the Zebree Project: New Approaches in Contract Archaeology in Arkansas, 1975,* edited by D. F. Morse and P. A. Morse, pp. 44–49. Research Report 8. Arkansas Archeological Survey, Fayetteville, Arkansas.

Milner, George R.
1990   The Late Prehistoric Cahokia Cultural System of the Mississippi River Valley: Foundations, Florescence, and Fragmentation. *Journal of World Prehistory* 4(1):1–43.

Milner, George R., Thomas E. Emerson, Mark W. Mehrer, Joyce A. Williams, and
Duane Esarey
   1984   Mississippian and Oneota Period. In *American Bottom Archaeology,* edited by C. J.
          Bareis and J. P. Porter, pp. 158–186. University of Illinois Press, Urbana.

Mooney, James
   1889   Cherokee Mound-Building. *American Anthropologist* 2:167–171.
   1900   Myths of the Cherokee. *Nineteenth Annual Report of the Bureau of American Ethnol-
          ogy,* Pt. 1. Smithsonian Institution, Washington, D.C.

Moorehead, Warren K.
   1906   Explorations at the Mouth of the Wabash. *Phillips Academy Bulletin* 3:62–86.

Morgan, William N.
   1980   *Prehistoric Architecture in the Eastern United States.* MIT Press, Cambridge, Massa-
          chusetts.

Morse, Dan F., and Phyllis A. Morse
   1983   *Archaeology of the Central Mississippi Valley.* Academic Press, New York.

Muller, Jon
   1978   The Kincaid System: Mississippian Settlement in the Environs of a Large Site. In
          Mississippian Settlement Patterns, edited by B. D. Smith, pp. 269–292. Academic
          Press, New York.
   1986   *Archaeology of the Lower Ohio River Valley.* Academic Press, New York.

Munson, Cheryl Ann
   1984   Preliminary Description of Caborn-Welborn Decorated. Paper presented at the 1984
          Paducah Ceramics Conference, May 30, Paducah, Kentucky. Manuscript on file, De-
          partment of Anthropology, Indiana University, Bloomington.

Munson, Cheryl Ann (editor)
   1994   Archaeological Investigations at the Southwind Site, a Mississippian Community in
          Posey County, Indiana. Prepared for the Division of Historic Preservation and Ar-
          chaeology, Indiana Department of Natural Resources. Manuscript on file, Depart-
          ment of Anthropology, Indiana University, Bloomington, and Division of Historic
          Preservation and Archaeology, Indiana Department of Natural Resources, Indian-
          apolis.

Niquette, Charles M., Paul P. Kreisa, R. Berle Clay, and G. D. Crites
   1991   *Excavations at the Andalex Village (15Hk22), Hopkins County, Kentucky.* Contract
          Publication Series 91-03. Cultural Resource Analysts, Lexington, Kentucky.

O'Brien, Michael J.
   1977   Intrasite Variability in a Middle Mississippian Community. Unpublished Ph.D. dis-
          sertation, Department of Anthropology, University of Texas, Austin.

O'Brien, Patricia
   1972   *A Formal Analysis of Cahokia Ceramics from the Powell Tract.* Monograph No. 3. Il-
          linois Archaeological Survey, Urbana.

Orr, Kenneth
   1951   Change at Kincaid: A Study of Cultural Dynamics. In *Kincaid: A Prehistoric Illinois
          Metropolis,* edited by Fay-Cooper Cole, Robert Bell, John Bennett, Joseph Caldwell,

Norman Emerson, Richard MacNeish, Kenneth Orr, and Roger Willis, pp. 293–359. University of Chicago Press, Chicago.

Pauketat, Timothy R.
1987   A Functional Consideration of a Mississippian Domestic Vessel Assemblage. *Southeastern Archaeology* 6(1):1–15.
1989   Monitoring Mississippian Homestead Occupation Span and Economy Using Ceramic Refuse. *American Antiquity* 54(2):288–310.

Pauketat, Timothy R., and Thomas E. Emerson
1991   The Ideology of Authority and the Power of the Pot. *American Anthropologist* 93:919–941.

Payne, John Howard
1932   The Green Corn Dance. *Chronicles of Oklahoma* 10:170–195.

Peebles, Christopher S., and Cyril B. Mann, Jr.
1983   Culture and Chronology in the Lubbub Creek Archaeological Locality. In *Prehistoric Agricultural Communities in West Central Alabama,* vol. 1, edited by C. S. Peebles, pp. 64–78. Interagency Archaeological Services, Atlanta, and U.S. Army Corps of Engineers, Mobile District.

Peterson, Roger Tory
1980   *A Field Guide to the Birds of Eastern and Central North America.* 4th ed. Houghton Mifflin, Boston.

Phillips, Phillip
1958   The Application of the Wheat-Gifford-Wasley Taxonomy to Eastern Ceramics. *American Antiquity* 24:117–125.
1970   *Archaeological Survey in the Lower Yazoo River Basin, Mississippi, 1944–1955.* Papers of the Peabody Museum of Archaeology and Ethnology Vol. 60. Harvard University, Cambridge, Massachusetts.

Phillips, Phillip, James A. Ford, and James B. Griffin
1951   *Archaeological Survey in the Lower Mississippi Valley, 1940–1947.* Papers of the Peabody Museum of Archaeology and Ethnology Vol. 25. Harvard University, Cambridge, Massachusetts.

Polhemus, Richard R.
1990   Regional Chronologies. In *Lamar Archaeology: Mississippian Chiefdoms in the Deep South,* edited by M. Williams and G. Shapiro, pp. 30–43. University of Alabama Press, Tuscaloosa.

Polhemus, Richard R., and James H. Polhemus
1966   The McCullough Bend Site. *Tennessee Archaeologist* 22(1):13–24.

Pollack, David
1998   Intraregional and Intersocietal Relationships of the Late Mississippian Caborn-Welborn Phase of the Lower Ohio River Valley. Unpublished Ph.D. dissertation, Department of Anthropology, University of Kentucky, Lexington.

Pollack, David, and Cheryl Ann Munson
1998   Caborn-Welborn Ceramics: Intersite Comparisons and Extraregional Interaction. In *Current Archaeological Research in Kentucky,* vol. 5, edited by C. Hockensmith,

K. C. Carstens, C. Stout, and S. J. Rivers, pp. 163–202. Kentucky Heritage Council, Frankfort.

Pollack, David, and Jimmy A. Railey
1987 *Chambers (15Mh09): An Upland Village in Western Kentucky.* Kentucky Heritage Council, Frankfort.

Porter, James Warren
1964a Comment on Weaver's "Technological Analysis of Lower Mississippi Ceramic Materials." *American Antiquity* 29(4):520–521.
1964b *Thin Section Descriptions of Some Shell Tempered Prehistoric Ceramics from the American Bottoms.* Research Report 7. Lithic Laboratory, Southern Illinois University Museum, Carbondale.
1966 Thin Section Analysis of Ten Aztalan Sherds. *Wisconsin Archaeologist* 47:12–27.
1971 Thin-section Identifications of Spiro Sherds. In *Spiro Studies,* Volume 3, Pottery Vessels, by James A. Brown. First Part of the Third Annual Report of Caddoan Archaeology—Spiro Focus Research, pp. 244–246. University of Oklahoma Research Institute, Norman.

Porter, James Warren, and Christine R. Szuter
1978 Thin-section Analysis of Schlemmer Site Ceramics. *Midcontinental Journal of Archaeology* 3(1):3–14.

Potzger, J. E., M. E. Potzger, and Jack McCormick
1956 The Forest Primeval of Indiana as Recorded in the Original U.S. Land Surveys and an Evaluation of Previous Interpretations of Indiana Vegetation. *Butler University Botanical Studies* 13:95–111.

Power, Marjory W. (Honerkamp)
1976 Delineation of the Angel Phase: A Middle Mississippian Occupation in Southwestern Indiana. *Southeastern Archaeological Conference Bulletin* 19:26–30.

Purdue, A. H.
1897 Some Mounds of Vanderburgh County, Indiana. *Proceedings of the Indiana Academy of Science for 1896* 6:68–70. Indianapolis.

Rachlin, Carol J.
1954 Research papers concerned with textile-impressed pottery. Manuscript on file, Glenn A. Black Laboratory of Archaeology, Indiana University, Bloomington.

Read, D. W.
1989 Statistical Methods and Reasoning in Archaeological Research: A Review of Praxis and Promise. *Journal of Quantitative Anthropology* 1:5–78.

Redmond, Brian G.
1990 The Yankeetown Phase: Emergent Mississippian Cultural Adaptation in the Lower Ohio River Valley. Unpublished Ph.D. dissertation, Department of Anthropology, Indiana University, Bloomington.
1991 *An Archaeological Investigation of Late Woodland Period Settlement in the East Fork White River Valley: Martin, Lawrence and Jackson Counties, Indiana.* Report of Investigation 91–15. Glenn A. Black Laboratory of Archaeology, Indiana University, Bloomington.

Rice, Prudence
 1987 *Pottery Analysis: A Sourcebook.* University of Chicago Press, Chicago.

Riordan, Robert V.
 1975 Ceramics and Chronology: Mississippian Settlement in the Black Bottom, Southern Illinois. Unpublished Ph.D. dissertation, Department of Anthropology, Southern Illinois University, Carbondale.

Rouse, I.
 1960 The Classification of Artifacts in Archaeology. *American Antiquity* 25(3):313–23.

Ruegamer, Lana
 1980 *A History of the Indiana Historical Society, 1830–1980.* Indiana Historical Society, Indianapolis.

Schurr, Mark R.
 1987 A "Partial Cremation" from the Angel Site, Vanderburgh County, Indiana. *Proceedings of the Indiana Academy of Science* 96:91–93.
 1989a The Relationship between Mortuary Treatment and Diet at the Angel Site. Unpublished Ph.D. dissertation, Department of Anthropology, Indiana University, Bloomington.
 1989b Fluoride Dating of Prehistoric Bones by Ion Selective Electrode. *Journal of Archaeological Science* 16:265–270.
 1989c Controlled Surface Collections from the Stephan-Steinkamp Site (12Po33). In *Current Research in Indiana Archaeology and Prehistory: 1987 and 1988,* edited by C. S. Peebles, pp 24–25. Research Reports No. 10. Glenn A. Black Laboratory of Archaeology, Indiana University, Bloomington.
 1992 Isotopic and Mortuary Variability in a Middle Mississippian Population. *American Antiquity* 57(2):300–320.

Schurr, Mark R., and Sherri L. Hilgeman
 1991 Fluorine Dating and Pottery Chronology at the Angel Site. In *Current Research in Indiana Archaeology and Prehistory: 1990,* edited by C. S. Peebles, pp. 21–22. Research Reports No. 12. Glenn A. Black Laboratory of Archaeology, Indiana University, Bloomington.

Scollar, I., and I. Herzog
 1991 *Bonn Seriation and Archaeological Statistics Package* (Version 4.1). Unkelbach Valley Software Works, Remagen, Germany.

Scollar, I., B. Weidner, and I. Herzog
 1985 A Portable Seriation Package with Dynamic Memory Allocation in PASCAL. *PACT* 11:149–157.

Sears, William H.
 1973 The Sacred and Secular in Prehistoric Ceramics. In *Variation in Anthropology: Essays in Honor of John C. McGregor,* edited by D. W. Lathrap and J. Douglas, pp. 31–42. Illinois Archaeological Survey, Urbana.

Shapiro, Gary
 1984 Ceramic Vessels, Site Permanence, and Group Size: A Mississippian Example. *American Antiquity* 49(4):696–712.

Shepard, Anna O.

1952 Letter to G. A. Black, dated June 16, 1952. Correspondence on file, Glenn A. Black Laboratory of Archaeology, Indiana University, Bloomington.

1956 *Ceramics for the Archaeologist.* Publication 609. Carnegie Institution of Washington, Washington, D.C.

Smith, Bruce

1986 The Archaeology of the Southeastern United States: From Dalton to DeSoto, 10,500 to 500 BP. *Advances in World Archaeology* 5:1–92.

Smith, Gerald P.

1969 *Ceramic Handle Styles and Cultural Variation in the Northern Sector of the Mississippi Alluvial Valley.* Occasional Papers 3. Anthropological Research Center, Memphis State University.

1990 The Walls Phase and Its Neighbors. In *Towns and Temples along the Mississippi,* edited by D. H. Dye and C. A. Cox, pp. 135–169. University of Alabama Press, Tuscaloosa.

Smith, Hale G.

1951 *The Crable Site, Fulton County, Illinois: A Late Prehistoric Site in the Central Illinois Valley.* Anthropological Papers No. 7. Museum of Anthropology, University of Michigan, Ann Arbor.

Smith, Kevin E.

1992 The Middle Cumberland Region: Mississippian Archaeology in North Central Tennessee. Unpublished Ph.D. dissertation, Department of Anthropology, Vanderbilt University, Nashville, Tennessee.

Smith, R. E., G. R. Willey, and J. C. Gifford

1960 The Type-Variety Concept as a Basis for the Analysis of Maya Pottery. *American Antiquity* 30:330–340.

Speck, Frank G.

1909 *Ethnology of the Yuchi Indians.* Anthropological Publications No. 1. University Museum, University of Pennsylvania, Philadelphia.

Steponaitis, Vincas P.

1983 *Ceramics, Chronology, and Community Patterns: An Archaeological Study at Moundville.* Academic Press, New York.

1984 Technological Studies of Prehistoric Pottery from Alabama: Physical Properties and Vessel Function. In *The Many Dimensions of Pottery: Ceramics in Archaeology and Anthropology,* edited by S. E. van der Leeuw and A. C. Pritchard, pp. 79–127. Universiteit van Amsterdam, Amsterdam.

Stimmell, Carole A., Robert B. Heimann, and Ronald G. V. Hancock

1982 Indian Pottery from the Mississippi Valley: Coping with Bad Raw Materials. In *Archaeological Ceramics,* edited by Jacqueline S. Olin and Alan D. Franklin, pp. 219–228. Smithsonian Institution Press, Washington, D.C.

Stinson, Floyd

1883 Mounds and Earthworks in Vanderburgh County, Indiana. *Annual Report of the Smithsonian Institution for the Year 1881,* p. 591. Smithsonian Institution, Washington, D.C.

Stuiver, M., and P. J. Reimer

1993   Extended 14C Database and Revised CALIB Radiocarbon Calibration Program (version 4.1). *Radiocarbon* 35:215–230.

Stuiver, M., P. J. Reimer, E. Bard, J. W. Beck, G. S. Burr, K. A. Hughen, B. Kromer, F. G. McCormac, J. v. d. Plicht, and M. Spurk

1998   INTCAL98 Radiocarbon Age Calibration 24,000—0 cal BP. *Radiocarbon* 40:1041–1083.

Swanton, John R.

1911   *Indian Tribes of the Lower Mississippi Valley and Adjacent Coast of the Gulf of Mexico.* Bulletin 43. Bureau of American Ethnology, Smithsonian Institution, Washington, D.C.

1928a   Sun Worship in the Southeast. *American Anthropologist* 30:206–213.

1928b   Religious Beliefs and Medical Practices of the Creek Indians. *Forty-second Annual Report of the Bureau of American Ethnology,* pp. 473–672. Smithsonian Institution, Washington, D.C.

1942   *Source Material on the History and Ethnology of the Caddo Indians.* Bureau of American Ethnology Bulletin 132. Smithsonian Institution, Washington, D.C.

1946   *The Indians of the Southeastern United States.* Bulletin 137. Bureau of American Ethnology, Smithsonian Institution, Washington, D.C.

Tankersley, Kenneth B., Cheryl Ann Munson, and Donald Smith

1987   Recognition of Bituminous Coal Contaminants in Radiocarbon Samples. *American Antiquity* 52(2):318–330.

Thomas, Cyrus

1894   Report of the Mound Explorations for the Bureau of Ethnology. *Twelfth Annual Report of the Bureau of Ethnology for 1890–1891.* Smithsonian Institution, Washington, D.C.

Thomas, David Hurst

1989   *Archaeology.* 2nd ed. Holt, Rinehart and Winston, Inc., Fort Worth.

Vaillant, G. C.

1930   *Excavations at Zacatenco.* Anthropological Papers Vol. 32, Pt. 1. American Museum of Natural History, New York.

van der Leeuw, Sander E.

1981   Preliminary Report on the Analysis of Moundville Phase Ceramic Technology. *Southeastern Archaeological Conference Bulletin* 24:105–108.

Vogel, Joseph O.

1975   Trends in Cahokia Ceramics: Preliminary Study of the Collections from Tracts 15A and 15B. In *Perspectives in Cahokia Archaeology,* pp. 32–125. Bulletin 10. Illinois Archaeological Survey, Urbana.

Walker, Winslow, and R. M. Adams

1946   Excavations in the Matthews Site, New Madrid County, Missouri. *Transactions of the Academy of Science of St. Louis* 31(4):75–120.

Waring, Antonio J., Jr.

1968a   The Southern Cult and Muskhogean Ceremonial. In *The Waring Papers: The Col-*

lected Works of Antonio J. Waring, edited by Stephen Williams, pp. 30–69. Papers of the Peabody Museum of Archaeology and Ethnology Vol 58. Harvard University, Cambridge, Massachusetts.

1968b Some Recent Thoughts on the Cult. A. The Striped Pole and Terrace Motif. In *The Waring Papers: The Collected Works of Antonio J. Waring*, edited by Stephen Williams, pp. 87–89. Papers of the Peabody Museum of Archaeology and Ethnology Vol. 58. Harvard University, Cambridge, Massachusetts.

Waring, Antonio J., Jr., and Preston Holder
1945 A Prehistoric Ceremonial Complex in the Southeastern United States. *American Anthropologist* 47:1–34.

Watson, Patty Jo
1990 Trend and Tradition in Southeastern Archaeology. *Southeastern Archaeology* 9(1):43–54.

Webb, William S., and William D. Funkhouser
1931 The Tolu Site in Crittenden County, Kentucky. *University of Kentucky Reports in Archaeology and Anthropology* 1(5):307–410.

Wesler, Kit W.
1988 Ceramics and Mississippian Chronology at Wickliffe Mounds, 15Ba4. Paper presented at the Southeastern Archaeological Conference, New Orleans.

1991a *Archaeological Excavations at Wickliffe Mounds, 15Ba4: North Village and Cemetery, 1988–1989.* Wickliffe Mounds Research Center, Report 4. Murray State University, Murray, Kentucky.

1991b Ceramics, Chronology, and Horizon Markers at Wickliffe Mounds. *American Antiquity* 56(2):278–290.

1991c Spatial and Chronological Perspectives on Ceramic Vessel Form at Wickliffe Mounds, 15Ba4. Paper presented at the annual meeting of the Kentucky Heritage Council Conference, Bowling Green.

Wetmore, Ruth
1983 The Green Corn Ceremony of the Eastern Cherokees. *Journal of Cherokee Studies* 8(1):46–56.

Wheat, J. B., J. Gifford, and W. Wasley
1958 Ceramic Variety, Type Cluster, and Ceramic System in Southwestern Pottery Analysis. *American Antiquity* 24:34–47.

Willey, Gordon R., and Phillip Phillips
1958 *Method and Theory in American Archaeology.* University of Chicago Press, Chicago.

Williams, Stephen
1954 An Archaeological Study of the Mississippian Culture in Southeast Missouri. Unpublished Ph.D. dissertation, Department of Anthropology, Yale University, New Haven.

Williams, Stephen, and Jeffrey P. Brain
1983 *Excavations at the Lake George Site, Yazoo County, Mississippi, 1958–1960.* Papers of the Peabody Museum of Archaeology and Ethnology Vol 74. Harvard University, Cambridge, Massachusetts.

Witthoft, John

    1946   The Cherokee Green Corn Medicine and the Green Corn Festival. *Journal of the Washington Academy of Sciences* 36(7):213–219.

    1949   *Green Corn Ceremonialism in the Eastern Woodlands.* Occasional Contributions No. 13. Museum of Anthropology, University of Michigan, Ann Arbor.

Wobst, H. Martin

    1977   Stylistic Behavior and Information Exchange. In *For the Director: Research Essays in Honor of James B. Griffin,* edited by C. E. Cleland, pp. 317–342. Anthropological Papers No. 61. Museum of Anthropology, University of Michigan, Ann Arbor.

Wolforth, Lynne Mackin

    1987   *Jonathan Creek Revisited: The House Basin Structures and Their Ceramics.* Western Kentucky Project Report No. 5. Department of Anthropology, University of Illinois at Urbana-Champaign.

Wolforth, Tom

    1983   Excavations at Angel Mounds, 1983 Season. Manuscript on file, Glenn A. Black Laboratory of Archaeology, Indiana University, Bloomington.

Index

About the Author

Sherri L. Hilgeman is assistant professor of anthropology at Indiana Southeast University. She received her M.A. from the University of Kentucky at Lexington and her Ph.D. from Indiana University at Bloomington.